ADVANCES IN ACCOUNTING

Volume 7 • 1989

ADVANCES IN ACCOUNTING

A Research Annual

Editor: BILL N. SCHWARTZ
School of Business and Management
Temple University

Associate Editors: PHILIP M. J. RECKERS
School of Accounting
Arizona State University

JAMES C. STALLMAN
School of Accountancy
University of Missouri

JAMES H. SCHEINER
College of Business Administration
University of Tennessee

VOLUME 7 • 1989

 JAI PRESS INC.

Greenwich, Connecticut   London, England

CONTENTS

PART I. FINANCIAL AND MANAGERIAL

LIST OF CONTRIBUTORS

E. Michael Bamber

Department of Accounting
Indiana University

Allen W. Bathke, Jr.

Department of Accounting
The Florida State University

Dennis M. Bline

Department of Accounting
University of Texas at San Antonio

Mehmet Canlar

Department of Accounting
Plymouth State College

Judith H. Cassidy

Department of Accounting
Louisiana State University

Timothy Doupnik

Division of Accounting
University of South Carolina

Alan H. Friedberg

Department of Accounting
Louisiana State University

Don E. Giacomino

Department of Accounting and
    Finance
Marquette University

G. William Glezen

Department of Accounting
University of Arkansas

Terry Gregson

College of Business Administration
University of Hawaii

James E. Groff   Department of Accounting
                                 University of Texas at San Antonio

Hugh Grove   Department of Accounting
                                 University of Denver

Bart P. Hartman   Department of Accounting
                                 Louisiana State University

John M. Hassell   Department of Accounting
                                 The Florida State University

David LaRue   Department of Accounting
                                 University of Virginia

Kenneth S. Lorek   Department of Accounting
                                 The Florida State University

Man Chand Maloo   Department of Accounting and
                                     Finance
                                 Towson State University

Ruth Ann McEwen   Department of Accounting
                                 Temple University

David E. Mielke   Department of Accounting and
                                     Finance
                                 Marquette University

Dennis Murray   Accounting Department
                                 University of Colorado at Denver

Philip M.J. Reckers   School of Accounting
                                 Arizona State University

Roy Regel   Department of Accounting
                                 University of Montana

Robert J. Rolfe   Division of Accounting
                                 University of South Carolina

Heibatollah Sami   Department of Accounting
                             Temple University

Jenice Stewart   School of Accountancy
                             University of Missouri

Jerry R. Strawser   Department of Accounting
                             Louisiana State University

Arlette C. Wilson   School of Accountancy
                             Auburn University

Charlotte J. Wright   School of Accountancy
                             Oklahoma State University

xiii

AIA STATEMENT OF PURPOSE

Advances in Accounting (AIA) is a professional publication whose purpose is to meet the information needs of both practitioners and academicians. We publish thoughtful, well-developed articles on a variety of current topics in financial and management accounting, accounting education and auditing.

Articles may range from empirical to analytical, from practice-based to the development of new techniques. Articles must be readable, relevant, and reliable. To be readable, articles must be understandable and concise. To be relevant, articles must be related to problems facing the accounting and business community. To be reliable, conclusions must follow logically from the evidence and arguments presented. For empirical reports, sound design and execution are critical. For theoretical treatises, reasonable assumptions and logical development are essential.

AIA welcomes all comments and encourages articles from practitioners and academicians.

Editorial correspondence pertaining to manuscripts should be sent to:

Professor Bill N. Schwartz, *Editor-in-Chief*
School of Business and Management
Temple University
Philadelphia, Pennsylvania 19122
(215) 787-8196

EDITORIAL POLICY AND MANUSCRIPT FORM GUIDELINES

1. Manuscripts should be typewritten and double-spaced on 8″ x 11″ white paper. Only one side of a page should be used. Margins should be set to facilitate editing and duplication except as noted:

   a. tables, figures and exhibits should appear on a separate page. Each should be numbered and have a title.

   b. footnotes should be presented by citing the author's name and the year of publication in the body of the text, e.g., Schwartz [1981]; Reckers and Pany [1980].

2. Manuscripts should include a cover page which indicates the author's name and affiliation.

3. Manuscripts should include on a separate lead page an abstract not exceeding 200 words. The author's name and affiliation should not appear on the abstract.

4. Topical headings and subheadings should be used. Main headings in the manuscript should be centered, secondary headings should be flush with the left-hand margin. (As a guide to usage and style, refer to William Strunk, Jr. and E. B. White, **The Elements of Style.**)

5. Manuscripts must include a list of references which contain only those works actually cited. (As a helpful guide in preparing a list of references, refer to Kate L. Turabian, **A Manual for Writers of Term Papers, Theses, and Dissertations.**)

6. In order to be assured of an anonymous review, authors should not identify themselves directly or indirectly. Reference to unpublished working papers and dissertations should be avoided. If necessary, authors may indicate that the reference is being withheld for the reasons cited above.

7. The author will be provided one complete volume of the **AIA** issue in which his or her manuscript appears and the senior author will receive twenty-five off-prints of the article.

8. Manuscripts currently under review by other publications should not be submitted. Complete reports and research presented at a national or regional conference of a professional association (e.g., AAA, DSI etc.) and "State of the Art" papers are acceptable.

9. **Four** copies of each manuscript should be submitted to the Editor-in-Chief at the Temple University address. Copies of any and all research instruments also should be included.

10. For additional information regarding the type of manuscripts that are desired, see **AIA Statement of Purpose.**

PART I

FINANCIAL AND MANAGERIAL

THE MARKET FOR CORPORATE
CONTROL AND ITS IMPLICATIONS
FOR ACCOUNTING POLICY CHOICE

James E. Groff and Charlotte J. Wright

ABSTRACT

A number of accounting research studies have attempted to assess the role of
managerial economic incentives in the choice of accounting methods. This has
been seen as an important part of the effort to develop a positive theory of
accounting policy choice. The results of these studies have been mixed, possibly
because a market for managerial labor exists that serves to lessen the incentive
for managers to make apparently "self-serving" accounting policy choices. In this
study it is suggested that economic incentive-motivated choices are more likely
to occur in an environment in which the managerial labor market has become
inoperative. It is argued that firms that are subjected to the disciplining forces
of the market for corporate control (i.e., are subject to takeover attempts) are
ones in which the managerial labor market has failed and are thus more likely
to be ones that show evidence of self-serving accounting choices. The research
tests whether accounting policy choices, which have been identified as possibly

Advances in Accounting, Volume 7, pages 3-21.
Copyright © 1989 by JAI Press Inc.
All rights of reproduction in any form reserved.
ISBN: 0-89232-960-2

economic incentive motivated, occur more frequently in a sample of firms that has been the target of takeover attempts than in a nontarget sample. The results support the hypothesis that accounting policy choices are affected by the economic incentives of managers.

INTRODUCTION

As part of the continuing effort to develop a positive theory of accounting, agency theory, specifically economic incentives or self-serving manager perspective, has been widely used to explain accounting policy choice.[1] This perspective suggests that, when faced with a choice from among competing but equally acceptable accounting policies, self-serving managers, acting rationally, make choices that maximize their own wealth rather than the wealth of stockholders. The economic incentives perspective has been criticized by Fama [1980] for failing to consider the manager disciplining effects of the market for managerial labor. According to Fama, managers, although free of direct stockholder supervision, are indeed not entirely free to act in their own self-interest. There are multiple disciplining forces working from both inside and outside of the firm. From within the firm, managers are monitored by other managers. Poor performance will not go undetected and will eventually result in their being disciplined by upper management or replaced by managers from below. From outside the firm, the signals sent by stockholders in bidding the value of firms' securities upward or downward provide information to the market for managerial labor toward the assessment of firms' management, thus affecting the outside opportunity wage of managers.

Although Fama's criticism appears to be valid for the large majority of firms, he retains the possibility that circumstances may arise in which the managerial labor market may fail (i.e., an entrenched Board of Directors). Manne [1965], Jensen and Ruback [1983], and Dodd [1983], argue that when the managerial labor market fails as a disciplining mechanism the market for corporate control may serve to discipline managers. According to Manne, Jensen and Ruback, and Dodd, entrenched managers acting in their own self-interest will ultimately be disciplined by the threat of a corporate takeover. The purpose of this research is to explore the relationship between this market for corporate control and accounting policy choice.

Attempts to establish the economic incentives of managers as a motivation for accounting policy choice have been inconclusive. Given Fama's criticisms, it seems likely that one reason evidence of managerial economic incentives-motivated accounting policy choice has not been more convincing is the likelihood that the market for managerial labor is functioning (and thus the economic incentives of managers and stockholders coincide) in the majority of firms. However, in those firms in which the managerial labor market fails, managers would be more likely to behave in a manner in which the economic incentives for the managers to make a particular accounting policy choice would be evident (e.g., to make accounting policy choices that maximize managers' wealth at the expense of stockholders). In this research, it is assumed that the market for managerial labor has failed if a firm is subjected to the disciplining actions of the market for corporate control (e.g., is the target of a takeover attempt). If the managerial economic incentives hypothesis does help explain accounting policy choices, accounting policies that potentially increase the compensation of managers at the expense of stockholders would be more prevalent among this group of firms (takeover targets) than among those firms in which the managerial labor market is functioning effectively. Thus, the current research tests for the existence of self-serving manager-motivated accounting policy choices in a sample of firms in which it is most likely that the economic incentive motive is operating. This should provide a more powerful test of the managerial economic incentives hypothesis, as it relates to accounting policy choice, than have previous studies and, consequently, contribute to the development of a positive theory of accounting policy choice.

The next section of this paper includes a brief description of the managerial economic incentives perspective, the market for managerial labor, and the market for corporate control followed by a review of the results of a number of studies that have used this hypothesis to explain accounting policy choice. Next, hypotheses are developed and the research design is described. The results and conclusions are presented in the final section.

REVIEW OF THEORETICAL VIEWPOINTS

The economic incentives of self-serving management perspective of accounting policy choice has been particularly popular since Watts and Zimmerman [1978] suggested that a positive theory of the determination of accounting standards be developed. To develop such a theory it is necessary to know why firms choose accounting policies rather than what policies they "should" adopt. Agency theory as set out by Jensen and Meckling [1976] provides the basis for the economic incentives approach to accounting policy choice. The central tenent of this approach is that managers, as rational individuals, make choices that are consistent with the maximization of their own rather than stockholders' utility. Managers' utility is generally assumed to be a function of their compensation, which is broadly defined to include salary, bonuses, and perquisites they are able to extract as managers of the firm. Stockholders' utility is considered to be a function of firm stock price alone. Among the policy choices managers must make are accounting policy choices, a number of which present options involving possible conflicts between the interests of managers and those of stockholders. These conflicts arise when *different* accounting policy alternatives, all of which are in conformity with Generally Accepted Accounting Principles (GAAP), maximize the managers' and stockholders' utilities. In these situations the economic incentives perspective suggests that rational (self-serving) managers choose accounting policies that maximize their compensation at the expense of stockholder wealth (i.e., firm worth). Empirical tests involving a number of accounting policy choices that may lead to conflicts between the interests of managers and stockholders have been performed to determine whether evidence of rational choice behavior on the part of managers exist. Among the accounting choices included in these tests are inventory cost flow assumption [Hagerman and Zmijewski 1979; Zmijewski and Hagerman 1981; and Abdel-khalik 1984], depreciation method choice [Hagerman and Zmijewski 1979; Zmijewski and Hagerman 1981; and Dhaliwal et al. 1982], accounting for investment tax credits and pensions [Hagerman and Zmijewski 1979; and Zmijewski and Hagerman 1981], the decision to capitalize certain interest costs [Bowen et al. 1981], and the choice of full cost or successful efforts methods of accounting by oil and gas producing companies [Collins et al. 1981]. These are discussed in more detail in the next section. Although the results have been mixed, these studies provide some evidence that the economic incentives of managers influence accounting policy choices.

Fama [1980] severely criticizes the self-serving manager approach for failing to consider the manager disciplining effects of the market for managerial labor and the market for corporate control. According to Fama, in the presence of an efficient market for managerial labor, managers are constantly engaging in competition with other managers both within their organizations and in the broader market for managers. Managers are not motivated to maximize current period utility; rather they are motivated to maximize the present value of their future earnings stream by obtaining the highest possible market price for their services in the managerial labor market. Within the firm, managers who extract too many perquisites are replaced by lower level managers willing to be more productive. In addition, firms are willing to hire more productive managers from other firms to replace less productive managers within the organization. Consequently, when the managerial labor market is functioning, the most productive managers, although not necessarily having the highest current period levels of compensation, have the highest present value of future compensation. The Board of Directors of a firm, through its power to hire and replace managers, is the agent for ensuring that this market for managerial labor functions within a firm.

An efficient stock market plays a role in this scheme as the metric by which managerial performance is gauged. Productive managers who engage in relatively little shirking[2] are acting to increase the value of the firm and consequently stockholder utility. Because stock prices are a function of the value of the firm, firms with productive managers experience relatively higher security prices than do firms in which managers are less productive. Thus, the level of stock returns reflects the quality of management. Because managerial services are purchased on the basis of quality, managers can maximize their worth in the managerial labor market by maximizing stockholder wealth. When this managerial labor market is effective, managers have little or no incentive to enhance their near term wealth at the expense of stockholders because the resultant decline in the value of their present employer firm is reflected by a decline in their own worth in the market for managers.

However, under certain circumstances the managerial labor market may fail to function as a disciplining mechanism for managers. If managers effectively control the actions of the Board of Directors and therefore do not fear replacement by more productive managers, they may be in a position to increase their utility more by engaging in self-serving behavior than by improving their position in the managerial labor market. This would be particularly true of senior managers who are nearing retirement. With a relatively short stream of future earnings, the present value of that stream is heavily dominated by near-term compensation. These managers have little opportunity or incentive to attempt to increase their worth in the managerial labor market through the performance of the firm in which they are employed. Any increase in managerial utility resulting from increased shirking comes at the expense of the stockholders of the firm. When the managerial labor market fails, the disciplining mechanism invoked for managers in this situation is the market for corporate control.

Manne [1965], Jensen and Ruback [1983], and Dodd [1983] among others describe the market for corporate control as a market in which alternative managerial teams compete for the rights to manage corporate resources. In this market, which is an important complement to the internal and external managerial labor markets described by Fama [1980], agents use mergers, tender offers, and proxy fights to obtain control of publicly held corporations. These agents identify firms in which managers are pursuing private goals rather than the goals of their stockholders, creating an opportunity for the more efficiently managed firms to acquire the less efficiently managed firms and combine to form more efficient and profitable entities. Thus, increased efficiency and profitability is achieved by replacing managers engaged in self-serving behavior and reestablishing a functional managerial labor market within the takeover target firm. Even if the takeover attempt fails, the management of the target firm is disciplined by the takeover threat because their defense must involve substitution of stockholder interests for their private goals (the pursuit of which first led to the takeover attempt).

In this research it is assumed that both a managerial labor market and a market for corporate control exist and function essentially as described by Fama, Manne, Jensen and Ruback, and Dodd. Additionally, it is assumed that an attempt by a firm to acquire control of a target firm through an interfirm tender office is ex post evidence that the managerial labor market has failed to function for the target firm.[3] This implies that the managers of the target firm have engaged in self-serving behavior in the periods prior to the takeover attempt. Finally, for firms that have not been subjected to takeover attempts it is assumed that the managerial labor market is functioning effectively.

The managerial labor market and agency literature suggest that one important way in which managers shirk is through their choice of manager-benefiting accounting policies [Abdel-khalik 1981; Hagerman and Zmijewski 1979; and Bowen et al. 1981]. If this is true then firms in which managers are pursuing private goals at the expense of the stockholders (firms that were the object of takeover attempts) should be firms that most frequently adopt manager-benefiting accounting policies. It is this proposition that is tested.

At least three additional, competing theories explaining motivations underlying takeover activity can be found in the literature: synergy, tax factors, and market share [Weston and Chung 1983]. The synergy theory indicates that some takeovers are motivated by potential operating or financing efficiencies that can be achieved. Vertical and horizontal takeovers may involve economies of scale and/or more efficient coordination of resources. Financial synergies may accrue from altering cash flow streams or from altering the overall debt structure of the combined entity. Second, tax considerations may serve as the motivation for some takeovers. For example, a profitable firm may acquire a target firm with accumulated tax losses that can then be used to shelter earnings of the acquiring firm. Some takeovers may be attractive because they allow the acquiring firm to achieve a stepped-up basis for tax purposes on certain depreciable assets. The market share theory holds that takeovers are motivated by a firm's desire to increase firm size, decrease the number of competitors in the industry, and, thus, increase the firm's share of the market in which it operates. The presence of these competing motivations for corporate control should limit neither the methodology nor the applicability of the results of this research. None of these alternative explanations for takeover activity would seem to be systematically associated with accounting policy choice. Therefore, the inclusion in the test sample of target firms whose takeover attempts are motivated by synergy, tax, or market share considerations should mitigate against finding significant differences in the accounting policy choices between the target and the match firms used in this study.

ACCOUNTING POLICY CHOICES

The linkage between managers' utility and accounting policy choice is developed in detail by Watts and Zimmerman [1978]. The primary route by which managers can increase their wealth through the choice of accounting standards is through the interaction of those standards with the firm's management compensation plan. Management compensation is typically a function of accounting income either directly or through some return on investment measure. Any accounting policy choice that increases a firm's reported income increases management compensation, other things being equal. Because, in most cases,[4] these accounting choices do not have direct cash flow implications they do not, in and of themselves, directly affect the value of the firm. However, there are a number of ways in which accounting policy choices that are on the surface neutral in their impact on cash flows may indirectly affect the value of the firm. Examples that have been cited in the literature include the impact of accounting choices on the choice of investment strategy [Collins et al. 1981] and on the amount of political costs borne by a firm [Watts and Zimmerman 1978]. The increased compensation to managers arising from the nature of accounting-based compensation schemes, which decrease firm cash flows, is one of the indirect effects of accounting policy choice. Market agents in an efficent stock market see past accounting income numbers and respond to the lower cash flows by bidding down the value of the firm's stock. Because stockholder utility is entirely a function of the value of their stock the increased manager wealth accrues at the expense of the stockholders.

When managers are presented with alternative accounting policies, each of which is acceptable under GAAP, it would be anticipated that managers who are *not* subject to the disciplining mechanism of the market for managerial labor would choose the accounting alternative that increases reported accounting income. This is the manager-benefiting choice and is evidence, ceteris paribus, of self-serving management. A number of these accounting policy choices will be discussed.

Inventory Cost Flow Choice

The choice of inventory cost flow assumptions has been widely discussed in the accounting literature because it is one of the few accounting policy choices that has direct cash flow implications. It is widely recognized that in times of rising prices (the historical norm in the United States since World War II), a firm can reduce its current period net income by adopting Last-In-First-Out (LIFO) as an inventory cost flow assumption in lieu of First-In-First-Out (FIFO). This deferral of income recognition through the use of LIFO results in a deferral of the associated taxes and a corresponding increase in period cash flows. Under certain circumstances these taxes can be deferred indefinitely. However, unlike most accounting policy choices, the tax laws require firms adopting LIFO for tax purposes to also use the method for external financial reporting. Consequently, tax savings and associated increases in cash flows are traded for lower reported accounting net income (versus what would be reported under FIFO). Use of FIFO is manager benefiting because it results in higher reported net income than would be reported under LIFO. Thus, according to the research hypothesis, takeover target firms would more frequently use FIFO than nontakeover target firms. Interestingly, the use of FIFO carries a double penalty for the stockholders because they suffer reduced cash flows from both higher taxes and higher management compensation payments.

Depreciation Method Choice

The choice of depreciation method does not carry the direct cash flow effect of the inventory cost flow assumption choice. Firms need not use the same method for external reporting that is used in the computation of income taxes. Therefore, assuming net investment is nonnegative, straight line depreciation will result in higher reported income than any of the accelerated methods. Because the use of straight line depreciation is manager benefiting, takeover target firms are expected to use straight line depreciation for external financial reporting more frequently than nontakeover target firms.

Investment Tax Credit Choice

Two alternative investment tax credit treatments are available. Under the flow-through method, accounting income, in the period of the purchase of an eligible asset, is increased by the amount of the tax credit. Under the deferral method, the tax credit is spread out over the life of the asset generating the tax credit. Because the flow-through method results in higher current period income, essentially all firms use it. The primary support for the deferral method is theoretical. Revenues and expenses are, in theory, correctly matched when the deferral method is used. Hagerman and Zmijewski [1979] identify the flow-through method as the merger-benefiting choice because income in the initial period is higher. Because total income over the life of the asset is identical, total compensation would be the same, however, the present value of the compensation stream would be larger under the flow-through method. Consequently, it would be expected that takeover target firms would more frequently use the flow-through method than would nontakeover target firms.

Other Conflict Inducing Accounting Choices

Several other accounting policy choices have been studied from an economic benefits/self-serving manager perspective. These are the choice of a pension cost amortization period, the decision to capitalize certain interest costs, and the choice between successful efforts and full cost accounting by oil and gas producing companies.

Firms are allowed to choose an amortization period for past service costs of pensions of between 10 and 40 years. The longer the amortization period the higher the reported income and the higher management compensation. Therefore, the manager- benefiting choice is a relatively longer amortization period. Hagerman and Zmijewski [1979] define amortization periods longer than 30 years as manager benefiting and amortization periods of 30 years or less as stockholder benefiting and find some evidence of manager-benefiting choices.

The decision to capitalize interest associated with capital expenditures was studied by Bowen et al. [1981]. In their study they use the data concerning interest capitalization that were disclosed for 1974. Because capitalizing interest increases current period income, thus increasing the present value of managers' compensation stream, the decision to capitalize rather than expense the relevant interest costs was viewed as manager benefiting.

The successful efforts versus full cost choice involves only oil and gas producing companies. The full cost approach allows oil and gas producing firms to capitalize exploration costs and certain costs associated with unsuccessful projects (e.g., dryholes). These capitalized costs are subsequently expensed over future production from successful wells. Firms using the successful efforts method expense exploration costs and dryhole costs as incurred. Full costing is the manager-benefiting method because current period reported income is higher than it would be under successful efforts. Collins et al. [1981] also argue that full cost is manager benefiting because it reduces the amount of variability in managers' earning streams.

This research focuses on the inventory valuation method, depreciation method, and investment tax credit choices for the following reasons:

1. Data concerning those choices are available on the Compustat tapes.
2. The classification of those choices into manager/stockholder benefiting was relatively unambiguous. (The classification of pension costs amortization period that has been used previously seemed particularly arbitrary.)
3. The interest capitalization data were disclosed for only one year (1974) of the current research period and thus insufficient data were available for this study.
4. Only four oil and gas producing companies were identified as tender offer targets and, as such, included in our test sample.

Because the objective of this research is to determine whether takeover target firms made manager-benefiting choices more frequently than nontakeover target firms it is necessary to identify a set of choices that can be classified into manager and stockholder benefiting. The omission of the more ambiguous or less accessible policy choices should not bias the results.

HYPOTHESIS AND RESEARCH DESIGN

Research Hypothesis

In this research the frequency with which two samples of firms adopt manager-benefiting accounting policy choices is compared. The two samples include a test sample (firms that have been the target of a takeover attempt) and a control sample (firms that have not been the target of a takeover attempt). It is assumed that for those firms in the test sample the managerial labor market has failed and the disciplining action of the market for corporate control has been invoked. The managerial labor market is assumed to be functioning in the control (nontakeover) sample. The overall research hypothesis (stated as the alternative) is:

HYPOTHESIS 1.   Firms in the target sample more frequently chose manager-benefiting accounting policies than did firms in the match sample.

Because three separate accounting policy choices are being considered, this hypothesis has three subhypotheses:

HYPOTHESIS 1A.   Target sample firms chose the FIFO inventory cost flow assumption more frequently than did match sample firms.

HYPOTHESIS 1B.   Target sample firms chose straight line depreciation more frequently than did match sample firms.

HYPOTHESIS 1C.   Target sample firms chose the flow-through method for accounting for investment tax credits more frequently than did match sample firms.

Sample Selection

Manne [1965], Jensen and Ruback [1983], and Dodd [1983] argue that the market for corporate control is functioning when an effort is made by an outside party to wrest control from those managers currently in control. The main vehicle for accomplishing this are mergers, tender offers, and proxy fights. Mergers are negotiated with target managers and approved by the target's board of directors before being voted on by the target's stockholders. Tender offers are offers to purchase shares made directly to target stockholders. The target stockholders then decide whether or not to tender their shares to the bidding firm. Proxy fights occur when an insurgent group, often led by a dissatisfied manager or large stockholder, attempts to gain control of the board of directors [Jensen and Ruback 1983]. Mergers may be preceded by tender

Table 1.   Reconciliation of Takeover Target Firms with Test Sample

Firms Originally Identified as	
Takeover Targets	121
Firms Eliminated Because	
Not on COMPUSTAT	22
Lack an Appropriate Match	9
Reguated Utilities	9
Financial Institutions	2
Target (Test) Sample	79

offers or proxy fights. Additionally, the term "merger" is often used rather loosely to refer to any takeover bid.

Tender offers are used in this research to identify instances in which the market for corporate control has been invoked for a number of reasons. First, the tender offer is the only takeover mechanism in which the managers of the target firms are consistently *not* involved in initiating the takeover or in negotiating its terms. Second, the announcement of a tender offer most likely represents the initiation of takeover activity. Dodd and Ruback [1977] report that, in their sample of firms that were the targets of tender offers, 72% were subsequently merged with the initial bidder or a subsequent bidder within 5 years of the initial tender offer. Dodd and Ruback [1977] also confirm that the date of a tender offer, rather than the date of the initiation of a merger, is consistently the date of the capital market reaction. This is of importance because the managers of a target firm can make value-increasing changes in the operation of the target firm [Bradley 1980]. Thus, the use of mergers as a signal of the failure of the managerial labor market could result in the assessment of managerial accounting choices made *after* management had some time to alter their behavior. Although there is no perfect mechanism whereby "uninvited" or "hostile" takeover bids are identifiable, the interfirm tender offer appears to be the most logical choice for the current research.

Accordingly, takeover target firms are defined as firms in which a tender offer was made for more than 50% of the outstanding shares of the firm. By searching the weekly listings of tender offers in the *Investment Dealer's Digest,* 121 firms that were the subjects of takeover attempts through tender offers during the period January 1, 1975 through December 31, 1979 were identified. To be included in the final test sample a firm had to have data available on the Compustat tapes of the year *preceding* the takeover attempt. Financial firms do not generally report either inventories or investment tax credits, accordingly all financial firms were dropped from the test sample. Regulated utilities were also dropped because those firms may be required by their

Table 2. Size, Leverage, and Profitability Comparisons:
Target and March Firms (in Thousands)

	Mean	Standard Deviation	Minimum	Maximum
Target Firms				
Total Assets	312.6	505.3	10.9	3268.4
Sales	451.2	755.9	0.9	4309.6
Income	15.5	25.7	-24.6	170.4
Debt/Equity	0.54	0.41	0.15	2.74
ROI	0.11	0.09	-0.21	0.44
Match Firms				
Total Assets	432.3	676.6	3.0	3233.5
Sales	524.7	722.1	5.0	3200.7
Income	24.2	34.1	-5.7	137.7
Debt/Equity	0.55	0.58	0.0	3.54
ROI	0.10	0.14	-0.8	0.35

regulatory authorities to use specific accounting methods. The final test sample included 79 of the original 121 target firms. Table 1 provides a reconciliation of the set of target firms.

A number of factors were taken into consideration in determining the selection criteria for firms in the control group. Watts and Zimmerman [1978] argue that the income effects of managements' choice of accounting methods are related to firm size. Hagerman and Zmijewski [1979], Bowen et al. [1981], and Zmijewski and Hagerman [1981] all find some empirical support for this hypothesized relationship. Dhaliwal [1980] argues that financial leverage and accounting methods are related. Evidence to support this argument was also reported by Deakin [1979], Leftwich [1981], and Holthausen [1981]. Capital intensity [Hagerman and Zmijewski 1979] and rate of return [Dhaliwal 1980] may also be related to managements' choice of accounting methods. Also an industry bias in the choice of accounting policies seems logical.

Accordingly, the match firms for the control group were identified as follows. First, all firms in the same industry as the target firm were identified based on their four digit SIC code. Means and standard deviations for total assets and average debt-to-equity were computed, by industry, over the test period. Potential matches were selected by identifying the industry member with the minimum sum of absolute standard deviations from the target firm's total assets and debt-to-equity. Because of the nature of the question being addressed it appears to be necessary to ensure that the control sample firms were not being disciplined by the market for corporate control; therefore the requirement was invoked that control firms could not have been the target of a takeover attempt for the period of five years subsequent to the takeover attempt relative to their

Table 3.   Size, Profitability, and Leverage Distributions:
Mann-Whitney U Test

	Mean Rank	U Statistic	Z Score	p > Z
Total Assets				
Target Firms	79.23			
Match Firms	79.77	6301.5	0.0713	0.9432
Sales				
Target Firms	77.33			
Match Firms	81.67	6452.0	0.5946	0.5521
Income				
Target Firms	75.89			
Match Firms	83.11	6565.5	0.9893	0.3225
Debt-to-Equity				
Target Firms	83.19			
Match Firms	75.81	5989.0	-1.0120	0.3116
Return on Investment				
Target Firms	75.76			
Match Firms	83.24	6576.0	1.0259	0.3050

test sample partners. Thus, if a potential match was identified as being a takeover target in the relevant evaluation period, it was dropped and the next closest match was selected. Summary statistics for the target and match samples are given in Table 2. The Mann-Whitney U test was used to test the null hypothesis that there was no dfference in total assets, sales, income, debt-to-equity, and return on investment distributions of the target and match group firms. These results are reported in Table 3.

Managerial Compensation Plans

Intuitively, it seems appealing to identify the target firms that actually had earnings-based managerial compensation plans in place prior to the takeover attempt.[5] Two characteristics of this study (the research period and the nature of the target firms) proved to be obstacles to obtaining such information. SEC 10K reports and proxy statements are the primary sources of information regarding compensation plans. Searches (both by hand and computerized), however, yielded incomplete data for periods preceding 1980. Collins et al. [1981] encountered similar difficulties and report mailing questionnaires to firms in their sample. This alternative was also ineffective because the majority of target firms in the sample were, indeed, taken over by other firms either during or after the test period.

A thorough evaluation of the literature indicates that information regarding managerial compensation plans of the target firms, although desirable, is not critical to this study. Gagnon [1967] and Williamson [1967] establish that managers, maximizing their own utility, will attempt to maximize nonmonetary as well as monetary compensation. Nonmonetary compensation results when managers are able to enhance their "security" and "reputation for excellence" by reporting higher profits. Thus, nonmonetary compensation schemes apparently exist but are not specifically identifiable. As for monetary compensation plans, Fox [1980] reports that 90% of the 1000 largest U.S. manufacturing firms use earnings-based bonus plans to remunerate management. Collins et al. [1981] report that the presence of earnings-based managerial compensation plans and firm size are significantly positively related (an observation supported by the findings of Dhaliwal et al. [1982] and Healy [1985]).

Thus, there appears to be no reason to believe that there would be any systematic difference in the compensation plans of the managers of the firms in the target and match samples. First, the nonmonetary compensation motivations of the managers should not differ. Second, because the presence of monetary compensation plans is significantly related to firm size, and Table 3 reveals that there is no statistical difference in the size of the target and the match firms, then it appears to follow that there should be no difference in the monetary compensation motives of the managers of the firms in the two groups. Thus, information regarding the compensation plans of the management of the target firms should not affect the interpretation of the results of this study.[6]

Accounting Method Data

Accounting policy choice data for each firm for each of the three accounting policies selected was obtained from the Compustat tapes. Because it is possible for managers to alter their accounting choices in the year of a takeover attempt, the accounting method data for both the target firm and its match sample partner were obtained for the year preceding the takeover attempt. Not every firm reported all three of the accounting policy choices considered.

Probit Analysis of the Relationship between
Accounting Choices and Firm Type

The research hypotheses are concerned with the frequency with which the two groups of firms made certain accounting choices. To test this a multivariate probit analysis was performed for each of three accounting choices. Multivariative probit analysis is appropriate in those situations in which the dependent variable is dichotomous (i.e., 0 or 1). The value of the dependent variable is predicted based on the probability that the dependent variable will take a 0 or 1 value given the values of the independent variables, $X_1, \ldots,$ X_k. Procedurally, Z_i is computed as a linear function of the independent variables,

$$Z_i = B_o + B_1 X_{1i} + \ldots + B_k X_{ki}$$

Z_i is assumed to be a continuous variable that is random and normally distributed and is estimated using a maximum likelihood technique.

In this study, the probit analysis was repeated three times with the dependent variable being defined as (1) the inventory method, (2) the depreciation method, and (3) the investment tax credit method adopted by the firms. The model used was defined as

$$Z_i = B_o + B_1 X_{1i} + B_2 X_{2i} + B_3 X_{3i} + B_4 X_{4i}$$

where Z_i is the accounting choice variable, X_{1i} is the total asset value for firm i, X_{2i} is the debt-to-equity ratio of firm i, X_{3i} is the return on investment for firm i, and X_{4i} is the firm type (either target or match) for firm i.[7]

RESULTS AND CONCLUSIONS

The first accounting choice studied was inventory method. Compustat lists a series of inventory valuation methods in the order of the relative amounts of inventory valued by each method. The classification rule adopted for firms reporting more than one method was to select the first method reported. The methods were first classified as being either FIFO, LIFO, or "other." Probit analysis requires that only one of two values can be assigned to the dependent variable, therefore it was necessary to identify the other methods as being either FIFO-like or LIFO-like. Because applying the "other" methods generally results in costs being higher than FIFO but lower than LIFO, there is no obvious method for making a dichotomous designation. However, for this research, combining the "other" methods and LIFO in a single category should decrease the likelihood that $\mathbf{H1_o}$ would be rejected (and Hypothesis 1A accepted).

Accordingly, the probit analysis was conducted using the inventory method adopted by a firm as the dependent variable for which a value of 1 had been assigned if the firm used FIFO and 0 if the firm used LIFO or any other method. The firm type variable was assigned a value of 1 if it was in the target group and a value of 0 if it was in the match group. The probit analysis results are presented in Table 4. These results are consistent with the hypothesis that the target firms chose the FIFO inventory cost flow method more frequently than

Table 4. Probit Analysis Results: Inventory Cost Flow Method[a]

Variable	Parameter Estimate	T Statistic
Constant	-1.1087	-4.20[b]
Total Assets	-0.0021	-1.09
Debt-to-Equity	0.6733	2.62[b]
Return on Investment	0.1939	0.20
Firm Type	0.4596	2.06[c]
(Target = 1, Match = 0)		

[a]Dependent variable: 1 = FIFO;   0 = all other methods.
[b]Significant at an α level of 0.01.
[c]Significant at an α level of 0.02.

Table 5. Probit Analysis Results: Depreciation Method Choice[a]

Variable	Parameter Estimate	T Statistic
Constant	0.3493	0.79
Total Assets	-0.2751	-1.50
Debt-to-Equity	1.1506	2.27[b]
Return on Investment	-1.2547	-0.48
Firm Type	1.1262	2.90[b]
(Target = 1, Match = 0)		

[a]Dependent variable: 1 = straight line; 0 = accelerated.
[b]Significant at an α level of 0.01.

the match sample firms. The firm type variable is positive and significant at an α level of 0.02. Interestingly, the significance of the debt-to-equity variable indicates that leverage also plays a role in the selection of inventory cost flow methods. (A factor that is notably controlled for in the multivariate probit analysis.)

The second accounting choice tested was depreciation method. Compustat uses three classifications for depreciation method: straight line only, accelerated only, and a combination of the two. Unlike the inventory choice in which the Compustat classification gives some clue as to the relative frequency of the method used, for depreciation method any mention of both methods results in the classification of "combination." Because it is impossible to make a distinction as to whether the choice of a combination of methods is more like straight line or accelerated and because probit analysis requires only two categories, this analysis was restricted to companies using only the straight line or accelerated method and their match partners. This restricted the total to 51 target firms and their match group partners. Table 5 presents the results of the probit analysis. Once again, the results are consistent with the alternative

Table 6. Probit Analysis Results: Investment Tax Credit Method Choice[a]

Variable	Parameter Estimate	T Statistic
Constant	1.1969	3.83[b]
Total Assets	-0.0022	-0.08
Debt-to-Equity	-0.2441	-0.98
Return on Investment	1.5429	1.09
Firm Type	0.6091	2.14[c]
(Target = 1, Match = 0)		

[a]Dependent variable: 1 = flow through; 0 = deferred.
[b]Significant at an α level of 0.01.
[c]Significant at an α level of 0.016.

hypothesis that target firms chose the straight line depreciation method more frequently than the match sample firms. The firm type variable is, once again, positive and significant at an α level of 0.01. Once again, the significance of the debt-to-equity variable indicates that leverage also plays a role in the selection of depreciation method.

The classification of investment tax credit treatment is unambiguous because there are only two choices, flow-through and deferral. The probit analysis results reported in Table 6 also support the alternative hypothesis that target firms are more likely to make the income-increasing choice than are match firms. The firm type variable is, once again, positive and significant at an α level of 0.016.

CONCLUSIONS

Using a matching approach and multivariate probit analysis, takeover target firms more frequently chose income-increasing accounting policies than did a matched sample of nontakeover target firms. These results provide support for the managerial economic incentives hypothesis as a motivation for accounting policy choice. This proposition is conditioned on the assumption that the market for corporate control functions as outlined by Manne [1965], Jensen and Ruback [1983], and Dodd [1983] and that firms in the test (target) sample are being subjected to the disciplining action of that market whereas the control (nontarget) sample firms are not. Those results are consistent with a number of earlier studies such as Hagerman and Zmijewski [1979] and Zmijewski and Hagerman [1981], which also found support for the managerial economic incentives hypothesis in accounting choices.

ACKNOWLEDGMENTS

The authors wish to thank the participants in the Oklahoma State University and University of Arkansas accounting workshops for their helpful comments. We particularly wish to thank the two anonymous reviewers whose comments contributed greatly to this paper. Of course, responsibility for any errors that may remain rest solely with the authors.

NOTES

1. The economic incentives perspective is most completely developed in Jensen and Meckling [1976] and its application to accounting theory is developed in Watts and Zimmerman [1978]. Holthausen and Leftwich [1983] survey a number of studies using this approach.

2. Shirking is any firm-related action by a manager that increases his/her compensation (broadly defined) without simultaneously increasing the value of the firm.

3. Manne [1965], in his seminal article, concludes that interfirm tender offers provide evidence that target firms are being suboptimally managed. The current use of tender offers is elaborated in greater detail in a future section of this paper.

4. The FIFO/LIFO choice is an exception that will be discussed.

5. Searches of SEC 10K reports, proxy statements, and the annual compensation survey published by *Business Week* yielded data indicating that 74 of the 79 firms in the match group did have earnings-based managerial compensation plans in place during the posttest period.

6. It should also be noted that the knowledge that the vast majority of the match firms did have earnings-based managerial compensation plans is actually more critical to the interpretation of the results of this study than is similar information regarding the target firms.

7. A chi-squared analysis was also performed on the data. The results were similar with the null hypotheses, each being rejected at an α level of <0.02. The results of the probit analysis are reported because the method explicitly controls for other firm characteristics, specifically, size, leverage, and profitability.

REFERENCES

Abdel-khalik, A. R., "Executives Pay and Accounting Income: The Effect of LIFO-Switching and Firm Ownership," Unpublished Working Paper [University of Illinois, 1984].

Benston, G. J., "The Self-Serving Management Hypothesis: Some Evidence," *Journal of Accounting and Economics* [April 1985], pp. 67-84.

Bowen, R. M., E. W. Noreen, and J. M. Lacey, "Determinants of the Corporate Decision to Capitalize Interest," *Journal of Accounting and Economics* [August 1981], pp. 151-179.

Bradley, M., "Interfirm Tender Offers and the Market for Corporate Control," *Journal of Business* [October 1980], pp. 345-376.

Collins, D. W., M. Rozeff and D. S. Dhaliwal, "The Economic Determinants of the Market Reaction to Proposed Mandatory Accounting Changes in the Oil and Gas Industry: A Cross-Sectional Analysis," *Journal of Accounting and Economics* [March 1981], pp. 37-71.

Deakin, E. B., "An Analysis of Differences between Non-major Oil Firms Using Successful Efforts and Full Cost Methods," *The Accounting Review* [October 1979], pp. 722-734.

Dhaliwal, D. S., G. Salamon and E. D. Smith, "The Effects of Owner vs Management Control on the Choice of Accounting Methods," *Journal of Accounting and Economics* [July 1982], pp. 78-84.

Dann, L. Y. and H. DeAngelo, "Standstill Agreements, Privately Negotiated Stock Repurchases, and the Market for Corporate Control," *Journal of Financial Economics* [April 1983], pp. 342-371.

Dodd, P., "The Market for Corporate Control: A Review of the Evidence," Unpublished Working Paper, Australian Graduate School of Management [August 1983].

Dodd, P. and R. Ruback, "Tender Offers and Stockholder Returns," *Journal of Financial Economics* [May 1977], pp. 351-373.

Fama, E., "Agency Problems and the Theory of the Firm," *Journal of Political Economy* [April 1980], pp. 288-307.

Fox, H., *Top Executive Compensation* [The Conference Board, New York, 1980].

Gagnon, J.-M., "Purchase Versus Pooling of Interests: The Search for a Predictor," *Journal of Accounting Research. Empirical Studies in Accounting: Selected Studies* [Supplement 1967], pp. 187-204.

Hagerman, R. L. and M. E. Zmijewski, "Some Economic Determinants of Accounting Policy Choice, *Journal of Accounting and Economics* [August 1979], pp. 141-161.

Healy, P. M., "The Effect of Bonus Schemes on Accounting Decisions," *Journal of Accounting and Economics* [April 1985], pp. 85-108.

Healy, P. M., S.-H. Kang and D. G. Palepu, "The Effects of Accounting Procedure Changes on CEOs' Cash Salary and Bonus Compensation," *Journal of Accounting and Economics* [August 1987], pp. 7-34.

Holthausen, R. W., "Evidence on the Effect of Bond Covenants and Management Compensation Contracts on the Choice of Accounting Techniques: The Case of Depreciation Switch-back," *Journal of Accounting and Economics* [March 1981], pp. 73-109.

Holthausen, R. W. and R. W. Leftwich, "The Economic Consequences of Accounting Choice: Implications of Costly Contracting and Monitoring," *Journal of Accounting and Economics* [August 1983], pp. 77-117.

Jensen, M. C., "Takeovers: Folklore and Science," *Harvard Business Review* [November-December 1984], pp. 109-121.

Jensen, M. C. and W. J. Meckling, "Theory of the Firm: Managerial Behavior, Agency Costs and Capital Structure," *Journal of Financial Economics* [September 1976], pp. 305-360.

Jensen, M.C. and R.S. Ruback, "The Market for Corporate Control: The Scientific Evidence," *Journal of Financial Economics* [April 1983], pp. 7-50.

Leftwich, R. W., "Evidence of the Impact of Mandatory Changes in Accounting Principles on Corporate Loan Agreements," *Journal of Accounting and Economics* [March 1981], pp. 3-36.

Linn, S. C. and J. J. McConnell, "An Empirical Investigation of the Impact of 'Antitakeover' Amendments on Common Stock Prices," *Journal of Financial Economics* [April 1983], pp. 361-399.

Manne, H.G., "Mergers and the Market for Corporate Control," *Journal of Political Economy* [April 1965], pp. 110-120.

Murphy, K. J., "Corporate Performance and Managerial Remuneration: An Empirical Analysis," *Journal of Accounting and Economics* [April 1985], pp. 11-42.

Watts, R. L. and J. L. Zimmerman, "Toward a Positive Theory of the Determination of Accounting Standards," *Accounting Review* [January 1978], pp. 112-134.

Weston, J. F. and K. S. Chung, "Do Mergers Make Money?" *Mergers and Acquisitions* [Fall 1983], pp. 40-67.

Williamson, O. E., *Prices: Issues in Theory, Practice, and Public Policy* [University of Pennsylvania Press 1967], pp. 11-31.

Zimmerman, J. L., "Taxes and Firm Size," *Journal of Accounting and Economics* [August 1983], pp. 119-149.

Zmijewski, M. E. and R. L. Hagerman, "An Income Strategy Approach to the Positive Theory of Accounting Standard Setting/Choice," *Journal of Accounting and Economics* [August 1981], pp. 129-149.

THE IMPACT OF
THE ACCOUNTING TREATMENT
OF LEASING CONTRACTS
ON USER DECISION MAKING:
A FIELD EXPERIMENT

Bart P. Hartman and Heibatollah Sami

ABSTRACT

Because the acceptability and use of differential accounting methods have been
subject to increasing criticisms, the accounting profession has attempted to define
more precisely the circumstances in which a particular alternative would be
acceptable. SFAS No. 13 is an example of the attempts to define and clarify
the conditions for treatment of long-term leases as capital or operating. This paper
reports the results of a field experiment designed to determine the effects of
differential lease-accounting methods on commercial loan officers' decisions
about the credit standing and interest rates assigned to a company. The results
indicate that the accounting treatment of lease contracts had a signficiant impact
on the interest rate charged and the assessed credit rating of the company.

Advances in Accounting, Volume 7, pages 23-35.
Copyright © 1989 by JAI Press Inc.
All rights of reproduction in any form reserved.
ISBN: 0-89232-960-2

23

INTRODUCTION

As criticism directed at the acceptability and use of differential accounting methods has increased, the accounting profession has attempted to define more precisely the circumstances in which a particular alternative would be acceptable. Statement of Financial Accounting Standards (SFAS) No. 13 [FASB 1976] attempts to define and clarify the conditions for use of the alternative accounting treatments for reporting leases. The purpose of this research was to investigate the effect of differential lease-accounting methods on loan officers' decisions about the creditworthiness of a company. Operationally, we focus on the effect of the accounting treatment on judgments about the interest rates that would be charged and credit ratings assigned to loan applicants.

The results of the study indicate that the accounting treatment of lease contracts had a significant impact on these loan officers' decisions. The interest rates charged on the loans were higher in instances in which lease information was reported by the capital lease accounting method than the operating lease method or for a control group with no leases. Similar results were obtained regarding credit ratings. The implication of these findings is that credit might be more costly to companies that capitalize their long-term lease contracts, thus, making it beneficial for companies to have lease contracts written in a manner that would qualify as operating leases.

The influence of the magnitude of the lease commitments was also investigated. The results indicated that the degree of reliance or lease financing did not have a significant effect on either the interest rate charged or the credit rating assigned within the levels of manipulation in this study.

Purpose of the Research

It has been argued that even if the economic reality of a company's condition does not change, the capitalization of lease contracts under SFAS No. 13 may cause the deterioration of the credit rating of the company within the debt market. Consequently, the company might prefer to avoid, where possible, capitalization of lease contracts. One avenue available to management is the packaging of the lease contract such that it could be accounted for as an operating lease [see Dieter 1979; Dieter and Wyatt 1980; Ferrara et al. 1980; and Abdel-Khalik et al. 1981, Ch.5]. On the other hand, if loan officers are sophisticated and fully understand a firm's financial reports with attendent lease footnotes, the accounting treatment of the lease contract should not matter. Whether the lease is capitalized or treated as an operating lease would not make a significant difference in credit rating as long as the users recognize comparable underlying economic conditions.

Whether the change in some financial ratios resulting from the treatment of the lease as capital versus operating would actually result in alteration of the credit standing of the company or whether the users are able to distinguish form from substance has not been resolved. This is the motivating question of this research.

Related Literature

Simply stated, the controversy is whether payments under all long-term leases should be capitalized or whether selective treatment is appropriate. Proponents of universal capitalization include Vatter [1966], Huefner [1970], Wyatt [1974], and Hendricksen [1982]. Their arguments suggest that a lease is a complete transaction resulting in economic resources and liabilities. Opponents of universal capitalization of all leases, such as Zises [1961], argue that disclosure of the lease terms provides sufficient information to financial statement users.

Financial Accounting Standards Board (FASB) favors capitalization of only those leases that transfer substantially all ownership risks to the lessee as stated in SFAS 13 [FASB 1976, para. 60]:

> The provisions of this Statement derive from the view that a lease that transfers substantially all of the benefits and risks incident to the ownership of property should be accounted for as the acquisition of an asset and the incurrence of an obligation by the lessee and as a sale or financing by the lessor. All other leases should be accounted for as operating leases. In a lease that transfers substantially all of the benefits and risks of ownership, the economic effect on the parties is similar, in many respects, to that of an installment purchase.

Palmon and Kwatinetz [1980] argue that these criteria are so vague and subject to interpretation as to invite manipulation.

Nelson [1963] conducted a case study to determine the effect of capitalization. He found a significant negative change in the ranking of the companies' performance after capitalization compared to their ranking before capitalization. Studies by May et al. [1978] and Ro [1978] investigated the effect of the lease disclosure requirements on the structure of security prices. Both studies revealed an anticipatory price adjustment over the 12 months prior to the release of information to the public. Abdel-Khalik et al. [1978] suggested the possibility of smaller risk premiums for those companies able to keep leases off their balance sheet. Two other studies found a significant relationship between capital leases and the market risk of lessees [Bowman 1980], and a nonsignificant effect of ASR 147 and the FASB capitalization requirements on the market-determined systematic risk of companies [Finnertz and Fitzsimmons 1980].

Abdel-Khalik et al. [1981] conducted a comprehensive study to determine the economic effects of SFAS No. 13. The results indicate that a majority of companies were structuring the terms of new lease contracts to avoid capitalization. The results also disclosed an apparent conflict between what some financial analysts and bankers said they did and what they actually might have done when considering lease disclosures. Most respondents reported that they did not downgrade their evaluation of companies that capitalized leases. However, when asked to evaluate financial statements of companies that differed only in the method of accounting for leases, a large number evaluated companies that did not capitalize leases as superior to companies that did capitalize leases.

Contradicting evidence also is available however. Wilkins and Zimmer [1983] conducted a field study of 52 loan officers from 35 international banks in Singapore. The results of their study indicated no significant differences to develop in subjects' decisions in relation to different methods of accounting for leases (capitalized vs operating). This contradictory evidence supports the need for further inquiry and reconciliation of differences.

METHODOLOGY

The research questions addressed in this study concerned the impact of the accounting treatment of long-term lease contracts on bank loan officers' judgments about interest rates and credit rating. A field experiment was chosen to investigate these questions because it provided an opportunity to manipulate the independent variables in a setting close to a real world situation.

The Research Instrument

A hypothetical set of financial statements including the audit report was developed from actual financial statements. This data set included detailed information for the 2 prior years of operation and a summary of the 5 prior years. For purposes of control, one set of financial statements did not include any lease transactions. To establish experimental treatments, this original set of financial statements was then modified to include one of the following:

1.   substantial lease contracts accounted as capital leases,
2.   substantial lease contracts accounted as operating leases,
3.   moderate lease contracts accounted as capital leases, or
4.   moderate lease contracts accounted as operating leases.

Thus, there were five sets of financial statements: the original set, two sets with substantial lease contracts, and two sets with moderate lease contracts.

The operational definition used for "substantial lease contracts" was that the capitalized present value of the lease contracts for the company approximated 50% of total debt after capitalization of the lease contracts. The operational definition of "moderate lease contracts" was that the capitalized present value of the lease contracts for the company approximated 15% of total debt after capitalizing the lease contracts. The percentages of 15 and 50 were chosen after a review of *Accounting Trends and Techniques,* which revealed a 3-61% range with an average of 24.63%. The instruments were pretested by a sample of bank loan officers and accounting faculty. The pretest results provided the basis for preparing the final draft of the instruments.[1]

The Research Design and Sample

The research design was a randomized control group posttest only. This design was chosen instead of a randomized control group pretest-posttest design because the pretest-posttest is difficult to execute in a field experiment, is uneconomical, and may result in an interaction of the treatment with the pretest.

A random sample of 500 bankers was selected from the Robert Morris Associates membership listing. The sample was randomly divided into one control and four experimental groups of 100 each.

Group 1, the control group, received financial statements with no leases at all. Groups 2 and 3 received financial statements that contained capitalized leases, with Group 2 having moderate (15% of total debt) lease commitment and Group 3 having a substantial (50% of total debt) amount of lease commitment. Groups 4 and 5 received the financial statements that contained operating leases with Group 4 receiving the moderate manipulation and Group 5 receiving the substantial manipulation.

The five sets of financial statements differed only with respect to the effects of the lease contracts. That is, the financial statements of Groups 2 and 3 had much higher debt/equity ratios than Groups 1, 4, and 5 because of the capitalized leases. Further, Group 3's debt/equity ratio was higher than that of Group 2. The changes in working capital were also quite different between the groups because of the existence and treatment of the leases in the financial statements.

If the bank loan officers properly use the available lease information, there should be no difference in the interest rates and credit ratings between Groups 2 and 4 and Groups 3 and 5. Groups 2 and 4 both contain moderate amounts of lease contracts, and are economically the same, whereas Groups 3 and 5 both contain substantial amounts of lease contracts and are economically the same. If, on the other hand, the users are not using all available accounting data, or are not using it properly, there may be significant differences.

Finally, the control group with no lease contracts was used to test whether the lease information was used at all. If it was used properly, there should be differences in results between the control group and all the other groups in regard to interest rate and credit rating. That is, an overall comparison should yield differences between the control group and the others.

The Experiment

Participants were randomly assigned to the control group or to one of the four treatment groups. Each participant received one of the five sets of financial statements. Each was asked to assume that 12% was the most current prime interest rate. They also were asked to determine the interest rate they would charge on a two million dollar, 2-year working capital loan to the hypothetical company.[2] In addition, the subjects were asked to rate the credit standing of the company on a nine-point scale corresponding to Moody's Bond Ratings (1 indicating C, the lowest rated class; 9 indicating Aaa, the best quality). As a reliability check the subjects were also asked to estimate the maximum dollar amount of a 2-year loan that they would approve for the hypothetical company at the prime rate.[3] Finally, the subjects were asked to indicate their banks' normal compensating balance requirements, the required compensating balance on the requested loan, and some demographic characteristics.[4]

The Sample

The instruments were mailed to a random example of 500 loan officers.[5] From the 104 responses received (20.8% reponse rate) 90 of them were usable (18% were usable response rate). From the 90 usable responses, 20 were from Group 1, 19 were from each of Groups 2 and 3, and 16 were from each of Groups 4 and 5. Ten responses were eliminated as the result of significant discrepancies in the reliability check (see note 3), and four others were incomplete. The demographic characteristics of the respondents are shown in Table 1.

Variable Definitions

The independent variables in the study were the accounting treatment of leases and the magnitude of the lease contract. The dependent variables were the required interest rate to be charged on a $2 million dollar, 2-year loan and the credit rating of the company.

Hypothesis Tested

Given identical lease terms, the effect of the lease contract should be the same whether it is treated as a capital or an operating lease. However, the credit standing of the company might vary as a result of unsophisticated or impaired financial statement analysis because capital leases appear in the body of the financial statements whereas operating leases appear only in the footnotes.

Table 1.   Respondent's Demographic Characteristics

Description	Number
Position	
Vice President (Credit and Loan Areas)	26
Executive Vice President	4
Senior Vice President	6
Vice President	16
Assistant Vice President (Credit and Loan Areas)	5
Credit Analyst	6
Credit and Loan Manager	6
Commercial Loan Officer	6
Others	15
Degree and Major	
Masters	30
Bachelors	44
High School	4
None	2
Years of Experience	
Average	11.21
Range	1-41
Loan Applications Evaluated per Month	
Average	29.4
Range	1-120
Dollar Amount of Loan Applications Evaluated	
Average	1.635mm[a]
Range	0.01mm-20.00mm
Percentages of Loans Evaluated	
Personal Loans	
Average	14.47
Range	0-90
Corporate Loans	
Average	85.53
Range	10-100
Time Spent to Respond (Minutes)	
Average	26.17
Range	10-70

[a]mm = million.

The first hypothesis was designed to test the overall experimental manipulation of the independent variables. The mean responses of each group were compared wtih each other and tested for differences. Thus,

HYPOTHESIS 1.   There are no significant differences in the interest rate or credit rating attributable to the amount, type, or existence of lease contracts in the financial statements.

Failure to reject this first hypothesis would point to weakness in the experimental manipulation of the independent variables, or to the fact that there really are no differences.

ANALYSIS AND THE RESULTS

The overall data were analyzed using Multivariate and Univariate Analysis of Variance (MANOVA and ANOVA), and orthogonal and nonorthogonal contrasts between calls.

The means and standard deviations of interest rate and loan amount for all groups are presented in Table 2. This table shows that the interest rate was higher for Groups 2 and 3 (the groups that received the capitalized lease information) as compared to Groups 1, 4, and 5 (the control group and the groups that received the operating lease information). Further, the credit rating is lower for Groups 2 and 3 as compared to those of Groups 1, 4, and 5. But the means of the interest rate and credit rating are fairly close for Groups 1, 4, and 5. These results indicate that on the average, the credit rating is lower and the cost of borrowing additional needed capital is higher for Groups 2 and 3 as compared to Groups 1, 4, and 5. To test for significance, an overall MANOVA analysis was conducted.

The overall MANOVA analysis based on Wilk's criterion indicated an F value of 3.77 that was significant at the 0.0004 level. This means that when both variables, interest rate and credit rating, are considered simultaneously, there is a significant difference among groups regarding either one of the two variables or both variables combined. Therefore, the responses were further analyzed through a completely randomized, one-factor design ANOVA,[6] the results of which are shown in Table 3. This table indicates a significant overall difference between the responses of the different groups with respect to both dependent variables. Based on these results, Hypothesis 1 was rejected, which indicated that the experimental manipulation of the independent variables was strong enough to observe significant differences in responses.

Having rejected Hypothesis 1, it becomes important to determine whether the influence of the accounting treatment prevails across leases of both high and low magnitude. The results of orthogonal and nonorthogonal contrasts are shown in Table 4. Orthogonal contrast 1 compared the control group to all other groups and found a significant difference for credit rating but not interest rates. Orthogonal contrast 2 compared Groups 2 and 3 (capitalized

Table 2.   Means and Standard Deviations for Interest Rate and Credit Rating

	Group 1	Group 2	Group 3	Group 4	Group 5
Interest Rate					
Means	12.697	13.026	13.382	12.609	12.375
Standard Deviations	0.593	1.017	1.278	0.652	0.508
Credit Rating					
Means	6.250	5.278	4.778	6.313	6.228
Standard Deviations	0.967	1.364	0.732	1.250	1.630

Table 3.   ANOVA Summary with Interest Rate and Credit Rating
as Dependent Variables

Source	df	SS	MS	F	p Value
Interest Rate					
Between Groups	4	10.93	2.73		
Error (within groups)	84	64.60	0.77	3.55	0.0100
Total	88	75.53			
Credit Rating					
Between groups	4	35.68	8.92	6.08	0.0002
Error (within groups)	83	121.75	1.47		
Total	87	157.43			

Table 4.   Orthogonal and Nonorthogonal Contracts

	Orthogonal				Nonorthogonal	
	1	2	3	4	5	6
Interest Rate	0.639	11.437[a]	1.5463	0.569	1.961	11.438[a]
Credit Rating	4.082[a]	18.670[a]	1.531	0.033	6.172[a]	13.139[a]

[a] Significant at $\alpha = 0.05$ or less.

lease groups) with Groups 4 and 5 (operating lease groups) and found significant differences in both credit rating and interest rates. No significant differences were found in orthogonal contrasts 3 and 4 that compared the two levels of the same type of lease contracts (15% capital to 50% capital, and 15% operating to 50% operating).

Nonorthogonal contrast 5 compared the 15% operating lease with the 15% capital lease. A significant difference with regard to credit rating was found but not for interest rate. Nonorthogonal contrast 6 compared the 50% operating lease with the 50% capital lease. The results indicated significant differences for both credit rating and interest rate.

CONCLUSIONS AND IMPLICATIONS

A summary of the results is shown in Table 5. The results indicate that different accounting methods for lease contracts make a significant difference in the credit standing of a company as measured by the interest rate on a $2 million, 2-year working capital loan and the credit rating of that company. This difference in the case of capitalization of lease contracts would apparently cause an increase in debt costs as compared to operating leases. These results are consistent with the results of the study by Abdel-Khalik et al. [1978, 1981] but contradict the results of the study by Wilkins and Zimmer [1983].

The Wilkins and Zimmer (WZ) study had several methodological and analytical differences from the present study. The WZ study was a repeated measures design in which each subject was asked to evaluate four loan applications. To deal with the confounding effect of order, all possible sets should have been presented (24 in their experiment) or the order of presentation should have been randomized [15, p. 194], but the researchers did neither. In our experiment, each subject evaluated only one loan application, so there was no possibility of ordering bias from repeated measures.

A second difference between the two studies was in the decision the subjects were asked to make. In the WZ study, the respondents were asked to indicate the maximum amount they would lend to each company. The responses to this question depend on several factors including the term of the loan and the interest rate to be charged, neither of which was included in the research instrument.

A third major difference occurred in the design of the studies. The WZ research design was a "Split-Split Pilot Design" in which the F test is most efficient and precise on the split-split plot and most conservative on the whole plot [Steel and Torrie 1960, p. 223; Hicks 1973, p. 217]. Consequently, in this type of design, the least important factor should be on the whole plot and the most important one on the split-split plot. However, WZ included the accounting method on the whole plot and the loan amount on the split-split plot.

The results of our study clearly indicate that the accounting treatment of long-term leases is apparently still an unresolved issue. These results tend to support the contention that whether a lease contract is reported as a capital lease or as an operating lease makes a diference in perceptions of the credit standing of the company, resulting in higher debt costs for companies with capital leases in their financial statements. The results provide a signal to the accounting profession, specifically the FASB, that loan officers' perceptions of credit worthiness are influenced by the accounting treatment of leases. Therefore, the FASB may wish to reconsider the accounting for leases by tightening the criteria for different accounting methods or by totally eliminating the option of treating the noncancellable long-term lease contracts as operating leases.

Table 5.   Summary of the Results of Tested Hypotheses

Testing	Interest Rate	Interest Rate
Overall effect ($\mu_1 = \mu_2 = ... = \mu_5$)	Significant	Significant
Capital Lease vs		
Operating Lease ($\mu_2 + \mu_3 = \mu_4 + \mu_5$)	Significant	Significant
Moderate (15%) Capital Lease vs		
Moderate (15%) Operating Lease ($\mu_2 = \mu_4$)	Nonsignificant	Significant
Substantial (50%) Capital Lease vs		
Substantial (50%) Operating Lease ($\mu_3 = \mu_5$)	Significant	Significant
Moderate (15%) Capital Lease vs		
Substantial (50%) Capital Lease ($\mu_2 = \mu_3$)	Nonsignificant	Nonsignificant
Moderate (15%) Operating Lease vs		
Substantial (50%) Operating Lease ($\mu_4 = \mu_5$)	Nonsignificant	Nonsignificant

SCOPE AND LIMITATIONS

This study concentrated only on the effect of different accounting treatments of long-term lease contracts on the credit standing of a company as measured by the rate of interest that is charged to the company on a specific amount of loan, and as measured by the rating of the credit standing of a company on a 9-point scale. Because neither industry information nor credit history information was provided within the research instruments, the results should be considered within that context and might not be applicable to the situations in which either industry or credit history or both types of information are present. Other factors such as size of company, executive profile, and personal relationship that may have an effect on the credit standing of a company were not considered in this study. These factors were omitted to achieve the control necessary to isolate the effect of the lease treatment. There may be many other ways to measure the credit standing of a company; also different accounting treatments of long-term leases may have some other effects on the position of a company within its enviroment that are beyond the scope of this study. Finally, the results of this study can be extended beyond the sampled population only to the extent that the sample is representative of its respective population.

ACKNOWLEDGMENT

The authors gratefully acknowledge the insightful comments and recommendations of the two anonymous reviewers. The paper has been significantly improved as a result of those suggestions. However, any remaining errors are the responsibility of the authors.

NOTES

1. A copy of the research instrument can be obtained by writing to either authors.
2. The interest rate was also used as task variable by Libby [1980] in evaluating the effect of reporting uncertainty on loan decisions.
3. For example, if a respondent indicated that the required interest rate on a $2 million, 2-year loan was 13% and the maximum amount of the 2-year loan approved for the company, at the prime rate of 12%, was $4 million, the responses were considered inconsistent.
4. The questions regarding the compensating balance were asked because some loan officers indicated in the pretest that there might be a compensating balance requirement by some banks. The compensating balance is the percentage of the loan that is required to be deposited in the company's non-interest-bearing account with the bank during the term of the loan. Consequently, the credit standing of the borrower might be reflected in the different compensating balance requirement as compared to the normal percentage rather than in the interest rate charged on the loan. However, a compensating balance requirement that is equal to the usual and normal requirement by the bank from all customers would indicate no need for adjusting the interest rate to make it representative of the credit standing of the company.
5. Four business days after mailing the instrument a follow-up letter was mailed to remind the subjects to respond. To test for nonresponse bias, responses received 4 business days after mailing the follow-up letter (allowing 2 days for delivery of the follow up letter and 2 days to respond) were segregated and compared to the previous responses. The analysis of these early-late responses through ANOVA did not reveal the existence of any significant difference.
6. The existence of a control group with no treatment did not allow the use of completely randomized design with a 2 × 2 factorial arrangement of treatments (capitalized vs operating and 50% vs 15%).

REFERENCES

Abdel-Khalik, A. R., R. B. Thompson, and R. E. Taylor, "The Impact of Reporting Leases Off the Balance Sheet on Bond Risk Premiums: Two Exploratory Studies." Accounting Research Center Working Paper, #78-2, University of Florida [February 1978].
Abdel-Khalik, A. R., R. B. Thompson, and R. E. Taylor, *The Economic Effects on Leases of FASB Statement No. 13, Accounting for Leases* [FASB 1978].
Bowman, R. G., "The Debt Equivalence of Leases: An Empirical Investigation," *The Accounting Review* 55(2) [1980], pp. 237-253.
Dieter, R., "Is Lessee Accounting Working?," *The CPA Journal* 49(8) [1979], pp. 13-19.
Dieter, R. and A. R. Wyatt, "Get it Off the Balance Sheet," *Financial Executive* 48(1) [1980], pp. 42-48.
Ferrara, W. L., J. B. Thies, and M. W. Dirsmith, *The Lease-Purchase Decision* [National Accounting Association, 1980].
Financial Accounting Standards Board, *Statement of Financial Accounting Standards No. 13: Accounting for Leases* [FASB 1976].
Finnertz, J. E., R. N. Fitzsimmons, and T. W. Oliver, "Lease Capitalization and Symmetric Risk," *The Accounting Review* 55(4) [1980], pp. 631-639.
Hendrikson, E. S, *Accounting Theory* [Irwin 1982].
Hicks, C. R., *Fundamental Concepts in the Design of Experiments* [Holt, Rinehart & Winston 1973].
Huefner, R. J., "A Debt Approach to Lease Accounting," *Financial Executive* 38(3) [1970], pp. 30-36.

Libby, R., "The Impact of Uncertainty Reporting on the Loan Decision," *Journal of Accounting Research* (Supplement) [1980], pp. 35-57.

May, R., J. Harkins and R. Rice., "Lease Disclosure: The Effect of Accounting Policy Change on Security Prices," Unpublished Manuscript [University of Washington, March 1978].

Meyer, J. L., *Fundamentals of Experimental Design* [Ally and Bacon 1979].

Nelson, A. J., "Capitalizing Leases—The Effect on Financial Ratios," *The Journal of Accountancy* 58(7) [1963], pp. 49-58.

Palmon, D. and M. Kwatinetz, "The Significance Role Interpretation Plays in the Implementation of SFAS No. 13," *Journal of Accounting, Auditing and Finance* 3(3) [1980], pp. 207-220.

Ro, B. T., "The Disclosure of Capitalized Lease Information and Stock Prices," *Journal of Accounting Research* 16(2) [1978], pp. 315-340.

Steel, R. G. and J. H. Torrie, *Principles and Procedures of Statistics* [McGraw-Hill 1960].

Vatter, W. J., "Accounting for Leases," *Journal of Accounting Research* 4(2) [1966], pp. 133-148.

Wilkins, T. and I. Zimmer, "The Effect of Leasing and Different Methods of Accounting for Leases on Credit Evaluations," *The Accounting Review* 59(4) [1983], pp. 749-764.

Wyatt, A. R., "Leases Should be Capitalized," *CPA Journal* 44(9) [1974], pp. 35-38.

Zises, A., "Disclosure of Long-Term Leases," *The Journal of Accountancy* 56(2) [1961], pp. 37-47.

AN EMPIRICAL EXAMINATION OF THE INFLUENCE OF SELECTED FACTORS ON PROFESSIONAL TAX PREPARERS' DECISION PROCESSES

David LaRue and Philip M. J. Reckers

ABSTRACT

The objective of this research is to provide some initial evidence on the decision processes of tax professionals in their role as advisors to taxpayers. Specifically examined for their influence on professional tax-preparer reporting recommendations were the probability of audit (detection), the size of the opportunity for tax savings, the overpayment/underpayment year-end tax status of the client, and the experience of the tax professional as a tax advisor. One hundred and ten Big 8 tax managers served as subjects in a role-playing experiment. In contrast to other recent research, the probability of audit when manipulated at realistic levels was not found to register significance. The experience of the professional was found significant, suggesting further attention

Advances in Accounting, Volume 7, pages 37-50.
Copyright © 1989 by JAI Press Inc.
All rights of reproduction in any form reserved.
ISBN: 0-89232-960-2

to cognitive theory may be appropriate. The opportunity for tax savings and the year-end payment status of the client entered into a higher order interaction that evidences a complex decision process.

INTRODUCTION

Tax evasion represents a major and growing problem facing policymakers. The IRS estimates that, for 1983 and every year since, the government has lost in excess of $100 billion through nonreported and underreported income [Friedrich 1983; Loftus 1985]. Recent surveys also reveal a second major change that has been occurring in taxation. At one time most taxpayers prepared their own returns. However, as the complexity of the law and the weight of the tax burden have increased, the tendency to rely on the advice of tax professionals has increased. Currently about half of all taxpayers use the services of professional tax preparers [Jackson and Milliron 1986]. The ability of this group to influence tax compliance may be dramatic. That is, professional tax preparers may act to enhance or dampen a taxpayer's propensity to be aggressive and/or engage in tax evasion. However, relatively little research specifically has examined the processes by which tax professionals reach their judgments and advice.

The objective of this research is to provide some initial evidence on the decision processes of tax professionals in their role as advisors to taxpayers. The research approach adopted by the authors differs from the approach commonly used in tax research. Instead of focusing on actual tax filings and the client files of tax professionals, and so forth, the authors used short scenarios containing hypothetical tax cases. Tax preparer subjects were asked to render tax advice on the scenarios. Among the advantages of this approach is that it allows a great deal of control over manipulated variables while simultaneously controlling for the potential effects of variables not of immediate interest. This method has been used extensively in research studying the decision processes of auditors over the past decade [e.g., Waller and Felix 1984; Kida 1984; Libby 1985].

The research builds on traditional economic theory that has often been utilized to explain the compliance/noncompliance behavior of taxpayers [see Kinsey 1984]. This general theory also may apply to tax professionals who fill an advocacy role for their clients and accordingly act in their clients' interests, subject to the restrictions of the profession's code of ethics. (The tax preparer also serves a public trust and is proscribed from participation in tax evasion or fraud.) This research, however, goes beyond economic theory, and also examines the influence of taxpayer year-end payment status and individual preparer characteristics on the advice the tax professional renders. The next section discusses the motivation for the factors examined in this research. This is followed by a description of the research method and the results.

BACKGROUND AND HYPOTHESES

Kinsey [1984] discusses the use of economic theory to understand an individual's tax compliance/noncompliance behavior and to determine the optimal level of tax evasion. Within this traditional economic framework, an optimal level of evasion is a function of the potential economic benefits and costs of the action. Economic benefits and costs, in turn, are a function of the amount of nonreported income, the tax rate, the probability of detection (audit), and the size of the penalty. This model also may apply to tax professionals who act on behalf of and in empathy with their clients. (Preliminary evidence that this model also applies to tax professionals is provided by Madeo et al. [1987].) In applying the economic model in this study we manipulated the probability of detection, the amount of nonreported income, and the potential size of the penalty. The latter two items are effectively manipulated simultaneously as this parallels real world conditions. That is, the size of tax penalties commonly relate to the amount of nonreported income. [See SEC 6659 and 6661 of the Internal Revenue Code of 1986, as amended.] Thus, manipulations to increase the amount of tax savings effected through adoption of an "aggressive" tax strategy will simultaneously increase the amount of penalty that is likely to be imposed if the untoward act is detected. This variable then appears on both sides of the equation, and thus a dual question arises with respect to such manipulations: Will they influence tax preparers recommendations and if so in what direction? In a recent study Kaplan et al. [1986] manipulated the amount of taxes that might be saved in scenarios similar to those used in this study. They reported that more "aggressive" but less supportable tax postures (that resulted in greater tax savings) were associated with less support from Big 8 tax professionals. Thus, in their study, the penalty side of the equation predominated—prospects of greater penalties caused reduced support for aggressive postures.

In the study by Kaplan et al. [1986], however, the stated probability of IRS audit (detection) reached 50%. Accordingly, it is questionable as to whether the influence observed can be replicated at lower levels of likelihood of detection or whether the benefits side of the equation will assume ascendency at lower levels of expectation. Thus, our first hypothesis, which relates to traditional economic theory, focuses on the effect of the amount of taxes that may be saved through a nonreporting of income opportunity, and its relationship to potential economic benefit versus cost under conditions of low levels of audit likelihood. We expect that at low levels of anticipated detection (all levels of audit probability posed in our cases were relatively low) the subjects will focus on the benefit side of the equation, in empathy with their clients, and thus greater opportunities for savings will be seen as warranting greater support. As Jackson and Jones [1985, p. 13] observe: "When the choice alternatives involve small probabilities, the focus on magnitudes has relevance in the design of the detection/penalty structure." Given that penalties remain modest in the U.S. system, benefit magnitudes are expected to predominate. Still, as Jackson and Jones [1985, p. 13] further note: "The I.R.S. currently appears to be more interested in focusing on improved detection through increased third party reporting and computerized matching of documents than in further increases in penalty (or other solutions), although the additional net benefits to be had from adoption of costly new detection procedures seems marginal."

To further explain our expectation in the face of the findings of Kaplan et al. [1986], we suggest that individuals may tend to categorically interpret probabilities. That is, high probabilities are not interpreted so much as highly probable but rather are seen as approaching certainty. Sanders [1986] found evidence of this in her recent empirical tax study, and we conjecture that a similar phenomenon prevailed in the study by Kaplan et al. [1986]. It seems tenable that their subjects categorically interpreted high probability manipulations as exhibiting greater certainty than was stated (or is likely in reality) and then overweighed the cost (penalty) side of the economic equation thus producing the results obtained. We expect that at more realistic and lower rates of detection subjects might emphasize the benefit side of the equation. Thus, our first hypothesis:

HYPOTHESIS 1.   Professional tax preparers will make more aggressive tax recommendations when there is an opportunity for greater tax savings.

We manipulated the probability of audit at two low levels (10 and 25%) to further evaluate the relative effect of changes in the likelihood of audit at relatively low levels. This basic element of the economic model is directly subject to government change and has a clearly specified directional influence. This manipulation thus serves both to examine the influence of this variable as a tool of government and as a benchmark against which to compare the other hypothesized influences that follow. Thus our second hypothesis is:

HYPOTHESIS 2.   Professional tax preparers will provide more aggressive advice to taxpayer clients when the probability of audit is relatively lower.

(Given our case manipulations, it was implicit that a condition of audit would almost invariably lead to detection of asset overvaluation, additional taxes, penalty, and interest.)

The tax professional also may act in empathy with the taxpayer in other ways. The tax advisor may render different advice to a risk-seeking client than would be rendered to a conservative client. Such varying professional response might be a conscious strategy by the tax professional or an unconscious bias.

The response may be supportive or the professional may try to mitigate (or dampen) client biases when deciding tax issues.

The influence of client biases on tax pprofessionals' decisions/advice has been examined with mixed results by Roark [1985], Sanders [1986], and Kaplan et al. [1986]. These authors attempted to examine the influence of client bias by manipulating within case scenarios client risk profile. They explicitly stated that the clients were risk assuming or risk averse. These manipulations were brief and somewhat palid and this may in part explain the mixed findings encountered across the different decision tasks by these researchers. Further, in the study by Kaplan et al. [1986], only a general risk propensity or aversion was provided. Alternatively, we attempted to manipulate related phenomena at a situation-specific level. Specifically, we examined whether advice to taxpayers who overpaid estimated taxes and withholding during the year was different than advice given to those who were underpaid at that point. Logically, the necessity of making a large payment on April 15 can be quite disruptive to family budgets and cash flows—and intuitively this certainly represents a more noxious prospect than that of receiving a large refund. It can be conjectured that individuals facing the prospects of large payments will seek relief by more aggressively approaching tax reporting alternatives. Importantly, government has the ability to regulate the year-end over/ underpayment status of its citizens through regulations related to employer withholdings and individuals' payments of estimated taxes. The new 1986 tax law, for instance, requires estimated payments equal to 90% of taxes due to avoid penalty, whereas previously the requirement was for only 80% to avoid penalty. Recently the government also considered requiring financial institutions to withhold taxes related to interest paid to depositors. Given the intuitive appeal of the logic of this matter and the government's ability to influence this factor, a select group of social scientists convened by the IRS in 1985 strongly encouraged more research in this area [see Loftus 1985]. These authorities further related this anecdotally supported phenomenon to prospect theory [see also Jackson and Milliron 1986 pp. 151-153]. In cases in which the professional works closely with the taxpayer, the professional might be expected to be sensitive to this client bias. This leads to our third hypothesis:

HYPOTHESIS 3. Professional tax preparers will provide more aggressive advice to taxpayer clients when the taxpayer has underpaid estimated taxes and withholdings during the year and faces further payments after year end.

In addition to the biases possibly evoked by the client's condition, the advice of the tax professional also might be influenced by characteristics of the tax professionals themselves, such as experience as a tax consultant, age, and perceptions of the equity and fairness of the tax code.

Regarding the first item, greater experience in technical fields has been found to lead to greater use of experience-developed schema and accompanying "conservatism" regarding reaction to transient environmental variation [see Gibbins 1984; and Kida 1984]. A schema is a knowledge structure that people use to organize and make sense of social and organizational information or situations. "Schemata organize experience into generalized cognitive structures that represent knowledge about how the world works . . . and schemata drive the selection and comprehension of environmental stimuli" [Waller and Felix 1984]. Abelson [1976] proposes that the development of knowledge structure and related behavior evolves through three stages. The first, episodic scripting, is elemental and is retained as a context-specific remembrance of a single experience. When a person has experienced many similar episodes in similar situations, the collection of episodic scripts evolves into a categorical script— a script still appropriate for a still relatively narrow class of situations. Finally, when enough experience is acquired and generalized across contexts, a generalized script or metascript to guide behavior in a range of related situations develops. Knowledge structures that thus have evolved through experience to the metascript level tend to be conservative. That is, a "conservative" response is more dependent on a learned response pattern (e.g., a standard operating procedure) than on minor environmental variations. In tax, greater experience could lead tax professionals to react less to transient taxpayer conditions such as overpayment or underpayment status. This suggests a possible interaction between tax experience and client payment status.

HYPOTHESIS 4.   Professional tax preparers with greater experience will react less to the client's overpayment/underpayment status; that is, they will display more "cognitive conservatism."

In the context of the above hypothesis, the subjects were partitioned so that the "less experienced" subjects (coded with a 1) were those with experience as a tax specialist of 4 years or less and the "more experienced" group (coded with a 2) was comprised of subjects with more than 4 years experience. This allowed a near equal split of the subjects who all were of the tax manager rank; most had significant prior auditing experience.

We also examined whether the advice rendered might be influenced by the age of the subject. In a review of the tax compliance literature around the globe, Lewis [1982] found that age is one of the most consistent influences over compliance behavior *among taxpayers,* with older subjects being more compliant. Although the age spread of our subjects was modest (they ranged from age 28 to 40), data were readily available and we felt impelled not to ignore the item but to treat age as a covariate. Thus, our fifth hypothesis is as follows:

HYPOTHESIS 5.   Professional tax preparers who are older will encourage more compliant behavior and less aggressive reporting by their clients.

Another factor frequently linked to evasion behavior *among taxpayers* is the perceived equity of the tax system. (Again see Lewis [1982] and/or Jackson and Milliron [1986] for reviews.) Succinctly, the federal income tax may be viewed to give rise to an exchange relationship between the government and its citizens. The citizen surrenders a part of his/her income in return for benefits from the government. If that exchange relationship is viewed as nonequitable, individuals will experience stress. To alleviate the stress, they will often adjust their inputs to the exchange (i.e., evade) [Adams 1965; Walster et al. 1978; Groenland and van Veldhoven 1983; Kinsey 1984; Jackson and Milliron 1986]. To the extent that tax preparers view the tax system as unfair, they will perceive their clients as "victims" of the system. To the extent empathy with the client also is great, these perceptions may translate into actions taken on behalf of the taxpayer client. Thus, our sixth hypothesis is:

HYPOTHESIS 6.   Professional tax preparers who perceive the tax system as less equitable will provide more aggressive advice to their clients.

It is also possible that neither all nor a majority of professional tax preparers view the income tax as giving rise to an exchange relationship. Alternatively, taxes may be perceived as compulsory exactions made by the federal government outside any quid pro quo relationship. It should be borne in mind that, although a benefits concept is well developed within a voluntary exchange model, this approach lacks a solution to the nonexcludability criterion of public goods. Neither taxpayers' nor tax professionals' attitudes regarding these matters need be consensual. A lack of majority subscription to the exchange perspective should lead to rejection of Hypothesis 6. Subscription to the confiscatory perspective should lead to more aggressive tax positions in general, everything else remaining the same (and as long as participation in the general consumption of government is not curtailed).

METHOD

This study employed an experimental method to examine recommendations made by tax professionals to their client-taxpayers. The subjects in the study were 100 tax professionals employed by a large public accounting firm. All subjects were tax managers. About half of the subjects had 4 years or less experience providing tax advice, whereas the other half had more than 4 years experience. Nearly all had prior audit experience with the firm.

This research was conducted at national training programs sponsored by the participating firm. Data were gathered at three separate training sites, on the final day of training. Data collection spanned 1 month. In each case, the material covered in the training course was identical, but unrelated to the specific scenarios posed in the research. In each instance, one of the researchers was present to conduct the research, provide directions, and maintain control and custody of the research instruments. Specifically, uncoded instruments were distributed to subjects in an obviously random fashion. Firm personnel, after endorsement of the project, left the training site. Subjects were ensured confidentiality and completed instruments were returned to the researcher administering the project in envelopes that the participants sealed.

Each subject responded to one case, that is, we employed a between-subjects design. Each case scenario described a real estate tax shelter in which the client had invested.[1] At issue were property valuation and allowable levels of depreciation. The study manipulated the tax payment status of the client at two levels (overpayment and underpayment), the probability of audit at two levels (10 and 25%), and the amount of excessive property valuation at two levels ($50,000 and $120,000).

The audit manipulation was effected by providing the subjects with information regarding audit priorities within the district director's office. In the debriefing questionnaire, subjects expressed strong belief that districts differentially challenge different types of tax shelters. Subjects were provided a 7-point ascending scale bounded by strongly disagree and strongly agree. They were asked "To what extent do you agree that the probability of audit on a particular issue may vary substantially from one jurisdiction to another?" The mean response was 5.1 with 76 of the respondents circling either a 6 or 7 on the 7-point scale. The subjects also expressed agreement that the cases were realistic. The mean response on a similar 7-point scale was 4.8 with individuals with 25% or more of their clients involved in real estate tax shelters providing a rating of 5.4.

Measured independent variables included experience as a tax consultant, the age of the subject, and the subject's perceptions regarding the equity of the tax code and its application. The specific form of the question used to assess the latter was:

Is the federal income tax system applied consistently and fairly across Americans?

Strongly Disagree	-3	-2	-1	0	+1	+2	+3	Strongly Agree

In retrospect, the wording of this question may have been ambiguous. Although selected from prior published research involving taxpayers rather than tax preparers (Arrington and Reckers [1985]; Kaplan and Reckers [1986, 1988]), to the extent that respondents may have perceived the fairness of the applicability of the law as distinct from the inherent fairness of the law, and to the extent that they responded to the question only in the context of the former, responses may not have provided a good and valid measure of equity perceptions. This may account for the insignificant results reported later relative to this measure.

In each case, the client was seeking advice regarding the amount of ACRS depreciation that could be claimed as a result of the tax shelter investment. The case had been designed to involve gray areas of the code and property valuation. Subjects responded to the following question:

How strongly would you recommend that Bill claim the ACRS deduction
with an established property basis of $300,000 for the property?
Strongly   Strongly
Discourage   0...1...2...3...4...5...6...7...8...9...10   Recommend

The figure of $300,000 was either $50,000 or $120,000 in excess of the best estimate of true value, depending on the treatment level.

RESULTS

Table 1 provides summary ANOVA statistics and cell means for ACRS recommendations. The amount of tax savings is marginally significant (0.08) in the predicted direction. (Thus weak support is found for Hypothesis 1.) Note that experience is treated as a factor and not as a covariate given the interaction hypothesized in Hypothesis 4. As can be seen only experience is significant among main effects at traditional levels (0.05). Also significant is the interaction of experience, payment status, and amount of tax savings afforded by the scenario. An experience by payment status interaction had been predicted, thus some support is found for Hypothesis 4. We had not anticipated quite the complexity observed here, however. Nonetheless, the interaction does appear explainable.

Table 2 presents the relevant interaction cell means. Ex post analysis revealed that the significant experience by payment status interaction, predicted in Hypothesis 4, exists only within the low tax savings condition, in which the less experienced tax preparers make significantly more aggressive recommendations when the client is underpaid at filing date, thus potentially exhibiting sensitivity to likely client distress in the face of necessary additional payments. It is consistent with cognitive theory that less experienced professionals working with less highly evolved cognitive structures would be more responsive to such environmental case superficialities as client payment

Table 1.   Summary Statistics

Source of Variation	Sum of Squares	df	F Score	Probability
ANOVA Results				
Covariates				
Age	2.400		0.501	0.48
Perceptions of Equity	14.831		3.097	0.08
Main Effects				
Experience	28.285	1	5.907	0.01
Amount of Savings	14.709	1	3.072	0.08
Payment Status	10.680	1	2.230	0.13
Probability of Audit	3.433	1	0.717	0.39
Significant Interactions				
Experience × Payment Status				
× Amount of Savings	21.267	1	4.441	0.03
Explained	120.285			
Residual	445.345			

Cell Means					
Experience	Low	High	Payment Status:	Over	Under
	6.94	5.78		6.11	6.81
Amount of Savings	Low	High	Probability of Audit	Low	High
	6.10	6.82		6.65	6.29

status. Among the more experienced tax preparers the client's payment status registered no influence, again, as cognitive theory would predict.

Within the high tax savings condition, however no significant interaction was found. Further, payment status also is insignificant individually and experience is significant at only 0.09 level. Thus, application of cognitive theory is not universally useful across all conditions and tax opportunities.

Among the covariates, the perceptions of the tax preparer subjects regarding the fairness and equity of the federal income tax system also registered marginal significance, lending some support for Hypothesis 6. As predicted, the greater the perceptions of inequity, the more aggressive were the recommendations rendered.

Neither the probability of audit nor age registered significance and thus Hypothesis 2 and 5 are not supported. Some additional comments on both of these may be in order, nonetheless.

Table 2.   Interaction Cell Means

	Experience		
	Low		High
High Tax Savings			
Overpaid Status	7.38		5.92
Underpaid Status	7.06		6.64
Low Tax Savings			
Overpaid Status	5.47	NS[a]	5.36
	SS[a]		NS
Underpaid Status	7.67	SS	5.18

[a]SS = statistically significant difference at 0.05; NS = not statistically significant at 0.10.

As previously noted, age is a common variable of interest in tax compliance research around the globe. "The most prevalent finding reported in the literature is that older tax *preparers* are more compliant" [Jackson and Milliron 1986, p. 130]. This variable has not been addressed previously with respect to tax*preparers*. Among taxpayers, it has been suggested that the relationship between age and deviance is attributable to both life-cycle variations and generational differences. Jackson and Milliron [1986] catalogue several researchers who, nonetheless, have found no significant relationship between age and deviance. Among the explanations are that (1) the relationship is curvilinear rather than linear (i.e., suggesting that the youngest [student subjects] and oldest both exhibit high compliance) but that researchers fail to look for curvilinear relationships, and that (2) "for researchers who use a limited set of the population, a lack of significant results may be attributable to a range restriction . . . the lack of variability in the restricted variable" [Jackson and Milliron 1986, p. 130]. We noted previously that our subjects exhibited just such a lack of variability with the range of ages being 28 to 40 years. Therefore, we are unsure whether the age variable, among tax preparers, is irrelevant and insignificant given the task or whether the exhibited age dispersion is too restrictive. Future research must address this concern.

Finally, we note that the recently reported work of Madeo et al. [1986] produces results regarding the effect of the probability of detection seemingly at odds with our results. In that prior work, the authors report a very significant effect resulting from their manipulation of the source of nonreported income. They manipulated source at three levels: mostly self-employment, equal salary and self-employment, and mostly salary. We believe that this manipulation was extreme, whereas ours was modest, and that this is the source of our differences in results. Tax preparers most certainly know that with the computerized cross-checks that are in place today, the individual who fails to report salary income stands a probability of detection of nearly 100%. Alternatively, the individual who is self-employed and tax-wise can evade a modest amount of taxes with virtual impunity. As such, we are not surprised that Madeo et al. [1986] found this variable to be the most significant in their model, using tax preparers. Our study, on the other hand, attempts to examine whether feasible increases in IRS detection ability regarding nonsalary income or nonemployee expenses offer any significant deterrence value. We found evidence that suggests that is does not.

DISCUSSION

These findings generally encourage future consideration of subjects' experience and client payment status. They further argue for the continued consideration of subjects' experience in future research not only as a covariate but consideration that would be sensitive to interactive influences between experience and other factors. A place for economic theory also is supported by these findings. Our findings, in combination with those of Kaplan et al. [1986], suggest that the factor related to the magnitude of savings (effected through underreporting of income) alternatively may register influence on the two sides of the economic equation depending on the probability of audit. That is, when the probability of audit is high (e.g., 50%), as was the case in the study by Kaplan et al. [1986], considerations of loss and penalty, which are then likely, may dominate, whereas when the probability of audit is low (10 and 25%), as was the case in this study, considerations regarding the benefits side of the economic equation may dominate. Further, we found no evident deterrence effect when audit probabilities were raised from 10 to 25%. This suggests that to the extent that taxpayers reporting choices are influenced or motivated by tax preparer advice, more docile compliance or less aggressive reporting is not likely to be achieved by increasing the prospects of IRS audit, within the limits manipulated. Further, within the realm of reality, we believe our treatment was strong as an increase from 10 to 25% is a very marked change. Certainly, our findings attest to the great complexity of influences potentially engaged in the professional's decision process.

More research is encouraged, but caution is noted in that we need to use the appropriate subjects. Over the past decade, auditing researchers repeatedly have enlisted the experimental assistance of audit seniors as subjects. Recent applications of cognitive theory in research conducted in that field now call to question the propriety of past decisions to use relatively inexperienced auditors in decision-modeling studies [see Kida 1984; and Gibbins 1984]. Our findings suggest that experience also may be a vital consideration in research among tax professionals.

Whether these results can be extended beyond the panel tested with the cases tested and the judgments examined needs to be addressed empirically. Further, client payment status was used in this study as an example of a client-related environmental condition that might affect professionals' advice. The influence of client condition, however, was thought to be conceivably contingent on the client being important enough to warrant considering his/her wishes. Although all clients are important, some are undoubtedly more important than others. We sought to provide a strong experimental treatment in this study to discern any potential influence of this variable that has had limited attention heretofore, and thus presented the client as an officer of an important audit client. We can only speculate as to the influence of this choice. We solicit other researchers to lend their talents and share in this search for a better understanding of these important matters.

NOTES

1. Jackson and Spicer [1985], nonetheless, did not find supporting evidence for this conjecture in their research funded by Arthur Young that focused on 270 jurors of modest income from Colorado Springs. Several methodological problems may have contributed to these results, however. Chang et al. [1987] do provide supporting evidence of this in their study of middle-income executives making compliance decisions.

2. Although the new tax law that took effect in 1987 will make substantial changes in the area of real estate tax shelters, neither the changes nor the subjects' perceived prospects for change are relevant to this study. All subjects understood that the relevant features of the case were not subject to retroactive change and advice was being given before the effective date of the new law.

REFERENCES

Abelson, R., "Script Processing n Attitude Formation and Decision Making," in *Cognition and Social Behavior* [Erlbaum, 1976].

Adams, J., "Inequity in Social Exchange," in L. Berkowitz (ed)., *Advances in Experimental Social Psychology* [Academic Press, 1965].

Arrington, C. and P. Reckers, "A Social Psychological Examination of Tax Evasion," *Accounting and Business Research* [Summer 1985].

Ayres, F. and B. Jackson, Report to the Peat, Marwick & Mitchell Foundation for Audit Research, "An Empirical Analysis of Factors Relating to the Degree of Aggression on Tax Return Positions by Professional Tax Preparers," Unpublished Report [1985].

Chang, O., D. Nichols, and J. Schultz, Jr., "Taxpayer Attitudes Toward Audit Risk," *Journal of Economic Psychology*, 8 [1987], pp. 299-309.

Friedrich, O., "Tax Cheating—Bad and Getting Worse," *Time* [March 28, 1983], pp. 26-32.

Gibbins, M. "Propositions about the Psychology of Professional Judgment in Public Accounting," *Journal of Accounting Research* [Spring 1984], pp. 103-125.

Groenland, E. and G. van Veldhoven, "Tax Evasion Behavior: A Psychological Framework," *Journal of Economic Psychology*, 3 [1983], pp. 129-144.

Internal Revenue Code of 1986, as Amended, Internal Revenue Service, Washington, D.C. [December 1987].

Jackson, B. and S. Jones. "Salience of Tax Evasion Penalties Versus Detection Risk," *The Journal of the American Tax Association* [Spring 1985].

Jackson, B. and V. Milliron, "Tax Compliance Research: Findings, Problems and Prospects," *Journal of Accounting Literature* [January 1986], pp. 125-165.

Jackson, B. and M. Spicer, "An Investigation of Under or Overwithholding of Taxes on Taxpayer Compliance," Arthur Young Tax Research Grant Report [New York: 1985].

Kaplan, S., P. Reckers, J. Boyd, and S. West, "An Empirical Examination of the Probability of Audit, Size of Loss and Client Risk Preference on Tax Preparer Judgments," Unpublished working paper, Working Paper Series, College of Business, Arizona State University [1986].

Kaplan, S. and P. Reckers, "An Application of Attribution and Equity Theories to Tax Evasion Behavior," *Journal of Economic Psychology* [Winter 1986].

Kaplan, S. and P. Reckers, "An Examination of Information Search during Initial Audit Planning," *Accounting, Organizations & Society* [forthcoming].

Kida, T., "The Impact of Hypothesis Testing Strategies on Auditors' Use of Judgment Data," *Journal of Accounting Research* [1984], pp. 332-340.

Kinsey, K., *Theories and Models of Tax Evasion* [American Bar Foundation, 1984].

Lewis, A., *The Pyschology of Taxation* [St. Martin's Press, 1982].

Libby, R., "Availability and the Generation of Hypothesis in Analytical Review," *Journal of Accounting Research* [Autumn 1985], pp. 648-667.

Loftus, E. F., "To File, Perchance to Cheat," *Psychology Today* [April 1985], pp. 35-39.

Madeo, S., A. Schepanski, and W. Uecker, "Modeling Judgments of Taxpayer Compliance," *The Accounting Review* [April 1987].

Roark, S., "An Examination of the Effect of Client, Subject and Firm Risk on Legal Tax Research," unpublished doctoral dissertation, Arizona State University [1985].

Roper Organization Inc., Third Annual Tax Study, Kansas City: Public Affairs Department [H&R Block, 1979].

Roper Organization Inc., The American Public and the Federal Tax System, Kansas City: Public Affairs Department [H&R Block, 1986].

Sanders, D., "An Application of Prospect Theory to Tax Compliance Judgments," unpublished dissertation, Arizona State University [1986].

Spicer, M. W., "A Behavioral Model of Income Tax Evasion," unpublished dissertation, The Ohio State University [1974].

Spicer, M. and L. Becker, "Fiscal Inequity & Tax Evasion," *National Tax Journal* [1980], pp. 171-176.

Tversky, A. and D. Kahneman, "The Framing of Decisions and the Psychlogy of Chocie," *Science* 211, pp. 453-458.

Waller, W. and W. Felix, "The Auditor and Learning from Experience: Some Conjectures," *Accounting, Organizations & Society* [1984], pp. 383-406.

Walster, E., G. M. Walster, and E. Bershield, *Equity: Theory & Research* [Allyn and Beacon, 1978].

THE RELEVANCE OF LEVEL OF AGGREGATION OF GEOGRAPHIC AREA DATA IN THE ASSESSMENT OF FOREIGN INVESTMENT RISK

Timothy S. Doupnik and Robert J. Rolfe

ABSTRACT

This study used a judgment modeling approach to evaluate the relevance of data on less aggregated geographic areas in assessing the riskiness of investing in multinational corporations (MNCs). The subjects were 54 Master of International Business students in their final semester of study. They were provided background information for a hypothetical MNC and then presented with cases in which data on the geographic areas in which the firm operated were systematically disaggregated. The response tasks were an evaluation of the level of risk associated with an investment in the hypothetical firm and the level of confidence attached to that risk assessment. Relevance was operationalized as a change in risk assessment or an increase in level of confidence resulting from

Advances in Accounting, Volume 7, pages 51-65.

a disaggregation of geographic area. Data were analyzed using a regression approach and hypotheses were tested using paired-samples t tests. Results show that disaggregated data at a continent level were more relevant than that at a global level and data at a country level were more relevant than that at a continent level. In addition, subjects were able to correctly differentiate between relatively high-risk and low-risk countries.

INTRODUCTION

Data aggregation has long been posited as resulting in a loss of information [see, for example, Orcutt et al. 1968; Ijiri 1971]. If true, this assumption has serious implications for the utility of financial statements. Lev [1968] describes financial statement preparation as a process of aggregation in which a relatively large number of individual account balances are aggregated in accordance with established rules so that only a relatively small number of items are reported. The presumed result of financial statement aggregation is a loss of information. More information would be conveyed if relatively more individual items were reported.

A specific area in which individual items are aggregated for external reporting purposes is in the information on foreign operations presented in the notes to the financial statements. Although Statement of Financial Accounting Standards (SFAS) No. 14 [FASB 1976] requires publicly held U.S. multinational corporations to present information on foreign operations by significant geographic area, a great deal of discretion is left to management in determining reportable geographic areas. This creates the possibility that the degree of aggregation of individual countries may not provide adequate information for assessing the riskiness of a firm's foreign operations. To counteract this, several researchers have called for the presentation of data on a less aggregated geographic area basis [see, for example, Arnold et al. 1980; Bavishi and Wyman 1980].

This study used an experimental framework to examine whether the level of aggregation of geographic area data is relevant in making investment decisions. Information is defined as relevant if it has the capacity to change a decision or if it reduces the uncertainty surrounding a decision already made [FASB 1980]. This was measured by changes in a decision maker's risk assessments of a firm with foreign operations and the confidence placed in those decisions. The results show that the level of aggregation of geographic area does influence the risk assessment and confidence of financial statement users.

DEVELOPMENT OF THE RESEARCH PROBLEM

SFAS No. 14 requires firms to present data on foreign operations by *significant* geographic areas if (1) revenues generated from total foreign operations are 10% or more of consolidated revenues or (2) identifiable assets of total foreign operations are 10% or more of consolidated total assets. A geographic area is regarded as significant if its revenues or identifiable assets are 10% or more of the related consolidated amounts.

Geographic areas can be either individual countries or groups of countries. Determination of geographic area is left to management's discretion. Factors to be considered include proximity, economic affinity, similarities in business environment, and interrelationship of the firm's operations in the various countries [FASB 1976, para. 34]. For each significant geographic area, firms must report revenue, operating profit, and identifiable assets.

Emmanuel and Gray [1977, p. 413] suggest that under SFAS No. 14, a firm wishing to provide minimum disclosure could argue that its "Japanese, Korean and Philippine operations which separately meet the 10 percent revenue rule are in fact one geographic area, that is Asia." In their view, adequate disclosure of information by geographic area depends on management's good intentions.

Unfortunately, studies by Arnold et al. [1980] and Bavishi and Wyman [1980] indicate that management has been reluctant to provide geographic area information on a relatively disaggregated basis. Arnold et al. [1980] examined 10K reports of 131 of the Fortune 500 firms with regard to geographic area disclosure. They found that only 17.6% of all disclosures were by country, 34.8% were at a continent or subcontinent level, and 12.8% were global in nature. "Other" was the geographic area used in 25.2% of all disclosures. Although each firm technically complied with the letter of SFAS No. 14, they may have violated its intent. The authors believe that the factors listed by the FASB for selecting appropriate geographic areas imply greater disaggregation than a single global category or continent. "Such data is important due to political (for example, expropriation) and economic (for example, currency exchange and translation) implications" [Arnold et al. 1980, p. 135]. They recommend disclosure of all countries in which 10% of total revenues is generated.

Bavishi and Wyman [1980] exmained geographic area disclosures of 296 of the Fortune 500. Seventy-three percent of their sample firms used only one or two geographic areas (other than the United States). Of 17 firms in the pharmaceutical industry, 12 different classification schemes were used, including:

U.S. - Americas and Far East - Europe and Mideast and Africa
and
U.S. - Europe and Africa - Canada and Latin America - Other

The lack of cohesiveness in these areas led them to ask: "Where is the 'proximity, economic affinity, similarities in business environment' apparent in a classification such as 'Europe/ Mideast/ Africa'?" They concluded that "the difficulty of assessing foreign risk of one company or comparing foreign risk between companies is apparent from the variety and vagueness of titles" [Bavishi and Wyman 1980, p. 159].

The broad geographic areas used by firms to divide the world mask differences in investment risk that exist between countries within those areas. The perceived risk of investing in Libya is likely to be far different from that for West Germany, yet both are encompassed by a single geograpic area in the examples previously cited. Even within a continent, such as Europe, there is likely to be a difference in perceived risk between a country such as West Germany and, say, Greece.

Implicit in the conclusions drawn by Arnold et al. [1980] and Bavishi and Wyman [1980] is the assumption that providing data on less aggregated geographic areas could increase the relevance of information to financial analysts and other financial statement users. This assumption is the basis for the research question addressed in this study:

> *Is data on less aggregated geographic areas more relevant than data on more highly aggregated geographic areas in assessing the riskiness of investing in a firm with foreign operations?*

Before making a policy decision that firms should provide less aggregated data, research is necessary to determine whether that data would be used. This question looks at two issues jointly, whether geographic area data are important in the investment decision process and whether users can differentiate between relatively low-risk and high-risk areas in the world.

METHODOLOGY

A decision-modeling approach was used to determine the impact of the level of aggregation of geographic area data on financial statement users' decisions. In this study, hypothetical cases were developed by combining all possible combinations of independent variables. The effect of each independent variable can be determined by analyzing the subjects' responses to changes in these variables.

Experimental Task

The experimental instrument used to gather the data for this study consisted of a set of cases describing the foreign operations of a hypothetical multi-

Exhibit 1.   Sample Cases

Geographic Area	Percentage of Total Assets and Operating Profit
Sample Case #1	
United States	40
Denmark	10
West Germany	10
Latin America (Could Be Anywhere in Latin America)	20
Asia and the Pacific	20

a. Level of Risk
          Low Risk   1 2 3 4 5 6 7 8 9   High Risk
b. Level of Confidence
          Low Confidence   1 2 3 4 5 6 7 8 9   High Confidence

Sample Case #2	
United States	40
Europe (Could Be Anywhere in Europe)	20
Latin America (Could Be Anywhere in Latin America)	20
Eastern Hemisphere (Other Than Europe)	20

a. Level of Risk
          Low Risk   1 2 3 4 5 6 7 8 9   High Risk
b. Level of Confidence
          Low Confidence   1 2 3 4 5 6 7 8 9   High Confidence

Sample Case #3	
United States	40
Greece	10
Portugal	10
Costa Rica	10
Ecuador	10
Middle East and Africa	20

a. Level of Risk
          Low Risk   1 2 3 4 5 6 7 8 9   High Risk
b. Level of Confidence
          Low Confidence   1 2 3 4 5 6 7 8 9   High Confidence

national corporation with common background information. Sample cases are presented in Exhibit 1. Because risk evaluation is an integral part of the investment decision process, change in risk evaluation served as an operational measure of the relevance of the level of aggregation of geographic area data. Subjects were asked to indicate the level of risk they associated with an investment in each company on a 9-point scale, with 1 signifying low risk (comparable to an investment in U.S. government securities) and 9 signifying high risk. They were told that risk was the possibility that the actual return from an investment would deviate from the expected return, which could be caused by many factors, including the economy in general, competition, technological development, and government interference. Subjects were also asked to indicate the level of confidence they placed in their risk assessment made in each case on a scale of 1 (low confidence) to 9 (high confidence). Change in level of confidence was used as a second measure of the relevance of less aggregated geographic area data. Thus, the two dependent variables were risk assessment and decision confidence.

Background Information

Subjects were told that the hypothetical firm is a diversified firm with manufacturing and distribution facilities in the United States, Latin America, Europe, and other locations in the Eastern Hemisphere. Summary financial statement data for the years 1981-1985 were provided. These data were constructed by taking average amounts for the 410 firms of the Fortune 500 that had complete data on the COMPUSTAT tape. This information was common to each of the cases that followed.

Independent Variables

The independent variables in this study were the geographic areas Europe, Latin America, and Eastern Hemisphere (other than Europe). These variables designated the geographic location of identifiable assets and operating profits. Three levels for each of the three independent variables were incorporated into the design by varying the level of aggregation and the level of risk. Two variables, Europe and Latin America, varied from a continent level of classification to a country level. The third independent variable, Eastern Hemisphere (other than Europe), varied from a global to a regional level. There were a total of 27 cases representing a full factorial design (3 × 3 × 3). The cases were presented in random order to avoid response bias.

The three treatment levels were neutral, high risk, and low risk. In some cases, subjects were told that 20% of total assets and operating profit were located in "Europe (could be anywhere in Europe)"—the neutral case. In other cases this 20% was evenly divided (disaggregated) between two countries located in Europe. Some of these cases contained countries that are relatively risky for foreign direct investment whereas others contained countries that are relatively less risky (the high-risk and low-risk treatment levels). For example, in sample case 1 shown in Exhibit 1, the 20% investment in Europe is shown as 10% in Denmark and 10% in West Germany (the low-risk treatment level) and in sample case 3, Greece and Portugal are the countries in which the 20% European investment is located (the high-risk treatment level for this independent variable). The same was done for the geographic area Latin

Table 1. Risk Ratings of the Countries Included in the Research Instrument

	Version 1			*Version 2*	
Europe			Europe		
Low Risk			Low Risk		
Netherlands	A+		Denmark	A+	
United Kingdom	A+		West Germany	A+	
High Risk			High Risk		
Spain	B[a]		Greece	C+	
Yugoslavia	C		Portugal	B+[a]	
Latin America			Latin America		
Low Risk			Low Risk		
Panama	B+		Costa Rica	A−	
Uruguay	B+		Ecuador	B	
High Risk			High Risk		
Chile	C+		Argentina	C	
Peru	C−		Guatamala	C	

[a] Relative to other countries in Europe, Portugal's rating of B+ and Spain's rating of B represented two of the highest risk ratings in that region.
Source: Coplin and O'Leary [1984], pp. 37-38.

America. For example, sample cases 1 and 2 include the neutral treatment level for this independent variable, and sample case 3 includes the low-risk treatment level with 10% of investment in Costa Rica and 10% in Ecuador.

For the remaining independent variable, Eastern Hemisphere (other than Europe), continents were selected that represent relatively high-risk and low-risk levels within that broad geographic area. Sample case 2 includes the neutral treatment level for this independent variable, sample case 1 includes the low-risk treatment level (Asia and Pacific), and sample case 3 includes the high-risk level (Middle East and Africa).

Country Selection

Countries were chosen for the cases on the basis of a direct investment risk index formulated by Coplin and O'Leary [1984] and used in *World Political Risk Forecasts* published by Frost and Sullivan. The direct investment risk index is developed through an assessment of a country's political stability, economic policy, and restrictions on international business and trade. Values of the index range from A+ through D−. Countries in Europe and Latin America with relatively good ratings were chosen to comprise the low-risk countries in those areas and countries with relatively poor ratings were chosen to comprise the high-risk countries.

"Asia and Pacific" was chosen to represent the relatively low-risk level of "Eastern Hemisphere (other than Europe)" and "Middle East and Africa" was chosen to represent the relatively high-risk level for that category. The average risk ratings for the countries located in those two areas were B+ and B—, respectively.

To ensure that the results of the study were not specific to the set of countries selected, two versions of the instrument were constructed with different countries used in the high- and low-risk levels. Subjects were randomly assigned to two groups receiving different versions of the instrument. The countries and their risk ratings are shown in Table 1.

Hypotheses

Two sets of hypotheses were developed related to the two dependent variables used in this study—risk assessment and decision confidence. With regard to risk assessment, it was expected that the high-risk cases would be perceived as more risky than the neutral cases, which in turn would be perceived as more risky than the low-risk cases. Formally, the risk hypotheses tested were

RH 1:   R(Eh) > R(En)
RH 2:   R(En) > R(El)
RH 3:   R(Eh) > R(El)

RH 4:   R(LAh) > R(LAn)
RH 5:   R(LAn) > R(LAl)
RH 6:   R(LAh) > R(LAl)

RH 7:   R(Oh) > R(On)
RH 8:   R(On) > R(Ol)
RH 9:   R(Oh) > R(Ol)

where

R = Subjective risk assessment
E = Europe
LA =Latin America
O = Eastern Hemisphere (other than
      Europe)
h = high-risk case
n = neutral case
l = low-risk case

These hypotheses were tested by calculating the mean risk assessment over the nine cases in which each treatment level was found and then testing for significant differences in means. For example, Hypothesis 1 was tested by comparing the mean risk assessment for the nine cases that included the high-risk level for Europe and the nine cases that included Europe neutral. Support for this hypothesis would imply (1) that disaggregation of the geographic area Europe provides relevant information and (2) that the decision makers are capable of correctly identifying the high-risk European countries.

If less aggregated geographic area data provide relevant information for assessing risk, then the subjects' confidence with regard to their risk assessments should increase as data becomes increasingly less aggregated. Specifically, confidence should be lowest in that case in which all three independent variables take on the neutral level (the most aggregated case) and the highest in those cases with zero neutral treatment levels (the least aggregated cases). The hypotheses tested with regard to decision confidence were

$$
\begin{array}{llll}
\text{CH 1:} & C(0) & > & C(1) \\
\text{CH 2:} & C(1) & > & C(2) \\
\text{CH 3:} & C(2) & > & C(3) \\
\text{CH 4:} & C(0) & > & C(2) \\
\text{CH 5:} & C(1) & > & C(3) \\
\text{CH 6:} & C(0) & > & C(3)
\end{array}
$$

where

C = level of confidence
0 = zero neutral independent variables
1 = one neutral independent variable
2 = two neutral independent variables
3 = three neutral independent variables

For example, with respect to Hypothesis 1, the mean confidence level for those cases in which less aggregated information was available for all three geographic areas (zero neutral independent variables) was expected to be significantly larger than the mean confidence level for those cases in which only two of the three geographic areas were disaggregated (one neutral variable).

The confidence hypotheses were tested by determining the mean level of confidence for those cases with zero neutral independent variables, one neutral variable, two neutral variables, and three neutral variables, respectively, and then testing for significant differences in means. Support for these hypotheses would imply that disaggregation of geographic area data provides relevant information through the reduction of uncertainty.

Subjects

The subjects were 54 students in the Master of International Business Studies (MIBS) program at the University of South Carolina. The MIBS students are relatively sophisticated users of financial information and are well-suited to the experimental task because of their international orientation. The subjects' average age was 26. Each had taken three finance courses and three accounting courses in their master's degree program. In addition, each of the subjects had completed a 6-month internship with a multinational enterprise in a foreign country (the United States for the foreign students in the program). Fifty-nine percent of the subjects had an internship in the accounting or finance areas and 43% had conducted financial statement analysis during their internship. The accounting courses were taken in the first two semesters of study and the questionnaire was administered at the end of the fourth semester after the students had returned from their internships.

ANALYSIS AND RESULTS

Several steps were taken to analyze the responses. As was previously explained, two versions of the research instrument containing different countries were administered. A multivariate analysis of variance was conducted between the two groups of subjects to determine whether the responses were specific to the countries depicted in the cases. No significant differences existed ($p = 0.429$). Accordingly, the two groups were combined for the subsequent analysis.

Regression analysis was used to examine the relationship between risk assessments and the independent variables. The specific research hypotheses discussed were tested with t tests.

Regression Analysis

Regression Analysis was implemented on a subject-by-subject basis to determine standardized β weight values and multiple correlation coefficients squared for each subject. As this was a factorial design, the independent variables of each subject's regression model were orthogonal, thereby allowing the standardized β weights to be used as measures of the importance each subject placed on each of the independent variables [Darlington 1968].

The average R^2 for all 54 subjects was 0.49. The individual R^2s were significant for each subject, which indicates that internally consistent decisions were made by all subjects. Only four subjects had significant interaction effects.

The independent variables were coded as zero when their value was neutral, $+1$ when there was low risk, and -1 when there was high risk. Given this coding scheme, an inverse relationship between the independent variables and the level of risk would be expected. As can be seen in Table 2, this result was obtained. All of the average β weights for the independent variables have the expected negative signs.

Higher β weights signify that subjects placed more emphasis on a particular variable in their assessment of risk. On average, Eastern Hemisphere (other than Europe) was the most important independent variable as it had the highest

Table 2.   Mean Standardized β-Weight Measurements

Independent Variable	Mean β	Number of Subjects Highest Weight N	(%)
1. Europe	−0.350	16	(29.6′)
2. Latin America	−0.240	11	(20.4)
3. Eastern Hemisphere (Other Than Europe)	−0.426	27	(50.0)

mean β weight (−0.426). It was followed by Europe (−0.350) and Latin America (−0.240) in order of importance. These results imply that disaggregation of the global geographic area Eastern Hemisphere (other than Europe) to a continent level had higher information content than diaggregation of the continental classifications Europe and Latin America to a country level. Moreover, disaggregation of the continent Europe to the country level provided more information than disaggregation of Latin America. This result indicates that the subjects perceived a greater difference in risk between the high-risk and low-risk countries in Europe than they did for the high-risk and low-risk countries in Latin America.

Hypothesis Testing

Paired *t* tests were used to test the research hypotheses. For Risk Hypothesis 1, this required calculation of the difference between the average risk decision across subjects when Europe had a neutral value and when it had a high-risk vlaue. Naturally, if a difference score is large, the risk assessment differed substantially. Paired samples *t* tests were used to determine whether these differences were significantly different from zero. As can be seen in Table 3, the only comparison that was not significant was that between high-risk Latin America and neutral Latin America (Risk Hypothesis 4). Accordingly, that hypothesis was rejected. All other risk hypotheses were supported.

Rejection of Hypothesis 4 indicates that no additional information was provided when the countries in Latin America were disclosed as being relatively high-risk countries. This implies that when told only that the firm had operations somewhere in Latin America, subjects automatically assumed that operations were located in the higher risk countries in that region. Conversely, when the countries were disclosed as relatively low-risk countries in Latin America, subjects perceived that as a relevant piece of additional information and adjusted their risk assessment downward (Risk Hypothesis 5).

Table 3.   Tests of Risk Hypotheses

Hypothesis	Comparison	t Score	Probability
Europe			
1	High Risk/Neutral	6.29	0.0001
2	Neutral/Low Risk	7.65	0.0001
3	High Risk/Low Risk	10.35	0.0001
Latin America			
4	High Risk/Neutral	0.85	0.4009
5	Neutral/Low Risk	6.63	0.0001
6	High Risk/Low Risk	6.71	0.0001
Eastern Hemisphere			
(Other Than Europe)			
7	Africa/Neutral	7.82	0.0001
8	Neutral/Asia	9.04	0.0001
9	Africa/Asia	15.45	0.0001

When subjects were told that operations in Europe, Latin America, and the Eastern Hemisphere (other than Europe) were in lower risk countries in those areas, their risk assessments were significantly lower than when they were not given this specific information. If U.S. multinational firms are more heavily invested in the lower risk countries in these areas, then this result implies that it may be in the firms' best interest to provide more diclosure than is done in current practice.

Consistent with the regression results already described, the magnitudes of the t scores in Table 3 show that disaggregation of Eastern Hemisphere (other than Europe) provided more information than disaggregation of the other geographic areas.

Difference scores for each subject were also used to test the hypotheses regarding decision confidence. The cases were divided into four categories: those with zero neutral independent variables, those with one neutral independent variable, those with two neutral independent variables, and that case with three neutral independent variables. The difference scores calculated indicated the extent to which confidence changed with the level of aggregation. Paired samples t tests were used to test whether these differences were significantly different from zero. As can be seen from Table 4, only hypothesis 3 cannot be supported. Thus, decreasing the level of aggregation generally resulted in an increase in subjects' decision confidence. However, providing more detailed data on only one variable did not significantly increase users' confidence in their risk decisions.

Table 4.   Tests of Confidence Hypotheses

Hypothesis	Comparison	t Score	Probability
1	Zero/One Neutral	3.25	0.0020
2	One/Two Neutral	3.63	0.0006
3	Two/Three Neutral	0.99	0.3277
4	Zero/Two Neutral	3.87	0.0003
5	One/Three Neutral	2.49	0.0161
6	Zero/Three Neutral	3.01	0.0040

SUMMARY AND CONCLUSIONS

This study used a judgment modeling approach to evaluate the relevance of level of aggregation of geographic area data to financial statement users. Results of the study show that the level of aggregation of geographic areas is relevant in evaluating the riskiness of foreign operations.

Regarding risk assessment decisions, disaggregated data at the continent level proved to be more relevant than that at the global level and disaggregated data at the country level proved to be more relevant than that at the continent level. Disaggregation of global data caused a greater change in risk assessment than did disaggregation of continent data, implying that more information was provided by disaggregating data at the global level than at the continent level. However, this result may be specific to the geographic areas used as the independent variables in this study. Of the nine comparisons made, only disaggregation of neutral Latin America into its high-risk components provided an insignificant amount of additional information to affect risk assessment.

In addition to showing the relevance of less aggregated geographic area data, the experimental results as shown in Table 3 demonstrate that the subjects employed in this study were able to correctly differentiate between high-risk and low-risk countries in Europe and Latin America and between high-risk and low-risk areas within Eastern Hemisphere (other than Europe). The subjects perceived a greater difference in risk between the two groups of countries in Europe than in Latin America, which implies that disaggregation of Europe may be more relevant than disaggregation of Latin America in assessing risk.

Disaggregation of geographic area data also proved to be relevant under the criterion of uncertainty reduction. Confidence increased as the level of aggregation declined. The level of confidence was greatest when all three independent variables were disaggregated. However, disaggregation of only one independent variable did not lead to a significantly different level of confidence. This implies that disaggregation of all geographic areas provides more relevant information than is provided through partial disaggregation.

Evaluation of the preceding results and the following conclusions requires consideration of the study's limitations. The primary limitation relates to external validity. Generalization of the results of this study to other groups, primarily financial analysts, is tenuous. Although student subjects do not have the experience in analyzing financial statements and assessing risk that financial analysts have, financial analysts may not have the knowledge and experience to evaluate investment risk between countries that the subjects in this study apparently had. A logical extension of this study would be to use financial analysts as subjects.

Second, the countries and percentages used in the cases may not be realistic. There may not be any U.S. multinational corporations with 10% of total assets located in countries such as Portugal and Peru. Unfortunately, because information at this level of disaggregation is not being provided by firms, the realism of the cases cannot be evaluated.

Finally, the extent to which the experimental task simulates the real world was not measured. Subjects may not respond in an experimental setting in the same fashion as they would in real situations.

The results of this study imply that if a U.S. MNC is investing in the lower risk countries in different parts of the world, then it might be advantageous to disclose that fact. This is particularly true for Latin America. This disclosure could result in financial statement users perceiving that firm as being less risky, which could result in higher stock prices and a lower cost of capital.

The policy implication from the results of this study is that perhaps the FASB should require firms to present less aggregated data on foreign operations. This suggestion raises the question of how to disaggregate, i.e., what criteria should be used to determine when data must be presented at the country level, continent level, or global level. To derive policy prescriptions, further research is needed to determine when the concentration of operations in a single country or continent is material enough to affect decision making.

ACKNOWLEDGMENT

The authors express their gratitude to Adrian Harrell for his helpful comments.

REFERENCES

Arnold, J., W. Holder and M. Mann, "International Reporting Aspects of Segment Disclosure," *The International Journal of Accounting* 16(1) [Fall 1980], pp. 125-135.
Bavishi, V. and H. Wyman, "Foreign Operations Disclosure by U.S.-Based Multinational Corporations: Are They Adequate?" *The International Journal of Accounting* 16(1) [Fall 1980], pp. 153-168.
Coplin, W. and M. O'Leary, "The 1984 Risk Index for International Business," *Planning Review* [May 1984], pp. 34-40.

Darlington, R., "Multiple Regression in Psychological Research and Practice," *Psychological Bulletin* 69(3) [1968], pp. 161-182.

Emmanuel, C. and S. Gray, "Corporate Diversification and Segmental Disclosure Requirements in the USA," *Journal of Business Finance and Accounting* [Winter 1977], pp. 407-418.

Financial Accounting Standards Board," "Financial Reporting for Segments of a Business Enterprise," *Statement of Financial Accounting Standards No. 14* [FASB 1976].

Financial Accounting Standards Board, "Qualitative Characteristics of Accounting Information," *Statement of Financial Accounting Concepts No. 2* [FASB 1980].

Ijiri, Y., "Fundamental Queries in Aggregation," *Journal of the American Statistical Association* 66(366) [December 1971], pp. 766-780.

Lev, B., "The Aggregation Problem in Financial Statements: An Informational Approach," *Journal of Accounting Research,* 6(2) [Autumn 1968], pp. 247-261.

Orcutt, G., H. Watts, and J. Edwards, "Data Aggregation and Information Loss," *The American Economic Review* 57(4) [September 1968], pp. 773-787.

NEW EVIDENCE ON THE ACCURACY OF MANAGEMENT FORECASTS AND TIME-SERIES FORECASTS OF ANNUAL EARNINGS

Allen W. Bathke, Jr., John M. Hassell,
and Kenneth S. Lorek

ABSTRACT

This paper examines the comparative accuracy of management and various time-series forecasts of annual earnings on a sample of 118 management forecasts disclosed voluntarily during the 1979-1982 time period. Our results suggest that controlling for the length of the forecast horizon is crucial to the assessment of relative accuracy between forecast agents. Specifically, we found that the mean absolute percentage errors of management forecasts (0.098) were smaller than both the composite time-series forecasts (0.116) and the firm-specific time-series forecasts (0.124) and that these differences were significant at the 0.001 level. We

Advances in Accounting, Volume 7, pages 67-84.
Copyright © 1989 by JAI Press Inc.
All rights of reproduction in any form reserved.
ISBN: 0-89232-960-2

partitioned our sample of management forecasts into those that were generated during the first two quarters of the forecast year (long-term) and those generated during the last two quarters (short-term). Interestingly, we reported virtual parity between the mean absolute percentage errors between management (0.204) and the composite time-series forecasts (0.200) for the long-term forecasts ($n = 39$), but the management forecasts were slightly more accurate than the firm-specific time-series forecasts (0.204 versus 0.220). On the other hand, the short-term forecasts ($n = 79$) revealed clear dominance of management (0.046) versus both the composite time-series forecasts (0.074) and the firm-specific time-series forecasts (0.076) with significant differences at the 0.001 level. These findings provide an ex post explanation for the inconsistent results that have been reported in previous studies comparing the accuracy of management and time-series forecasts of annual earnings.

INTRODUCTION

The purpose of this study is to address an apparent anomaly that exists in the findings of the comparative accuracy forecast agent literature. Specifically, inconsistent findings are prevalent in those studies that compared the accuracy of forecasts of annual earnings made public by management (MGMT) versus those generated by autoregressive-integrated-moving-average (ARIMA) time-series models.[1] We offer a plausible explanation for such inconsistent findings—that the comparative accuracy of MGMT versus ARIMA forecasts is dependent on the length of the forecast horizon. Our results suggest that controlling for the length of the forecast horizon is crucial to an overall assessment of the relative accuracy between MGMT and ARIMA forecasts. We find that shorter term MGMT forecasts issued during the last two quarters of the forecast year are more accurate than corresponding ARIMA forecasts. However, no significant differences are found for longer term forecasts issued during the first two quarters of the forecast year. Subsequent sections of this paper include a background section and sections on the methodology, empirical results, and a final section that discusses the limitations, results, and some concluding remarks.

BACKGROUND

Few studies have provided evidence on the comparability of MGMT forecasts of annual earnings vis-à-vis sophisticated extrapolative techniques such as Box-Jenkins [1976] ARIMA models. Cameron [1986], in a survey paper on the management earnings forecast literature, concluded that slightly more complex models such as Box-Jenkins appear to provide mixed results when compared to MGMT forecasts. The studies on which such inferences are drawn have been based typically on relatively small sample sizes employing substantially older test periods. In fact, comparisons between MGMT forecasts and extrapolative techniques have concentrated on naive, mechanical predictors such as the random walk model or moving average processes. The two major exceptions to this characterization are the studies by Lorek, McDonald, and Patz (LMP) [1976] and Imhoff and Pare (IP) [1982], which use ARIMA models.

Abdel-khalik and Thompson [1977-1978] have questioned the external validity of the results reported by LMP due to the relatively small sample of 40 MGMT forecasts that was examined. LMP's forecasts were obtained from a subpopulation of 201 MGMT forecasts originally compiled by McDonald [1973]. Because McDonald restricted his examination to those MGMT forecasts that could have been included conceivably with the issuance of the preceding year's annual financial statements, only those MGMT forecasts that were issued no later than 120 days after the end of a firm's fiscal year were included. The 40 MGMT forecasts of the LMP study were selected using a stratified random sampling procedure such that an equal number (n = 4) of relatively accurate (percentage error less than 10%) and relatively inaccurate (percentage error greater than 10%) forecasts was obtained for each year in the 1966-1970 test period. LMP found no statistically significant differences between the relatively accurate MGMT forecasts and the firm-specific ARIMA forecasts in spite of the fact that the mean of these differences indicated that the MGMT forecasts were 4.5% more accurate. However, with respect to the relatively inaccurate group, the ARIMA forecasts were superior at the 0.01 significance level. Moreover, the mean of the differences favored the ARIMA forecasts by an impressive 11.4%. Overall, across the entire sample of MGMT forecasts, the ARIMA forecasts were significantly more accurate. Whether the superiority of the time-series models would have persisted had the entire subpopulation ($n = 201$) of MGMT forecasts been used is a matter of conjecture. Thus, a potential sampling variation problem may have contributed to LMP's results.

The major finding of IP concerned the inability to reject the null hypothesis of no difference among six forecast agents in predicting annual earnings when using a standardized forecast error metric. IP's sample was comprised of 46 MGMT forecasts also issued 8 to 12 months prior to year-end during the 1971-1974 period. Included among the forecast agents were the three premier ARIMA models popularized by Brown and Rozeff [1979], Foster [1977], Griffin [1977], and Watts [1975], firm-specific ARIMA models, annual analyst earnings forecasts reported in the *Earnings Forecaster,* and MGMT earnings forecasts appearing in the *Wall Street Journal.* When IP allowed their ARIMA models to incorporate actual first quarter results (Type B forecasts), they reported no statistically significant differences across all forecast agents. The generation of the so-called Type B forecasts by the ARIMA models was an attempt by IP to compensate for the possibility that the actual first quarter results may have been publicly available. Close inspection of IP's results show that the absolute percentage errors of the Foster (0.119), Brown-Rozeff (0.140), Griffin-Watts (0.121), and firm-specific ARIMA models (0.137) actually were lower than that of the MGMT forecasts (0.149). Unfortunately, the relatively small sample size ($n = 46$) and the period examined (1971-1974) make it difficult to generalize to more current time periods.

The aforementioned papers by LMP and IP stand in marked contrast to earlier work in which naive, extrapolative predictors have been consistently outperformed by MGMT forecasts.[2] Other researchers have investigated the relative accuracy of ARIMA forecasts and those forecasts of annual earnings produced by financial analysts (FAF). Specifically, Brown et al. [1987] reported statistical dominance of FAF of quarterly earnings over those generated by ARIMA models. This finding is based on a relatively large sample ($n = 235$) and is apparently robust across alternative error metrics, truncation schemes, and forecast horizons. Moreover, this finding corroborates the earlier work of Brown and Rozeff [1978] and Collins and Hopwood [1980], which were both supportive of FAF dominance over ARIMA forecasts.

In contrast to FAF superiority over time-series based forecasts, there appears to be very little difference in accuracy between forecasts of financial analysts and management. Recently, Givoly and Lakonishok [1984] reviewed the forecast agent literature and concluded that the difference in accuracy between FAF and MGMT forecasts appears inconsequential. Whatever differences are reported typically favor MGMT forecasts but not necessarily in a significant fashion.[3] These findings are suggestive of an apparent anomaly in the forecast agent literature. Specifically, Cameron [1986] and Givoly and Lakonishok [1984] conclude that MGMT forecasts typically outperform FAF although in an economically insignificant manner, and Brown et al. [1987] provide strong support favoring FAF versus ARIMA forecasts. From these fndings one might infer that MGMT forecasts are superior to ARIMA forecasts. However, the dominance of ARIMA over MGMT forecasts reported by LMP and the insignificant differences reported by IP are inconsistent with the preponderance of evidence in the literature that is supportive of FAF dominance over ARIMA forecasts and virtual parity between FAF and MGMT forecasts.

The LMP and IP results may simply be an artifact of sampling variation or test period specificity. However, the comparative accuracy of MGMT versus ARIMA forecasts may also be highly dependent upon the length of the forecast horizon. Specifically, early in the year the ability of ARIMA models to better exploit subtle patterns in the data relative to management may compensate for the broader information set enjoyed by management. However, as more information becomes available to management during the year, management forecasts may begin to dominate the ARIMA models. We noted earlier that both

LMP and IP restricted the MGMT forecasts in their samples to those issued during the first 120 days of the forecast year. However, most studies comparing FAF versus ARIMA forecasts and FAF versus MGMT forecasts did not make this restriction. In the current study, we attempt to offer a reasonable explanation for the apparently anomalous results already reported by *not* restricting our MGMT forecasts to those issued in the first 120 days of the forecast year. In this manner, we are able to assess the impact of the length of the forecast horizon on the comparative accuracy of MGMT and ARIMA forecasts.

METHODOLOGY

Sample Selection

The Dow Jones News Retrieval Service (DJNRS) was the source for our MGMT earnings forecasts. It provides a data base of articles appearing in the *Wall Street Journal* and *Barrons* as well as additional unpublished sources of MGMT forecasts appearing on the *Broad Tape*. Hassell and Jennings [1986] provide a detailed discussion of how this data base may be accessed in a context similar to the present one. For the current study, hundreds of articles published between June 1979 (the inception of the DJNRS data base) and December 1982 were retrieved using several keywords indicative of MGMT earnings forecasts. We examined each article to determine whether it contained a usable annual EPS (net income) forecast from MGMT.

Our sample consists of 118 MGMT forecasts that satisfied the following criteria: (1) the forecast was disclosed by or attributed to a corporate official during the period July 1979 to December 1982; (2) it was a specific point estimate or could be converted to a point estimate (see subsequent discussion) of either primary EPS before extraordinary items ($n = 106$) or net income before extraordinary items ($n = 12$)[4]; (3) the forecast was issued 1 to 365 days prior to year-end (e.g., between January 1 and December 31 for calendar year-end firms); and (4) quarterly EPS before extraordinary items or net income before extraordinary items (see subsequent discussion) was available for a minimum of 32 quarters prior to the date of the MGMT forecasts. These extensive quarterly earnings time-series data bases were necessary for parameter estimation when using the Box-Jenkins models.[5]

Many articles in the DJNRS contained MGMT forecasts that were not point estimates but could be converted into usable point estimates. If the article contained a range estimate, we employed its midpoint. If the forecast indicated that prior year's EPS (net income) would increase a certain percentage, the prior year's amount was multiplied by the percentage to obtain the forecast of EPS (net income). All MGMT EPS forecasts were adjusted for stock splits and dividends through December 31, 1982.

By including two types of MGMT forecasts in the sample—(1) primary EPS before extraordinary items and (2) levels of net income before extraordinary items—we excluded specifically MGMT forecasts of EPS after extraordinary items, fully diluted EPS, and net income after extraordinary items. We felt that earnings before extraordinary items were more closely related to future levels of earnings and provided a more appropriate object of prediction.[6] By reading each article that contained a MGMT forecast, we were able to ensure the comparability of the time-series forecasts with the MGMT forecasts. That is, we used the appropriate input series in the Box-Jenkins estimation process—primary EPS before extraordinary items for the EPS forecasts and levels of net income before extraordinary items for the net income forecasts. By adopting these procedures we avoided the apples versus oranges problem alluded to by Givoly and Lakonishok [1984, p. 126]:

> The data base used by these studies, particularly the later ones, was susceptible to measurement errors, such as inconsistent definitions of the earnings variable in the expectational data and the actual earnings data (fully diluted vs. primary earnings-per-share, inclusions vs. exclusions of the extraordinary items, etc.).

Because we allowed MGMT forecasts issued 1 to 365 days prior to year-end to enter the sample, we were able to provide evidence on the relative predictive ability of the two forecast agents (MGMT versus Box-Jenkins) across varying lead times in the forecast horizon. Table 1 (Panel A) provides information on the dispersion of the announcement dates of the MGMT forecasts in the sample. Note that our sample is dominated by MGMT forecasts that appeared in the last quarter of the forecast year ($n = 65$), which represents more than half (55%) of the sample. Table 1 (Panel B) also provides information on the relative frequency of the MGMT forecasts across the 4 years in the analysis (1979-1982).

Our data base highlights the decline in usable MGMT earnings forecasts in 1982. Using a different procedure to obtain such forecasts over a slightly longer time period (1978-1983), Baginski [1987] also observed a similar decline in the number of usable MGMT forecasts during the latter part of his sample period. Based on a sample review of articles from DJNRS, it appears that companies generated a smaller number of MGMT forecasts during 1982 relative to the 1979-1981 period. Not only were managers less inclined to issue forecasts in 1982, but when they did, they were less specific and issued more open-ended ones.

Panel C of Table 1 presents certain macroeconomic factors that describe the economic climate in existence during the holdout period. The marked decline in before tax profits in 1982 for manufacturing as well as wholesale and retail companies coupled with an unemployment rate of 9.5% in that same year underscores the economic recession that the country was experiencing.

Table 1.   Distribution of Management Earnings Forecasts
and Macroeconomic Factors

Panel A: Days Prior to Year End

QTR IV 1-91 days	QTR III 92-182 days	QTR II 183-274 days	QTR I 275-365 days	Total
65	14	29	10	118

Panel B: By Year of the Forecast

1979	1980	1981	1982	Total
30	32	41	15	118

Panel C: Macroeconomic Factors during the Forecast Period[a]

1. Profits in Billions (Before Tax)—Manufacturing Companies

1979	1980	1981	1982
85.6	72.9	86.7	59.0

2. Profits in Billions (Before Tax)—Wholesale and Retail Companies

1979	1980	1981	1982
27.1	23.6	32.8	27.6

3. Unemployment Rate

1979	1980	1981	1982
5.8%	7.0%	7.5%	9.5%

4. Gross National Product (in Billions)

1979	1980	1981	1982
1479.4	1475.0	1531.8	1485.4

[a] Source: Department of Commerce, Bureau of Economic Analysis.

These factors evidently contributed to a reduction in GNP in 1982 relative to 1981. Faced with declining profits and rising unemployment levels, it is understandable why management seemingly appeared to have been more reluctant to provide projections of earnings in this uncertain economic environment.

Considerable evidence regarding the time-series properties of earnings numbers has appeared in the last decade of time-series research in accounting.[7] We employed the three parsimonious univariate time-sharing models that have been popularized by Brown and Rozeff [1979] (BR), Foster [1977] (F), and Griffin [1977] and Watts [1975] (GW) and estimated firm-specific (FS) time-series models to generate forecasts of annual earnings. Initially, we considered only employing the parsimonious time-series models for two reasons. First, Foster [1977] has attributed the identification of complex, firm-specific

ARIMA models to potential search bias and sampling variation. Second, and more importantly, the parsimonious models have not been outperformed by firm-specific alternatives.[8]

Based on the empirical literature, we believed that firm-specific models would not outperform the parsimonious models. However, we included the firm-specific models for two reasons. First, in an ideal situation in which sufficient data are available to identify the model structure and in which the data are free from measurement error, identifying the specific model structure rather than relying on a parsimonious structure should enhance predictive ability. Second, in a practical setting, investors or others seeking efficient forecast models may be willing to expend the additional time and resources to identify firm-specific models rather than relying on a parsimonious structure. Thus we included firm-specific models as well as the parsimonious models. In customary *(pdq)* × *(PDQ)* notation, the parsimonious models may be characterized as follows:

Model	(pdq) × (PDQ)
1. Brown-Rozeff	(100) × (011)
2. Foster	(100) × (010) with drift
3. Griffin-Watts	(011) × (011)

where

p = number of regular autoregressive parameters
d = number of consecutive differences
q = number of regular moving-average parameters
P = number of seasonal autoregressive parameters
D = number of seasonal differences
Q = number of seasonal moving-average parameters

Although our tables report the forecast accuracy of the BR, F, and GW parsimonious time-series models individually, our statistical tests, in which we compare the accuracy of parsimonious time-series models versus MGMT forecasts, will be based on composite time-series forecasts (COMP). Complete information on the statistical tests for each parsimonious model as all as COMP and FS models is presented in Appendix B. Although an infinite number of ways exist to form a composite forecast, Moriarity and Adams [1984] and Makridakis et al. [1982], among others, have shown that simple averages of forecasts are more accurate than individual forecasts in diverse settings. Specifically, Makridakis et al. [1982] found that a simple average of six different time-series forecasts outperformed all individual models as well as more complex weighting schemes (i.e., weighted averages). The theoretical rationale for combinational forecasting is similar to combining securities under portfolio theory to diversify away unsystematic risk. In this way, the likelihood of making a larger estimation error is reduced compared to the estimation error generated by a single point estimate. Therefore, we generated COMP time-series forecasts for comparative purposes with MGMT forecasts using an equally weighted combination of the predictions generated by the F, BR, and GW parsimonious models.

Error Metrics and Hypotheses

We employed three different error metrics that have been popularized in the accounting literature: (1) absolute value of percentage error (APE), (2) absolute value of relative prediction error (ARPE), and (3) absolute value of the standardized forecast error (AFSE). These metrics are defined below:

$$APE = |(A-F)/A|$$
$$ARPE = |(A-F)/F|$$
$$ASFE = |(A-F)/\sigma_A|$$

where

A = actual annual earnings
F = forecasted annual earnings
σ_A = standard deviation of annual earnings.

The absolute values of the error metrics were used to avoid positive forecast errors from counterbalancing negative ones. APE is the most frequently employed error metric in forecasting studies that have appeared in the accounting literature. It is consistent with a linear loss function that does not penalize larger forecast errors proportionately more than smaller errors. ARPE was used by LMP and IP and is based on the notion that expected earnings provide the relevant benchmark in assessing accuracy. We employed ASFE to control partially for potential variability in earnings across sample firms.[9]

Initially, we assessed the null hypothesis that there was no difference in forecast errors between MGMT forecasts, COMP forecasts, and firm-specific (FS) forecasts of annual earnings. In subsequent analyses, we refined the above hypothesis by controlling for the length of the forecast horizon. Specifically, we assessed the comparative forecast accuracy of MGMT forecasts generated in the first, second, third, or fourth quarter versus the COMP and FS forecasts generated in the corresponding quarter.

EMPIRICAL RESULTS

In Panel A of Table 2 we present the earnings forecast results across the entire sample of firms ($n = 118$), quarter during which the MGMT forecasts were announced (first, second, third, or fourth), year of the forecast (1979, 1980, 1981, 1982), and error metric (APE, ARPE, and ASFE). We present the aggregate results to illustrate simply the relative insensitivity of our findings to the specific error metric used as well as to demonstrate the superiority of MGMT forecasts on an aggregate basis. Specifically, the smallest errors across all three error metrics were generated by the MGMT forecasts. The MAPE of the MGMT forecasts (0.098) was smaller than the F (0.122), BR (0.128), and GW (0.118) models as well as the COMP (0.116) and FS forecasts (0.124). We note that the equal weighting scheme used to generate the COMP forecasts did reduce marginally the MAPE of COMP forecasts versus those of the individual premier models, which is consistent with the literature on composite forecasting previously cited. As a result of the consistency of these findings, we provide only MAPE results in subsequent partitioning of the data. In Panel B of Table 2, we employed a Wilcoxon matched pairs signed ranks test to assess the overall difference in accuracy between the MGMT, COMP, and FS forecasts.[10] The Wilcoxon test revealed that the differences in forecast errors described above were significant at the 0.001 level. Panel B also shows that no significant difference existed between the COMP and FS forecast errors ($p = 0.379$).

Partitioning of our sample by considering the length of the forecast horizon allows us to assess the comparative forecasting issue with greater precision. Therefore, in Table 3 we disaggregated the overall results reported in Table 2 into the specific quarters during which the MGMT forecast was made publicly available: Quarter I (275-365 days prior to year-end) $n = 10$, Quarter II (183-274 days prior) $n = 29$, Quarter III (92-182 days prior) $n = 14$, and Quarter IV (1-91 days prior) $n = 65$. Annual earnings predictions from the Box-Jenkins models were formed by aggregating the appropriate number of n-step-ahead quarterly earnings forecasts. Specifically, all Quarter I management forecasts ($n = 10$) were compared with four step-ahead Box-Jenkins forecasts because first quarter actual earnings numbers for the 10 firms in question were not publicly available prior to the disclosure of the MGMT forecasts. In this case the Box-Jenkins annual earnings forecast would be the sum of the one, two, three, and four step-ahead quarterly earnings forecasts.

The remaining MGMT forecasts were carefully matched to the appropriate n-step-ahead Box-Jenkins forecast of annual earnings based on the timing of the MGMT forecasts disclosure and the announcement date of the relevant quarterly earnings number. For example, if a MGMT forecast was issued during the second quarter, then the forecast date was matched against the release date for the first quarter earnings number. If actual first quarter earnings were available prior to the MGMT forecast issuance date, then the Box-Jenkins annual earnings forecast was compiled by summing the actual first quarter earnings with the forecasts for the second (one step-ahead), third (two steps-ahead), and fourth (three steps-ahead) quarterly earnings forecasts. Table 3

Table 2.   Comparative Analysis of Mangement and Box-Jenkins
Forecasts of Earnings

Panel A: Forecast Errors for Entire Sample[a] (n = 118)

			Type of Forecast			
Error Metric[b]	MGMT	F	BR	GW	COMP	FS
MAPE	0.098	0.122	0.128	0.118	0.116	0.124
MARPE	0.085	0.124	0.135	0.118	0.117	0.131
MASFE	0.276	0.360	0.384	0.366	0.306	0.387

Panel B: Wilcoxon Matched Pairs Signed Ranks Statistic on MAPE[c]

	COMP	FS
MGMT	-3.354[d]	-3.890[d]
COMP		-0.880

Notes: [a] The error metrics were all truncated at 100%. The relative rankings and overall results were unaffected by alternative truncation schemes (i.e., 200%, 300%) as well as no truncation.

  [b] MAPE   =   mean absolute percentage error.
  MARPE   =   mean absolute relative prediction error.
  MASFE   =   mean absolute standardized forecast error.
  MGMT   =   Management forecast of annual earnings.
  F   =   Foster's time-series model forecast of annual earnings.
  BR   =   Brown-Rozeff's time-series model forecast of annual earnings.
  GW   =   Griffin-Watts' time-series model forecast of annual earnings
  COMP   =   Composite time-series model forecast of annual earnings
  FS   =   Firm-Specific time-series model forecast of annual earnings.

  [c] A negative Wilcoxon statistic indicates that the "row" forecast is more accurate than the "column" forecast.

  [d] Significant at the 0.001 level. Note that similar results were obtained using the MARPE and MSFE error metrics.

provides detailed information on the specific matching of MGMT forecasts with n-step-ahead Box-Jenkins forecasts. Note that 22 of the 29 Quarter II MGMT forecasts were matched with 3 step-ahead Box-Jenkins forecasts whereas 7 of these forecasts were matched with 4 step-ahead ones. This is because 7 of the 29 Quarter II MGMT forecasts were disclosed prior to the public announcement of the first quarter annual earnings numbers. Detailed information on the Quarter III and IV MGMT forecasts and their appropriate n-step-ahead Box-Jenkins forecasts is also provided in Table 3.

Although our methodology matches precisely the respective MGMT and Box-Jenkins forecasts on the basis of the relationship between the MGMT forecast disclosure date and the availability of quarterly earnings numbers prior to that date, we recognize that a potential bias against a small percentage of Box-Jenkins forecasts may exist. It is conceivable that MGMT forecasts generated within short intervals of an actual quarterly earnings announcement date may have been formed partially on the basis of insider information with

Table 3.   n Step-Ahead Time-Series Forecasts

Management Forecast Issued in	Step-Ahead				Total
	4-Step	3-Step	2-Step	1-Step	
Quarter I (275-365 days from Y/E)	10				10
Quarter II (183-274 days from Y/E)	7	22			29
Quarter III (82-182 days from Y/E)		5	9		14
Quarter IV (1-91 days from Y/E)			17	48	65
Total	17	27	26	48	118

respect to the actual quarterly earnings number. Indeed, for those forecasts issued later in the quarter, disclosure of the previous quarter's earnings is within 3 days of the management forecast in the majority of cases (52%). Thus, almost assuredly management had knowledge of the actual quarterly earnings number when making the annual earnings forecast. Detailed information on the elapsed time between the issuance of the management forecast and the disclosure of the previous quarters earnings is provided in Appendix C. Previous researchers have made simplifying assumptions such as IP's Type A versus Type B categories wherein all MGMT forecasts generated in the first quarter were compared to both 4 step-ahead Box-Jenkins forecasts (Type A) and 3 step-ahead forecasts (Type B). We relied on the more precise matching procedure described above rather than this alternate approach.

The partitioning of the overall forecast results by the quarter in which the MGMT forecast was generated is reflected in Table 4. In Panel A we provide the MAPEs by quarter for each forecast agent. Quarter I forecasts ($n = 10$) reveal that the COMP model (0.169) actually outperformed the MGMT (0.194) and FS (0.203) forecasts. Of course the small sample of Quarter I forecasts precludes statistical testing of these differences. Nevertheless, it is interesting to observe the lack of dominance of MGMT when a relatively long-term forecast horizon is examined (275-365 days from year-end). We note that our Quarter I MGMT forecasts are similar to those that were tested by LMP and IP in the sense that they were issued quite early in the forecast year. Recall that neither study reported dominance of MGMT forecasts versus the time-series models.

Table 4. Forecast Results by Quarter of Management Forecast

Panel A: Partitioning by Quarter					
MGMT	F	BR	GW	COMP	FS
	< Quarter I (275-365 days from Y/E) MAPES ($n = 10$) >				
0.194	0.160	0.180	0.204	0.169	0.203
	< Quarter II (183-274 days from Y/E) MAPES ($n = 29$) >				
0.207	0.233	0.248	0.207	0.211	0.226
	< Quarter III (92-182 days from Y/E) MAPES ($n = 14$) >				
0.106	0.131	0.154	0.135	0.140	0.136
	< Quarter IV (1-91 days from Y/E) MAPES ($n = 65$) >				
0.033	0.069	0.060	0.061	0.060	0.063

Panel B: Statistical Testing of Short-Term versus Long-Term forecasts

< Long-Term Forecasts ($n = 39$) >

	MAPE			Wilcoxon Statistics[a]	
MGMT	COMP	FS		COMP	FS
0.204	0.200	0.220	MGMT	-0.943	-1.833[b]
			COMP		-1.260

< Short-Term Forecasts ($n = 79$) >

	MAPE			Wilcoxon Statistics[a]	
MGMT	COMP	FS		COMP	FS
0.046	0.074	0.076	MGMT	-3.499[c]	-3.682[c]
			COMP		-0.095

[a] A negative sign on the Z statistic indicates that the "row" forecast is more accurate than the "column" forecast.
[b] Significant, $p = 0.10$, two-tailed test.
[c] Significant, $p = 0.001$, two-tailed test.

Virtual parity exists between the MAPEs of MGMT forecasts (0.207) and COMP forecasts (0.211) in the Quarter II forecasts ($n = 29$) whereas the FS errors are larger (0.226). In fact, the previously reported overall dominance of MGMT forecasts appears confined entirely to the Quarter III and IV forecasts. Specifically, in the Quarter III forecast ($n = 14$), the MAPEs of MGMT (0.106) were more accurate than COMP (0.140) and FS (0.136) forecasts. This pattern of MGMT dominance persisted in the Quarter IV forecasts ($n = 65$) in which MGMT (0.033) outperformed COMP (0.060) and FS (0.063) forecasts in a similar fashion.

The forecasts issued during the first two quarters were aggregated and labeled long-term forecasts ($n = 39$). We did likewise for those forecasts issued during the last two quarters, which we labeled short-term forecasts ($n = 79$).[11] The results of this aggregation process are presented in Panel B of Table 4. We observe clearly that virtual parity exists between the MAPEs of MGMT (0.204) and COMP (0.200) forecasts for the long-term forecasts, and, as expected, the Wilcoxon test revealed insignificant differences in the MAPEs ($p = 0.346$). Note that these results are in sharp contrast to the significant differences reported on the entire sample of forecasts. Additionally, the MGMT forecasts were more accurate than the FS forecasts ($p = 0.10$) and the FS and COMP forecasts were insignificantly different ($p = 0.208$).

Finally, the short-term forecasts revealed clear dominance of MGMT forecasts (0.046) versus COMP (0.074) and FS (0.076) forecasts with significant differences at the 0.001 level. Again, the FS and COMP forecasts were not significantly different ($p = 0.925$). The current results suggest that the earlier findings of LMP and IP with respect to the lack of dominance of MGMT versus time-series models may be attributable partially to the relatively long-term nature of the MGMT forecasts that those studies examined.

DISCUSSION OF LIMITATIONS, RESULTS, AND CONCLUDING REMARKS

The results of the current study must be interpreted relative to several caveats. First, our sample of MGMT forecasts was obtained by searching the DJNRS data base using several keywords indicative of MGMT forecasts of annual earnings. Although we have no a priori reason to suspect any systematic biases in the sample selection process, a self-selection bias may affect the generalizability of our findings. Second, the regulatory environment pertaining to the potential legal liability of management for inaccurate projections of earnings was altered in June 1979 when the Securities and Exchange Commission promulgated a safe-harbor rule for MGMT forecasts. Thus, our results may not be strictly comparable to earlier work that was conducted on data generated in a less certain legal liability environment. Third, macroeconomic variables including GNP levels, unemployment rates, and aggregate profit levels for the 1979-1982 period were dissimilar to the economic climate existing in the early 1970s on which earlier work was based. Collectively, these factors suggest that the results of the current study may not be strictly generalizable to MGMT forecasts generated across different time periods and economic conditions.

The testing of our initial hypothesis resulted in a significant difference in forecast accuracy between MGMT forecasts of annual earnings and ARIMA forecasts. No significant difference was found between COMP and FS forecasts. The MAPEs of the MGMT forecasts (0.098) were smaller than those generated by COMP (0.116) and FS (0.124) forecasts, and the differences between the MGMT and COMP and MGMT and FS forecasts were significant at the 0.001 level. In subsequent analyses, we reported that the MGMT forecast dominance was confined to short-term forecast horizons, specifically those generated in Quarters III and IV ($n = 79$). The MAPEs for these forecasts were MGMT (0.046), COMP (0.074), and FS (0.076). On the other hand, no significant differences were found between MGMT (0.204) and COMP (0.200) when comparing the long-term forecasts ($n = 39$), but MGMT forecasts were more accurate than FS forecasts (0.204 versus 0.220).

These results may lend support to the notion that management's knowledge of the impact of recent events (e.g., labor contracts, sales orders, capital budgeting decisions) manifests itself over relatively short forecast horizons. Alternatively, management's knowledge of year-end adjustments, accruals, and deferrals may partially explain its dominance in the short-term forecasts reported in the paper. Because univariate time-series models do not incorporate any of these recent events and/or year-end adjustments into the formation of forecasts, the short-term results are not surprising. However, the inability of management to develop significantly more accurate long-term forecasts is interesting and may partially be the result of overreaction to short-term phenomena and/or lack of sufficient inside information to allow management to generate more accurate longer term forecasts. Because the previous work of LMP and IP consisted of samples of MGMT forecasts that were long-term in nature, it is perhaps understandable why their findings were not supportive of MGMT dominance.

The fact that a majority of the forecasts that entered our sample (55%) were generated in Quarter IV of the forecast year may provide an ex post explanation of our results. The Quarter IV results are consistent with the management of certain firms waiting to forecast annual earnings until it felt that it had a competitive advantage over other forecast agents. To the extent that few firms manifested such superiority in earlier quarters, the results might be a reflection on the extent to which inside information was obtained by management and/ or the efficacy of their forecasting methodologies. An interesting extension of the current research would be to examine the relative accuracy of MGMT and COMP forecasts of quarterly earnings. Such an analysis would pinpoint whether differential accuracy exists across all four quarters or is confined to a specific quarter.

Appendix A.   Firm-Specific Box-Jenkins AIRMA Models

Panel A:	Total Number of Parameters	Frequency
	5	3
	4	3
	3	22
	2	59
	1	31
		118

(continued)

82 ALLEN W. BATHKE, JR., JOHN M. HASSELL, and KENNETH S. LOREK

Appendix A. (continued)

Panel B: < Differencing Combinations and $(pdq) \times (PDQ)$ Structures >

1. Frequency of Models with No Differencing $(d = D = 0)$

(100) × (100)	9
(100) × (000)	5
Other Combinations	6
	20

2. Frequency of Models with Consecutive Differencing $(d = 1)$

(012) × (100)	5
(011) × (100)	4
(011) × (000)	3
(010) × (100)	3
Other Combinations	9
	24

3. Frequency of Models with Seasonal Differencing $(D = 1)$

(100) × (011)	12
(100) × (012)	6
(100) × (110)	3
Other Combinations	9
	30

4. Frequency of Models with Consecutive and Seasonal Differencing $(d = D = 1)$

(011) × (011)	12
(010) × (011)	11
(011) × (010)	4
(013) × (011)	3
Other Combinations	14
	44

Appendix B. Wilcoxon Sign-Ranks Z Statistics (Significance Level) for all Forecasts[a] $(n = 118)$

	FS	F	BR	GW	COMP
MGMT	-3.890 (0.001)	-2.917 (0.004)	-3.840 (0.001)	-3.563 (0.001)	-3.354 (0.001)
FS		0.184 (0.854)	-1.076 (0.282)	0.691 (0.490)	0.880 (0.379)
F			-0.960 (0.337)	-0.074 (0.941)	-0.071 (0.935)
BR				1.508 (0.131)	2.432 (0.015)
GW					0.329 (0.742)

[a] A negative sign on the Z statistic indicates that the "row" forecast is more accurate than the "column" forecast.

Appendix C. Management Forecasts Issued Prior to the Release of the
Previous Quarter's Earnings (*n* = 31)

Elapsed Time from Release of Forecast to Disclosure of Previous Quarter's Earnings

	3 Days or Less	4-8 Days	9-18 Days	19-32 Days	33-49 Days
Number of Forecasts	16	3	6	5	1
(Percentage)	(52)	(10)	(19)	(16)	(3)

NOTES

1. See the background section for a summary of these works.
2. See Cameron [1986 pp. 74-75] for a summary of these results.
3. See Jaggi [1980] as an example of a study that shows dominance of MGMT forecasts versus FAF.
4. We originally discovered 61 MGMT earnings forecasts of net income before extraordinary items. However, only 12 of these forecasts did not have a corresponding EPS forecast for the same firm. We eliminated the 49 duplicate forecasts and did not allow them to enter our sample twice.
5. We followed the recommendations of McKeown and Lorek [1978] who provided detailed information on the sensitivity of the number of observations to the estimation of quarterly earnings time-series models.
6. Given the nonrepetitive and unusual nature of extraordinary items, inclusion of such factors in the earnings series could conceivably reduce the autocorrelation of the series in question making identification of an appropriate time-series model problematic.
7. See Bao et al. [1983] for an in-depth review of this literature.
8. See Brown and Rozeff [1979] for comparisons of firm-specific ARIMA models versus the parsimonious models. Appendix A details the specific ARIMA model structures that were identified on our sample of firms.
9. See Imhoff and Pare [1982, p. 433] for a discussion of this issue.
10. See Hollander and Wolfe [1973] for a discussion of the Wilcoxon nonparametric test. Note that we provide information only on the MAPE metric. However, similar results were obtained when using MARPE and MASFE metrics.
11. Aggregation was clearly necessary to obtain reasonable sample sizes for statistical testing.

REFERENCES

Abdel-khalik, A. R. and R. Thompson, "Research on Earnings Forecasts: The State of the Art," *The Accounting Journal* [Winter 1977-1978], pp. 180-209.

Bao, D. H., M. T. Lewis, W. Lin and J. Manegold, "Applications of Time-Series Analysis in Accounting: A Review," *Journal of Forecasting* [October-December 1983], pp. 405-423.

Box, G. E. P. and G. M. Jenkins, *Time Series Analysis: Forecasting and Control,* 2nd ed. [Holdon Day, 1976].

Baginski, S., "Intraindustry Information Transfers Associated with Management Forecasts of Earnings," *Journal of Accounting Research* [Autumn 1987], pp. 196-216.

Brown, L. and M. Rozeff, "The Superiority of Analyst Forecasts as Measures of Expectations: Evidence from Earnings," *Journal of Finance* [March 1978], pp. 1-16.

Brown, L. and M. Rozeff, "Univariate Time-Series Models of Quarterly Accounting Earnings Per Share: A Proposed Model," *Journal of Accounting Research* [Spring 1979], pp. 179-189.

Brown L., P. Griffin, R. Hagerman and M. Zmijewski, "Security Analyst Superiority Relative to Univariate Time-Series Models in Forecasting Quarterly Earnings," *Journal of Accounting and Economics* [March 1987], pp. 1-16.

Cameron, A., "A Review of Management's Earnings Forecast Research," *Journal of Accounting Literature* 5 [1986], pp. 57-81.

Collins, W. and W. Hopwood, "A Multivariate Analysis of Annual Earnings Forecasts Generated from Quarterly Forecasts of Financial Analysts and Univariate Time-Series Models," *Journal of Accounting Research* [Autumn 1980], pp. 390-406.

Foster, G., "Quarterly Accounting Data: Time Series Properties and Predictive Ability Results," *The Accounting Review* [January 1977], pp. 1-21.

Givoly, D. and J. Lakonishok, "Properties of Analysts' Forecasts of Earnings: A Review and Analysis of Research," *Journal of Accounting Literature* [Spring 1984], pp. 117-148.

Griffin, P., "The Time Series Behavior of Quarterly Earnings: Preliminary Evidence," *Journal of Accounting Research* [Spring 1977], pp. 71-83.

Hassell, J. and R. Jenkins, "Relative Forecast Accuracy and the Timing of Earnings Forecast Announcements," *The Accounting Review* [January 1986], pp. 58-75.

Hollander, M. and D. Wolfe, *Nonparametric Statistical Methods* [Wiley, 1973].

Imhoff, E. and P. Pare, "Analysis and Comparisons of Earnings Forecast Agents," *Journal of Accounting Research* [Autumn 1982], pp. 429-439.

Jaggi, B., "Further Evidence on the Accuracy of Management's Forecasts Vis-à-vis Analysts' Forecasts," *The Accounting Review* [January 1980], pp. 96-101.

Lorek, K., C. McDonald and D. Patz, "A Comparative Examination of Management Forecasts and Box-Jenkins Forecasts of Earnings," *The Accounting Review* [April 1976], pp. 321-330.

Makridakis, S., A. Anderson, R. Carbone, R. Fildes, M. Hibon, R. Lewandowski, J. Newton, E. Parzen and R. Winkler, "The Results of Extrapolation (Time Series) Methods: Results of a Forecasting Competition," *Journal of Forecasting* [1982], pp. 111-153.

McDonald, C., "An Empirical Examination of the Reliability of Published Predictions of Future Earnings," *The Accounting Review* [July 1973], pp. 502-510.

McKeown, J. and K. Lorek, "A Comparative Analysis of the Predictive Ability of Adaptive Forecasting, Re-estimation, and Re-identification Using Box-Jenkins Time Series Analysis on Quarterly Earnings Data," *Decision Sciences* [October 1978], pp. 658-672.

Moriarity, M. and A. Adams, "Management Judgment Forecasts, Composite Forecasting Models, and Conditional Efficiency," *Journal of Marketing Research* [August 1984], pp. 239-250.

Watts, R., "The Time-Series Behavior of Quarterly Earnings," unpublished paper, University of New Castle [1975].

THE PREDICTION ACCURACY OF ALTERNATIVE INCOME REPORTING MEASURES:
AN EMPIRICAL INVESTIGATION

Jenice P. Stewart

ABSTRACT

There has been an upsurge in accounting research on the information content of cash flows (CF). This paper describes empirical evidence about signals provided by alternative earnings measures of various measures of "cash flow." Included among definitions of CF are cash flow from operations (CFO) and cash flow after investments (CFAI). Evidence is provided on three issues. First, recurring income per share is computed and its underlying time-series behavior is investigated. Second, evidence on the forecast accuracy of alternative random walk (RW) earnings models in estimating cash flows 1 year ahead is presented. Finally, the FASB's assertion that recurring earnings per share (EPSr) is superior to net income per share (EPSp) in predicting future CF is examined. The results

Advances in Accounting, Volume 7, pages 85-112.
ISBN: 0-89232-960-2

can be summarized as follows. First, the behavior of EPSr is in many cases similar to the defined behavior of EPSp. Second, EPSr more accurately predicts CFAI; however, EPSp more accurately predicts CFO. The superiority of the prediction accuracy of the alternative RW with drift income models was not robust enough to produce significant results using the Mann-Whitney Wilcoxon tests. Overall, these results are not consistent with the FASB's and accounting literature's assertion that EPSr provides better forecasts of future cash flows than does EPSp.

INTRODUCTION

In the past two decades, extensive literature on the underlying process of income and on forecasting earnings has developed. The predictive ability of income research has appeared in the accounting literature mainly because of the emphasis by the Financial Accounting Standards Board (FASB) [1978] and The American Institute of Certified Public Accountants (AICPA) [Study Group on the Objectives of Financial Statements 1973] on the usefulness of accounting income numbers in predicting cash flows.[1] Earlier research on the predictability of income concentrated on the underlying process of historical cost income [Ball and Wats 1972; Ball and Brown 1969; Albrecht et al. 1977; Brooks and Buckmaster 1976]. However, financial analysts [Mortimer 1979; Francis 1980], accounts [Strauss and Arcady 1981; Paton 1922, 1940], and users of financial reports [Mims 1979; SEC 1980] argue that recurring income may be more useful in assessing future cash flows than net income. Recurring earnings, an undisclosed variable, are those components of income that have a reasonably stable pattern over time, that is, sustainable revenues, expenses, and gains and losses associated with long-term earnings projects.

More recently, there has been a renewed interest in the recurring, "permanent" [Beaver et al. 1980], or "persistent" [Lipe 1986] component of earnings. Beaver et al. [1980] and Lipe [1986] argue that future cash flow (CF) measures are composed of random walk and recurring revisions. In addition, the FASB, as part of its conceptual framework [FASB 1979], recognized the need for research on the usefulness of recurring income in predicting cash flows. Therefore, the objective of this study is to investigate the underlying process of recurring income and compare the 1-year-ahead forecasting accuracy of net income and recurring income.

Improved earnings models are potentially useful to the investor in assessing future cash flows. Recurring income would be useful to the financial analyst in determining the intrinsic value of a security that is used to assess whether the security is under- or overvalued [Francis 1980]. Paton [1940] contends that recurring income is more useful than net income in assessing an entity's future earnings power. Users of financial reports state that they would have better been able to predict the downturn in General Motor's earnings if recurring income had been reported [Mims 1979]. In contrast, historical cost income has been cited as presenting only the change in earned capital, which may not be useful in assessing an entity's cash flows [Mautz 1966; Hendriksen and Budge 1974]. Accountants contend that the single-step method of reporting income can be misleading because too much emphasis is placed on the bottom line [Paton 1940; Strauss and Arcady 1981].

SIGNIFICANCE OF THE STUDY

Prior market studies have generally been concerned with the relationship between accounting signals and user decisions [Bowen et al. 1986]. This study, like most prior studies, is concerned with the relationship between earnings measures and prediction accuracy of cash flow. This investigation, however, differs from previous market studies in the variables examined. Previous studies investigating the predictive ability of income numbers have concentrated on an unclassified earnings statement. For example, earlier studies have employed the Box-Jenkins [Watts and Leftwich 1977; Albrecht et al. 1977] and exponential smoothing [Gordon et al. 1966; Ball and Watts 1972; Brooks and Buckmaster 1976] methodologies in examining net income. Those time series forecasting studies employing exponential smoothing have included only the use of annual reported net income. For example, Brooks and Buckmaster [1976] used exponential smoothing to determine whether annual net income follows an exponential, submartingale, or other underlying process over time. Ball and Watts [1972] used exponential smoothing primarily to observe the behavior of net income, deflated net income, and sales over time. Gordon et al. [1966] applied exponential smoothing to annual net income numbers in testing the smoothing hypothesis. This study differs from previous predictive ability studies because exponential smoothing is used to detect an undisclosed compoent of earnings, recurring income. Thus, this study advocates a classified, recurring and nonrecurring, earnings report that may assist the user in maximizing return on his investment portfolio.

Other market research has been concerned with the information content of earnings in assessing stock price or cash flows using interval estimates. For example, Rayburn [1986], Wilson [1986], and Bowen et al. [1986] investigate the relationship between abnormal returns of accurals and cash flows. However, this study is concerned not with an interval estimate, but with a point estimate of CF derived from alternative accrual earnings measures. Interval estimates imply prediction of abnormal returns, that is, the difference between expected and actual returns. Point estimation is concerned with predicting the actual measure of a variable. Thus, this study does not predict abnormal returns of cash flow variables, but tests the prediction accuracy of accrual income

measures. Lev and Ohlson [1982] state that there are many information content
studies based on interval estimates but few based on point estimates. They argue
that accounting and/or accrual variables must manifest themselves on a
valuation level as well as value changes. They conclude that much research
effort, analytical as well as empirical, is needed to address this issue. The
accruals included in prior studies were abnormal returns, whereas this
investigation includes predicting point estimates of CF.

Some studies on the prediction accuracy of accrual earnings have
concentrated on the evaluation of various earnings forecasting methods
[Brandon et al. 1986; Johnson and Schmitt 1974]. This study is not an attempt
to assess alternative forecasting methodologies, but includes assessing the
predicting accuracy of alternative earnings measures in predicting cash flows.

Third, the cash flows measures used in this study differ from those of Rayburn
[1986]. Rayburn uses data prior to 1971 when the Statement of Changes in
Financial Position was not generally available, thus her measure of cash flow
may contain more accruals and may be less exclusively related to operations than
the measure cash flow from operations (CFO). I also consider an additional
measure of cash flow, cash flow after investment activities (CFAI). CFAI is used
in practice and is supported by the FASB [1986] as an important component
in many firm valuation models and in lending and bond rating decisions. Additionally, this study adopts a view that is opposite to the "institutional environment" adopted by Rayburn [1986]. That is, in this study cash flows are the
primitive concept. This means that the variability and timing of future cash flows
are attributes of concern to investors. From this perspective it is reasonable to
ask whether recurring income more accurately predicts cash flows than net income?

Finally, Wilson [1986] and Lipe [1986] investigate the relations between
components of earnings (gross profit, general and administrative expense,
depreciation expense, interest expense, income taxes, and other income), which
are routinely disclosed in financial reports. Unlike Lipe's and Wilson's
components of earnigns defined as "persistent" or "permanent income,"
recurring earnings, as defined in this study, are not disclosed in financial
reports. Rather, the objective of this article is to determien if recurring income
should be a required disclosure in financial reports because of its superior
prediction accuracy above net income. That is, this study has an implication
not reflected in the Wilson [1986] and Lipe [1986] articles: Recurring income
(additional information) may be consistent with market partipants rationally
reacting to differences in the time-series properties of cash flows.

THEORETICAL UNDERPINNING

The empirical and analytical linkages between income classification
alternatives and predictability (or accuracy) in assessing cash flow variables

have been discussed in the accounting and finance literature. For example, classification has been cited as the basis for giving accounting numbers meaning [Mattessich 1964]. Accounting can result in a more precise language through classification [Gilman 1939; Whorf 1956; Sapir 1956]. That is, the more precise or delineated (through classification) a language, the more consistently interpreted and reliable are the data. Thus, an earnings statement format that results in more classifications than is currently practiced in accounting may result in a change in market participant's behavior.

A classified earnings statement may not only influence a reader's expectations but alternative reporting procedures or disclosures have been shown to have an effect on the user's predictions. For example, management is believed to smooth income in selecting among alternative reporting procedures to influence the investor's subjective expectations regarding earnings and dividends. Studies employing alternative inventory valuation disclosures have resulted in statistically significant differences in investment decisions [Dopuch and Ronen 1973], stock price predictions [Jensen 1966], and advertising expenditure decisions [Bruns 1965]. In addition, alternative ways of arraying data on the income statement, all-inclusive versus current operating performance, have been addressed as a significant issue in accounting since 1966 [see Accounting Research Bulletin (ARB) 43, Chapter 8, and Accounting Principles Board (APB) 9 and 30]. Hence, the results of this investigation may have implications regarding market participant's behavior.

The present study includes an empirical investigation of two income numbers, net income and recurring income, to determine if alternative classifications of income affect predictions of cash flows, and, if so, which is the more accurate predictor. The alternative earnings models are compared in three ways. First, the underlying behavior of recurring income is examined and compared to net income. Second, the relative prediction accuracy of two RW earnings models is assessed by comparing their performance in forecasting cash flows. The forecast accuracy is computed using point, not interval estimates. Third, a Mann-Whitney Wilcoxon test is applied to the forecasts of the alternative random walk (RW) earning models to assess the significance of forecasting accuracy differences. Finally, the findings of the three comparisons are reported. The last section of this paper includes a summary and conclusion of the study.

TIME-SERIES MODELS

The two earnings measures advocated in the accounting literature as useful predictors of CF are net income [Watts and Leftwich 1977; Albrecht et al. 1977; Ball and Brown 1969] and recurring income [Paton 1940; Mortimer 1979; Beaver et al. 1980; Strauss and Arcady 1981; Hendriksen 1982; Lipe 1986].

Recurring income is defined in this study as earnings that are systematically related to long-term earnings projects [FASB 1979]. These income measures are included in the RW with drift models, advocated in the accounting literature as a good proxy for the behavior of earnings [see Albrecht et al. 1977; Watts and Leftwich 1977]. The specific structural forms of these RW with drift income models [Fried and Givoly 1982; Lorek 1982] are provided as:

RW with Drift Model 1: Net Income

$$E(CF_t) = \alpha + \beta_1 EPSp_{t-1} + \beta_2 Sp + e_t \qquad (1)$$

where

E = expected value
$EPSp$ = annual primary earnings per share
t = time period
Sp = the (arithmetic) average growth in EPSp computed over the years $t-6$ to $t-1$
e = identically distributed random variables
CF = cash flow variable = CFO and CFAI, which were computed from COMPUSTAT as follows:

$$CFO = WCFO - REC - INV - OCA + AP + TP + OCL$$

where

$WCFO$ = working capital from operations (Item No. 110)
REC = change in accounts receivable during the period (Item No. 2)
INV = change in inventories during the period (Item No. 3)
OCA = change in other assets during the period (Item No. 68)
AP = change in taxes payable during the period (Item No. 71)
OCL = change in other current liabilities during the period (Item No. 72)

$$CFAI = CFO + PSPPE + PSI - \Delta PPE - \Delta INVMT$$

where

$PSPPE$ = proceeds from sale of property, plant, and equipment (Item No. 107)
PSI = proceeds from sale of investments (Item No. 109)
PPE = amount of capital expenditures during the period (Item No. 128)
$INVMT$ = increase in investments in other corporations during the period (Item No. 129).

Previous empirical studies [Fried and Givoly 1982; Penman 1983] indicate that net income of time t is best predicted using past earnings in a RW with drift model. Furthermore, as a general model, RW with drift was found to perform as well as the firm-specific Box-Jenkins models in describing the time series characteristics of earnings [Watts and Leftwich 1977; Albrecht et al. 1977]. However, the above model implies that past earnings are not only the best predictor of income in period t, but also the best predictor of CFs one period ahead.

RW with Drift Model 2: Recurring Income

The other earnings measure advocated as having predictive value is recurring income. Recurring income was computed as a function of the exponential smoothing trend and α level combination that minimized mean squared error (MSE) using the 12 most recent historical years of normal income (i.e., net income before extraordinary items, discontinued operations, change in accounting principle, unusual in nature, and infrequent in occurrence items). Exponential smoothing is used to delete any unsystematic change in amount of a normal earnings item. The unsystematic change should be determined by management. However, because an unexpected change, a nonrecurring item, is usually not disclosed in financial reports [Hendriksen and Budge 1974] it is estimated in this study via exponential smoothing. Although there may be factors exogenous to the firm that may impact recurring earnings that a mechanical univariate time series model, such as exponential smoothing, would exclude, Cragg and Malkiel [1968], Elton and Gruber [1972], and Imhoff and Pare [1982] found that mechanical or univariate time series models can be just as accurate in predicting earnings as human forecasts. Hence, the specific structural form of the recurring RW with drift model [Fried and Givoly 1982; Lorek 1982] is:

$$E(CF_t) = \alpha + \beta_1 EPSr_{t-1} + \beta_2 Sr + e_t \tag{2}$$

where

    EPSr = recurring earnings divided by the number of shares used to calculate primary earnings per share. (That exponential smoothing model [first, second, or third order] and α level—ranging from 0.05 to 0.95 in increments of 0.05—combination that minimizes MSE when tracking [Casey 1979] the most recent 12 years of normal income [Bowerman and O'Connell 1979; Brown 1963] is recurring income.)

    Sr = the (arithmetic) average growth rate in EPSr computed over the years $t-6$ to $t-1$.

Exponential smoothing also includes the same flexibility in tracking a time-series as that of management. For example, exponential smoothing can be used to estimate future values of a time-series based solely on past observed values of that time-series, whether the historical trend is random, linear, or quadratic. Single exponential smoothing is used to tract a time-series with a random trend. To predict future periods in a time-series using first-order or single exponential smoothing, first S_t, the smoothed estimate or statistic is computed [Bowerman and O'Connell 1979, p. 122]:

$$S_t = \alpha Y_t + (1 - \alpha)S_{t-1} \tag{3}$$

where

α = the smoothing constant
Y_t = income of time period t
S_t = smoothed estimate or statistic.

Once S_t has been computed, then the one-period-ahead forecast is computed [Bowerman and O'Connell 1979]:

$$\hat{Y}_{t+1} = S_t \qquad (4)$$

where

$\hat{}$ = estimated or forecasted data.

Alpha, referred to as the smoothing constant, measures the contribution that the observations Y_t, Y_{t-1}, Y_{t-2}, ..., Y_1 make to the most recent estimate, S_{t+1}. For example, the forecast using single-order exponential smoothing can be written [Bowerman and O'Connell 1979, p. 123]:

$$S_t = \alpha Y_t + \alpha(1 - \alpha)Y_{t-1} + \alpha(1 - \alpha)^2 Y_{t-2} + \ldots + \alpha(1 - \alpha)^{t-1} Y^1 + (1 - \alpha)^t S_0 \qquad (5)$$

The coefficients of the observations, α, $\alpha(1 - \alpha)$, $(1 - \alpha),^2$, $\alpha(1 - \alpha)^{t-1}$ decrease geometrically with the age of the observations and measure the contributions that the observations Y_t, Y_{t-1}, Y_{t-2}, ... Y_1 make to the most recent estimate of S_t.

Second-order exponential smoothing introduces additional formulas that estimate the linear trend so that it can subsequently be used to forecast short-to-intermediate-period(s)-ahead. The second-order exponential smoothing statistic is computed as follows [Bowerman and O'Connell 1979, p. 146]:

$$S_t^{[2]} = \alpha S_t + (1 - \alpha)S_{t-1}^{[2]} \qquad (6)$$

where

$S_t^{[2]}$ = double smoothed statistic

$S_{t-1}^{[2]}$ = trend, the initial trend is computed using a least-squares procedure.

In Equation (6), the double smoothed statistic $S_t^{[2]}$ is found by applying the smoothing operation to the output of the single smoothing equation. The first S_t and second $S_t^{[2]}$ smoothed statistics are then used to compute the forecast for second-order exponential smoothing as follows [Bowerman and O'Connell 1979, p. 147]:

$$\hat{Y}_{t-1} = 2 + \frac{\alpha}{1 - \alpha} \ S_t - 1 + \frac{\alpha}{1 - \alpha} \ S_t^{[2]} \qquad (7)$$

where

Y_{t+1} = forecasted earnings one period ahead.

Triple exponential smoothing would be useful in forecasting data with a quadratic or curvilinear trend. Triple exponential smoothing involves the use of the smoothed statistics S_t, $S_t^{[2]}$, and $S_t^{[3]}$. S_t and $S_t^{[2]}$ computations were illustrated in Equations (3) and (6). The initial value of $S_t^{[3]}$ is computed using 12 years of historical data, after which the third smoothed statistic $S_t^{[3]}$ is computed as follows [Bowerman and O'Connell 1979, p. 173]:

$$S_t^{[3]} = \alpha S_t^{[2]} + (1 - \alpha) S_{t-1}^{[3]} \qquad (8)$$

$S_t^{[3]}$ is found by applying the smoothing operation to the output of the double smoothing equation. The equation used to derive the one-period-ahead forecast of earnings using triple exponential smoothing is as follows [Bowerman and O'Connell 1979, p. 177]:

$$Y_{t+1} = [6(1 - \alpha)^2 + (6 - 5\alpha)\alpha + \alpha^2]\, \frac{S_t}{2(1 - \alpha)^2}$$

$$- [6(1 - \alpha)^2 + 2(5 - 4\alpha)\alpha + 2\alpha^2]\, \frac{S_t^{[2]}}{2(1 - \alpha)^2}$$

$$+ [2(1 - \alpha)^2 + (4 - 3\alpha)\alpha + \alpha^2]\, \frac{S_t^{[3]}}{2(1 - \alpha)^2} \qquad (9)$$

Thus, exponential smoothing can be used to accommodate time-series with no trend (single), with a linear trend (double), and with a quadratic trend (triple).

Exponential smoothing, rather than some other time-series forecasting technique, was used in converting normal earnings to recurring earnings for three reasons. First and foremost, exponential smoothing can be justified on the basis of its relative prediction accuracy in relation to Box-Jenkins. For example, Groff [1973, p. 30] found that Box-Jenkins models were "either approximately equal to or greater than the errors of the corresponding exponentially-smoothed models for most series." Granger and Newbold [1977] and Brandon et al. [1986] conclude, after conducting time-series forecasts, that exponential smoothing models were the best predictors for short-time-series over Box-Jenkins methodology. Additionally, Box-Jenkins and exponential smoothing are from the same general ARIMA methods [Makridakis and Wheelwright 1978]. Second, exponential smoothing is preferred over other moving-average models because moving average is less attractive, requires more data points and calculations, and is less accurate than exponential smoothing techniques [Makridakis and Wheelwright 1978]. Third, the α level of exponential smoothing indicates whether the income-generating proces is a random walk with drift model (α levels between 0.8 and 0.98 [Muth 1960]), random walk model (α is greater than 0.98, which implies that income in $t-1$ is the best predictor of income in t), or a mean reverting model (the α level is less than 0.3 or 0.4 [Bowerman and O'Connell 1979]). Additionally, the exponential smoothing model used implies either no trend (single), a linear trend (double), or a quadratic trend (triple) [Bowerman and O'Connell 1979; Brown 1963]. The optimal firm-specific smoothing model (i.e., minimizes MSE) is used to estimate recurring income 1 year ahead.

One year ahead or annual windows were incorporated in this study for three reasons. Two of the reasons are based on arguments advance by BBD [1986], whose study defines cash flow as does this study. First, "as with earnings, considerable cash flow data likely become available to market participants throughout the fiscal year" [BBD 1987, p. 732]. Second, conversion to a more refined measure of cash flow is not practical for shorter than annual time periods [BBD 1987, p. 732]. Rayburn [1986] also uses annual rather than quarterly data for similar reasons. Third, Hoskin et al. [1986, p. 2], who investigate the information content of components of firm disclosures, justify using annual data on reducing data-gathering costs. Hence, the annual window is used in this study for the above reasons.

The preceding two variables, EPSp and EPSr, represent the independent variables of the study. Each of these two independent variables is used to predict each dependent or CF variable one period ahead. The dependent variables are those CF measures defined and supported by BBD [1986, 1987], Largay and Stickney [1980], and Gombola and Ketz [1983] when examining the information content of accruals.

RESEARCH DESIGN

Hypotheses

The following two hypotheses are based on the expectation that recurring income is a more accurate predictor of cash flows than is net income.

HYPOTHESIS 1.   Recurring earnings is more accurate than primary earnings per share when used to predict CFO 1 year ahead.

HYPOTHESIS 2.   Recurring earnings is more accurate than primary earnings per share when used to predict CFAI 1 year ahead.

Sample Selection and Data Acquisition

Annual income and cash flow data were taken from the annual *COMPUSTAT* file of the New York Stock Exchange (NYSE) industrial firms [1982]. The 153 firms included in this study are listed in Table 1 and have the following characteristics.

1. *They are based in the United States.* Only U.S. firms were selected in an attempt to provide for homogeneity in application of the same generally accepted accounting principles.
2. *They have consistent year ends.* That is, only firms that have consistent monthly year ends for the data base period, 1966 through 1982, were included in the sample to allow for homogeneity of 12 months between year ends.
3. *Annual cash flow data for the years 1966-1982 were available on COMPUSTAT.* The statistical technique used in computing recurring income is sensitive to both few and missing observations [Ball and Watts 1972].
4. *Banks, utilities, and life insurance or property and casualty companies are not included.* This is because "special items," a variable used to compute recurring income, is not disclosed in the financial reports of these entities.
5. *Firms that have had major capital structure changes (mergers and consolidations) between the years 1966 and 1982 are excluded from the study.* This is to allow for some consistency with respect to within-firm risk class from year to year.

Table 1. Sampled Firms

Sample Firm Number	Industry Number (SIC)	Company Number (Standard and Poors)	Company Name	Year End
1	100	797151	San Carlos Milling	December
2	100	912673	U S Sugar Corp	September
3	1000	43413	Asarco Inc	December
4	1021	49249	Atlas Cons Mining & Dev	December
5	1021	81851	Benguet Corp-Cl B	December
6	1021	717265	Phelps Dodge Corp	December
7	1031	200435	Cominco Ltd	December
8	1040	131069	Callahan Mining Corp	December
9	1040	134411	Campbell Red Lake Mines	December
10	1040	257075	Dome Mines Ltd	December

(continued)

Table 1.   (Continued)

Sample Firm Number	Industry Number (SIC)	Company Number (Standard and Poors)	Company Name	Year End
11	1040	374586	Giant Yellowknife Mines Ltd.	December
12	1040	437614	Homestake Mining	December
13	1211	656780	North American Coal	December
14	1311	811267	Scurry-Rainbow Oil Ltd	September
15	1381	379352	Global Marine Inc	December
16	1381	423452	Helmerich & Payne	September
17	1499	929160	Vulcan Materials Co	December
18	1600	20771	Alpha Portland Inds	December
19	1600	390662	Great Lakes Intl Inc	December
20	1600	618448	Morrison-Knudsen	December
21	2010	440452	Hormel (Geo. A.) & Co	October
22	2050	24069	American Bakeries Co	December
23	2063	594729	Michigan Sugar	September
24	2065	890516	Tootsie Roll Industries Inc	December
25	2065	982526	Wrigley (Wm.) Jr Co	December
26	2085	811850	Seagram Co Ltd	July
27	2200	387478	Graniteville Co	December
28	2300	364802	Garan Inc	September
29	2300	972091	Wilson Brothers	December
30	2400	189000	Clopay Corp	December
31	2450	158501	Champion Home Builders Co	February
32	2520	361614	GF Corp	December
33	2750	248019	De Luxe Check Printers	December
34	2750	257867	Donnelley (R.R.) & Sons Co	December
35	2841	742718	Procter & Gamble Co.	June
36	2844	423236	Helene Curtis Industries	February
37	2844	459506	Intl Flavors & Fragrances	December
38	2860	305477	Fairmount Chemical Co Inc	December
39	2860	744635	Publicker Industries Inc	December
40	2911	28861	American Petrofina-CL A	December
41	2911	228219	Crown Central Petroleum CP-A	December
42	2911	302290	Exxon Corp	December
43	2911	453038	Imperial Oil Ltd-CL A	December
44	2911	626717	Murphy Oil Corp	December
45	2911	718507	Phillips Petroleum Co	December
46	3000	42465	Armstrong Rubber	September
47	3000	216831	Cooper Tire & Rubber	December
48	3000	318315	Firestone Tire & Rubber Co	October
49	3000	382550	Goodyear Tire & Rubber Co	December
50	3000	730026	Plymouth Rubber Co-CL A	November
51	3079	688605	O'Sullivan Corp	December
52	3140	818869	Shaer Shoe Corp	October
53	3199	869716	Swank Inc	December

(continued)

Table 1. (Continued)

Sample Firm Number	Industry Number (SIC)	Company Number (Standard and Poors)	Company Name	Year End
54	3241	374532	Giant Portland & Masonry CE	December
55	3241	745075	Puerto Rican Cement Co Inc	December
56	3250	826750	Sikes Corp-CL A	February
57	3310	125005	CCX Inc	June
58	3318	217687	Copperweld Corp	December
59	3310	224399	Crane Co	December
60	3310	668367	Northwestern Steel & Wire Co	July
61	3310	760779	Republic Steel Corp	December
62	3310	949357	Welded Tube of America	January
63	3320	525030	Lehigh Valley Inds	December
64	3330	13716	Alcan Aluminium Ltd	December
65	3330	761763	Reynolds Metals Co	December
66	3410	228255	Crown Cork & Seal Co Inc	December
67	3429	276317	Eastern Co	December
68	3443	124800	CBI Industries Inc	December
69	3444	770553	Robertson (H.H.) Co	December
70	3444	977878	Wolverine Aluminum Corp	December
71	3452	784626	SPS Technologies Inc	December
72	3499	105655	Braun Engineering	December
73	3499	871565	Synalloy Corp	September
74	3520	244199	Deere & Co	October
75	3520	627151	Murray Ohio Mfg Co	December
76	3540	172172	Cincinnati Milacron Inc	December
77	3540	489170	Kennametal Inc	June
78	3540	540210	Lodge & Shipley Co	December
79	3550	730162	Pneumatic Scale Corp	November
80	3560	90527	Binks Mfg Co	November
81	3573	253849	Digital Equipment	June
82	3573	459200	Intl Business Machines Corp	December
83	3573	754713	Raymond Industries Inc	December
84	3573	848355	Sperry Corp	March
85	3622	286065	Electronics Corp of America	December
86	3630	439272	Hoover Co	December
87	3630	637215	National Presto Inds Inc	December
88	3630	758114	Reece Corp	December
89	3630	963320	Whirlpool Corp	December
90	3640	266867	Duro-Test Corp	July
91	3651	296677	Esquire Ratio & Electron Inc	December
92	3662	34393	Andrea Radio Corp	December
93	3662	421596	Hazeltine Corp	December
94	3662	860486	Stewart-Warner Corp	December
95	3670	922204	Varian Associates Inc	September
96	3674	882508	Texas Instruments Inc	December

(continued)

Table 1.   (Continued)

Sample Firm Number	Industry Number (SIC)	Company Number (Standard and Poors)	Company Name	Year End
97	3679	268420	Eeco Inc	December
98	3679	500440	Kollmorgen Corp	December
99	3711	27627	American Motors Corp	July
100	3711	171196	Chrysler Corp	December
101	3711	345352	Ford Motor Co of Canada Ltd	December
102	3711	370442	General Motors Corp	December
103	3711	459578	Intl Harvester Co	October
104	3721	97023	Boeing Co	December
105	3728	909313	United Aircraft Products Inc	November
106	3760	539821	Lockheed Corp	December
107	3760	573275	Martin Marietta Corp	December
108	3861	277461	Eastman Kodak Co	December
109	3861	847660	Speed-O-Print Bus Machines	December
110	3990	776338	Ronson Corp	December
111	4210	690326	Overnite Transportation	December
112	4511	1765	AMR Corp-Del	December
113	4511	276191	Eastern Air Lines	December
114	4511	419848	Hawaiian Airlines Inc	December
115	4511	482516	KLM Royal Dutch Airlines	March
116	4511	667281	Northwest Airlines Inc	December
117	4511	692515	Ozark Air Lines Inc	December
118	4511	957586	Western Air Lines Inc	December
119	4700	137051	Canal-Randolph Corp	October
120	4811	30177	American Tele & Telegraph	December
121	4811	171870	Cincinnati Bell Inc	December
122	4811	843486	Southern New Eng Telephone	December
123	4922	694325	Pacific Gas Transmission	December
124	4922	835415	Sonat Inc	December
125	4922	882593	Texas Oil & Gas Corp	August
126	5050	480827	Jorgensen (Earle M.) Co	December
127	5311	228093	Crowley Milner & Co	January
128	5311	556139	Macy (R.H.) & Co	July
129	5331	147129	Casablanca Inds Inc	June
130	5331	809123	SCOA Industries Inc	January
131	5411	72797	Bayless (A.J.) Markets Inc	December
132	5411	172576	Circle K Corp	April
133	5411	501044	Kroger Co	Decemberr
134	5411	786514	Safeway Stores Inc	December
135	5411	825101	Shopwell Inc	December
136	5411	862097	Stop & Shop Cos	January
137	5411	885851	Thriftimart Inc-CL A	March
138	5621	974212	Winkelman Stores Inc	January
139	5712	859145	Sterchi Brothers Stores Inc	February

(continued)

Table 1. (*Continued*)

Sample Firm Number	Industry Number (SIC)	Company Number (Standard and Poors)	Company Name	Year End
140	5912	543162	Longs Drug Stores Inc	January
141	5944	382748	Gordon Jewelry Corp	August
142	5961	648210	New Process Co	December
143	6200	319336	First Boston Inc	December
144	6798	619103	Mortgage Growth Investors	November
145	6799	2050	ASA Ltd	November
146	6799	573057	Martek Invs Inc	December
147	6799	911315	United Park City Mines	December
148	7011	27591	American Motor Inns	July
149	7011	553012	MGM Grand Hotels Inc	August
150	7011	982135	Wrather Corp	December
151	7392	654098	Nielsen (A.C.) Co-CL A	August
152	7830	456632	Inflight Services Inc	June
153	7990	254687	Disney (Walt) Productions	September

Error Metrics

There are two sets of error metrics included in this study. The first error metric was developed as a result of the exponential smoothing computation of recurring earnings. The model specifications of exponential smoothing that minimized the mean squared error (MSE) in tracking the 12 most recent years of normal income represented the first set of error metrics. The MSE metric is used in computing recurring income rather than the mean absolute deviation (MAD) error metric because the RW with drift model is the statistical forecasting technique that is used to detect the usefulness of, or the relationship of, each independent variable in predicting each dependent variable. RW with drift models use the least-squares or MSE principle, thus the MSE error metric is considered the optimal exponential smoothing model to allow for consistency in determining the optimal or most useful model.

The second set of error metrics used in this study includes the forecast accuracy of each of the earnings models. The forecast accuracy of both models will include mean absolute relative error (MARE), the primary variable of interest, and an average relative error (ARE), a measure of model bias [Fried and Givoly 1982].

The relative prediction error was defined as [Fried and Givoly 1982, p. 90]:

$$e_{it}^k = (A_{it} - P_{it}^k)/|A_{it}| \qquad (10)$$

where

k = expectation model
i = observation index ($i = 1, \ldots, N$)
t = year
A = actual cash flow value
P = predicted cash flow value.

The MARE is computed as [Fried and Givoly 1982, p. 90]:

$$|e_t^k| = (1/N) \sum_i |e_{it}^k| \qquad (11)$$

The corresponding measure of bias in the model, average relative error (ARE), is computed as [Fried and Givoly 1982, p. 90]:

$$e_t^k = (1/N) \sum_i e_{it}^k \qquad (12)$$

If A (actual cash flow value) was ≥ -0.2 and ≤ 0.2, then the observation was deleted from the study. This methodology was followed by Elton et al. [1981] and Collins et al. [1987] to prevent large error distribution bias.

It is common in the forecasting literature to "pull in" or "truncate" outliers. A truncation rule of setting all errors, of the individual firm, greater than 200% exactly equal to 200% was used in this study. (Truncation was used by Foster [1977], BBD [1987], and Brown et al. [1987].) To ensure that the results are not the result of the deflator/truncation choice, two additional specifications of the truncation rule were included in this study. The two additional truncation rules were no truncation and truncate at 300%. Results qualitatively equivalent to the results presented in this paper were obtained across the three truncation and two deflator (MARE and ARE) methodologies.

Statistical Methods

If one earnings measure (EPSp or EPSr) is the more accurate predictor of cash flows, then the more accurate model should exhibit a smaller MARE. RW with drift is used to investigate the association between each earnings model (EPSp and EPSr) and each CF (CFO and CFAI) measure. The RW with drift model has been shown to be the best means of detecting the relationship between an independent and dependent variable when certain key assumptions are met [Johnston 1960; Lorek 1982]. These assumptions are (1) homoscedasticity, (2) the relationship between the independent and dependent variable is linear, and (3) the dependent variables are statistically independent. If heteroscedastic disturbance is found in the error terms of the RW with drift model, this indicates that the resulting equation will not be a minimum variance estimator. However, the objective of using RW with drift was not to develop a model that produces the least or minimum variance, but to determine which model or predictor variable better assessed the dependent variable. Therefore, a violation of the constant variance assumption should not materially affect the results of this study. However, a test of heteroscedasticity was conducted using the F test statistic of the Goldfeld-Quandt F test [Judge et al. 1982].

Lack of independence in the error terms over time (serial correlation) can cause the parameters of the model to be inaccurately estimated. Because the data included in the RW with drift models are cross-sectional rather than time-series, there was no need to test for serial correlation in the models [Judge et al. 1982].

RW with drift was used to test the linear relationship between each independent and dependent variable for each year (1978-1982) across firms. An investigation of the normality of residuals was conducted to determine whether a parametric or nonparametric statistic is more appropriate in testing the prediction accuracy of the RW with drift models of EPSp and EPSr. The Kolmogorov-Smirov D test statistic [Gibbons 1976] was used to determine if the residuals were normally distributed. Because the residuals were found to be nonnormally distributed, the Mann-Whitney Wilcoxon test was used to test the usefulness of the two RW with drift earnings models [Gibbons 1976]. The Mann-Whitney Wilcoxon test was applied to all deflator/truncation error metrics, across companies as well as within each SIC.

RESULTS

Recurring Income

In computing recurring income, exponential smoothing was used as a surrogate for management to eliminate from normal earnings amounts that are unsystematic in relation to normal earnings of the most recent 12 years. The frequencies of optimal exponential smoothing models used to compute recurring income are illustrated in Table 2 (MSE metric). The findings indicate that in most cases recurring earnings exhibit a RW pattern (i.e., $\alpha = 0.95$; see Tables 2 and 3). RW with drift has been found to be the underlying behavior of traditional net income [Gordon et al. 1966; Ball and Watts 1972; Brooks and Buckmaster 1976]. This finding indicates that recurring income, in many cases, behaves similarly to net income and/or that those shocks that affect net income also affect recurring income.

However, recurring income exhibits a random or no trend and mean reverting pattern [Brooks and Buckmaster 1976], or emphasizes noise reduction for those firms exhibiting a triple exponential pattern and for many (55) of the observations exhibiting a single exponential smoothing pattern. In

Table 2. Exponential Smoothing Models of Recurring Earnings
Employing the Mean Squared Error (MSE) Metric

	Model Order			
α	1	2	3	Total
0.05	55	7	8	70
0.10	10	2	7	19
0.15	9	5	8	22
0.20	13	6	8	27
0.25	12	12	10	34
0.30	13	9	14	36
0.35	11	8	13	32
0.40	14	11	13	38
0.45	11	13	11	35
0.50	10	9	13	32
0.55	22	11	2	35
0.60	17	8	3	28
0.65	12	16	1	29
0.70	8	10	4	22
0.75	11	8	2	21
0.80	10	5	3	18
0.85	9	6	3	18
0.90	9	5	3	17
0.95	187	39	6	232
Total	443	190	132	765

Table 3. Exponential Smoothing Models of Recurring Earnings
Employing the Mean Absolute Deviation (MAD) Error Metric

	Model Order			
α	1	2	3	Total
0.05	46	9	7	62
0.10	7	2	6	15
0.15	10	1	5	16
0.20	11	6	13	30
0.25	10	7	10	27
0.30	21	9	10	40
0.35	16	5	4	25
0.40	15	7	20	42
0.45	11	13	11	35
0.50	14	12	5	31
0.55	17	8	5	30
0.60	17	7	2	26
0.65	7	10	1	18
0.70	20	9	5	34
0.75	11	5	2	18
0.80	13	19	8	40
0.85	17	24	2	43
0.90	11	24	0	35
0.95	148	46	4	198
Total	422	223	120	765

these instances recurring income did not exhibit a RW, but a curvilinear trend and a mean reverting behavior.

The optimal exponential smoothing model, in some cases, tended to be industry related. For example, the mining industry dominated those firms exhibiting a curvilinear pattern. For those firms whose recurring earnings were computed using single exponential smoothing with $\alpha \leq 0.6$, the manufacturing industry dominated. This finding suggests that recurring income within industries may follow similar income-generating processes.

Predictive Ability Results

Table 4 represents the forecasting error of each RW with drift earnings model, EPSp and EPSr, in predicting CFAI. Two features of the table merit discussion. First, the MARE findings show that EPSr is a superior predictor of CFAI than EPSp in every year. However, the MARE forecast error distribution is tighter (i.e., has the smallest standard deviation) for EPSp than EPSr.

Second, the forecast error of each earnings model measured by MARE is greater than ARE for each year. The ARE reveals that both earnings models tended to overpredict every year. This finding of optimistic bias in each model conforms to those reported by previous studies [Brown et al. 1987; Fried and Givoly 1982].

Table 4.   Earnings' Forecast Accuracy of CFAI

Year(s)	MARE[a]	S.D.	ARE[a]	S.D.
		Net Income Model		
CFA1 78-82	0.963	0.749	0.583	1.073
CFA1 78	0.978	0.768	0.596	1.094
CFA1 79	1.040	0.738	0.640	1.107
CFA1 80	0.920	0.753	0.576	1.042
CFA1 81	0.845	0.717	0.463	1.009
CFA1 82	1.027	0.761	0.630	1.114
		Recurring Model		
CFA1 78-82	0.116	1.480	0.574	1.075
CFA1 78	0.197	1.468	0.568	1.097
CFA1 79	0.151	1.056	0.607	1.104
CFA1 80	0.081	1.475	0.570	1.054
CFA1 81	0.056	1.454	0.468	1.007
CFA1 82	0.207	1.499	0.629	1.116

[a]The size of these forecast errors are similar to those of BBD [1986].

Table 5.   Earnings' Forecast Accuracy of CFO

Year(s)	MARE[a]	S.D.	ARE[a]	S.D.
		Net Income Model		
CFO 78-82	0.914	0.799	0.404	1.104
CFO 78	0.960	0.802	0.438	1.136
CFO 79	0.917	0.793	0.402	1.106
CFO 80	0.928	0.832	0.523	1.094
CFO 81	0.875	0.813	0.347	1.095
CFO 82	0.891	0.761	0.306	1.092
		Recurring Model		
CFO 78-82	1.027	0.590	0.397	1.177
CFO 78	1.056	0.583	0.415	1.253
CFO 79	1.031	0.575	0.382	1.297
CFO 80	1.026	0.649	0.514	1.102
CFO 81	1.023	0.586	0.359	1.126
CFO 82	0.999	0.561	0.313	1.105

[a]The size of these forecast errors are similar to those of BBD [1986].

Table 5 illustrates the forecasting error of each earnings model in predicting CFO 1-year-ahead. The MARE results demonstrate that EPSp is a better predictor of CFO than EPSr in every year. However, the MARE forecast error distribution is tighter (i.e., has the smallest standard deviation) for EPSr than for EPSp. Table 5 also reveals that the bias in forecast error is positive, that is, both earnings models tended to underpredict CFO every year.

Table 6.   Test of Heteroscedastic Disturbance
Goldfeld-Quandt Test F Statistic[a]

Year	CFO		CFAI	
	EPS	REPS	EPS	REPS
1978	0.1764	0.1648	0.1566	0.4137
1979	0.1603	0.1724	0.5041	0.2600
1980	1.9113[b]	2.2163[b]	0.3111	0.0003
1981	0.6047	0.7371	0.9188	1.4784
1982	0.7829	0.7302	0.7411	0.9115

[a]$d.f. = 64.$
[b]Significant at $p \le 0.01.$

Table 7. Wilcoxon p value Using MARE Results

Variable/Year	Sample	Agriculture and Forestry	Mining	Contract and Construction	Manufacturing	Transportation and Communication	Wholesale and Retail Trade	Finance and Real Estate	Services
CFO 78	0.6381	0.6985	0.8682	0.6625	0.9161	0.8682	0.6268	0.7237	0.9362
CFO 79	0.8803	0.6985	0.9010	1.0000	0.9258	0.8682	0.9856	0.7237	0.9362
CFO 80	0.6709	0.6985	0.9339	1.0000	0.8318	0.8357	0.8430	0.7237	0.9362
CFO 81	0.7349	0.6985	1.0000	1.0000	0.9240	0.9339	0.7048	0.7237	0.9362
CFO 82	0.8551	0.6985	0.9339	0.6625	0.6956	0.7089	0.8095	0.7237	0.9362
CFAI 78	0.9504	n/a[a]	0.9476	1.0000	0.9585	0.9698	0.9755	0.5403	0.9362
CFAI 79	0.9549	n/a[a]	0.8777	1.0000	0.9530	0.9698	0.9264	0.5403	0.8345
CFAI 80	0.9549	n/a[a]	0.7609	1.0000	0.8746	0.8955	0.7350	0.5403	0.6650
CFAI 81	0.9168	n/a[a]	0.8391	0.6985	0.9469	0.8598	1.0000	n/a	0.8852
CFAI 82	0.9975	0.6985	0.7973	0.6625	0.8002	0.9476	0.9770	0.5403	1.0000

[a] n/a = No observations were available after deleting observations with zero or −0.02 ≤ actual CF Value ≤ 0.02 CFAI or CFO.

Table 8. Wilcoxon *p* value Using ARE Results

Variable/Year	Sample	Agriculture and Forestry	Mining	Contract and Construction	Manufacturing	Transportation and Communication	Wholesale and Retail Trade	Finance and Real Estate	Services
CFO 78	0.8909	0.6985	1.0000	0.6625	0.7455	0.8682	0.7595	0.7237	0.3785
CFO 79	0.9154	0.6985	0.9010	1.0000	0.8958	0.8682	0.6787	0.7237	0.6889
CFO 80	0.6827	0.6985	0.9010	1.0000	0.8889	0.8357	0.9282	0.7237	0.9362
CFO 81	0.8824	0.6985	0.8682	1.0000	0.8822	0.9339	0.7566	0.7237	0.9362
CFO 82	0.8551	0.6985	0.9339	1.0000	0.9397	0.7089	0.9451	0.7237	0.9362
CFAI 78	0.8471	n/a[a]	0.8955	1.0000	0.9154	0.9698	0.8777	0.5403	0.9362
CFAI 79	0.7193	n/a[a]	0.7976	1.0000	0.9119	0.9698	0.9755	0.5403	1.0000
CFAI 80	0.8236	n/a[a]	0.7583	1.0000	0.9718	0.9476	0.8294	0.5403	0.8852
CFAI 81	0.9060	n/a[a]	0.8375	0.6985	0.9744	0.8598	0.9183	n/a	0.8852
CFAI 82	0.8150	0.6985	0.9310	1.0000	0.8551	0.9476	0.9770	0.5403	1.0000

[a] n/a = No observations were available after deleting observations with zero or $-0.02 \leq$ actual CF Value ≤ 0.02 CFAI or CFO.

Test of the Assumptions of RW with Drift

The results of the Goldfeld-Quandt Test F statistic for heteroscedastic disturbance are displayed in Table 6. The recurring and net income RW with drift models do not exhibit significant heteroscedastic disturbance in the residuals except for the year 1980, in predicting CFO. Thus, it is concluded that the RW with drift model is an appropriate forecasting model for CF.

The Usefulness of Each Model

The residuals of the RW with drift models (EPSp and EPSr) exhibited a significant nonnormal distribution. Thus, the nonparametric Mann-Whitney Wilcoxon statistic was used to test the significance of the RW with drift models (EPSp and EPSr). The resultant Wilcoxon p values using the MARE and ARE error metrics are illustrated in Tables 7 and 8. In all cases, the null hypotheses were not rejected at the $p \leq 0.05$ level of significance. This implies that EPSr is equally as accurate as EPSp in predicting CF 1 year ahead. The nonsignificant Wilcoxon statistics were also exhibited within industries.

CONCLUSIONS AND OBSERVATIONS FOR FUTURE RESEARCH

This study sought to operationally define recurring earnings and to compare the predictive ability of EPSp and EPSr in forecasting CFO and CFAI 1 year ahead across 153 companies (years 1978-1982). Specifically, the goal was to determine the legitimacy of the arguments that recurring income is more accurate in predicting cash flows and thus alternative ways of presenting information may affect a user's predictions. To the extent that firms were systematically excluded, the conclusions of the study are limited to the subpopulation of COMPUSTAT firms that the sample represents.

Recurring income was computed using the optimal exponential smoothing model to delete unsystematic variations from normal income. The results of exponential smoothing indicate that in most cases recurring income exhibits a RW with drift underlying pattern (i.e., α equal to 0.95) that is similar to that of net income. However, many firms did not exhibit a RW with drift, but a mean reverting pattern (i.e., $0.50 > \alpha$). For example, under first-order exponential smoothing, the cell with the second greatest frequency was at an α level of 0.05. The exponential smoothing results also indicate that the behavior of recurring income may be industry related. The mining industry dominated third-order exponential smoothing and the manufacturing industry dominated first-order exponential smoothing. That is, recurring income of the mining industry tends to be curvilinear, whereas recurring income of the manufacturing industry tended to be mean reverting for the years 1978-1982. These findings of the industry effects are similar to those of Watts and Leftwich [1977, p. 262] and Watts [1970, p. 113].

Recurring income was converted to EPSr using as the denominator "common shares used to calculate primary earnings per share." $EPSp_{t-1}$ and $EPSr_{t-1}$ were used to predict CF 1 year ahead using an RW with drift model. Then EPSp and EPSr RW with drift forecasts were compared to the actual value of each dependent variable 1 year ahead. A MARE and ARE error metric was developed to compare the forecast accuracy and measure the error bias of each variable EPSp and EPSr in predicting cash flows 1 year ahead.

A test for heteroscedastic disturbance in the residuals of the RW with drift models was conducted using the Goldfeld-Quandt F test statistic. The F test revealed almost no heteroscedastic disturbance.

With regard to the RW with drift models, EPSr was a more accurate predictor of CFAI and EPSp was a more accurate predictor of CFO. However, the Mann-Whitney Wilcoxon tests revealed that both models, EPSp and EPSr, were found to be equally accurate in forecasting each of the CF variables for each year, 1978-1982. These findings imply that the additional costs incurred if EPSr is a required disclosure may not outweight the benefits, because EPSr is not significantly more accurate in predicting CF than EPSp. These findings are consistent with Statement of Financial Accounting Concepts (SFAC) 5 [1984]. That is, the FASB in its *Discussion Memorandum* "Reporting Earnings" [1979] included the disclosure of recurring income as a possible means of providing information more useful than net income in assessing future cash flows. However, when SFAC 5 was issued, the FASB did not require or recommend the disclosure of recurring income. This implies that the Board did not deem the disclosure of recurring income as more useful in assessing cash flows than the current earnings disclosures.

However, in this study recurring income was estimated using a statistical technique as a surrogate of management. It may be that managements' estimation of recurring income would have been different than that acquired when using exponential smoothing. If so, recurring income may be more useful to users of financial reports than is net income.

The findings of this study contradict the theory that alternative ways of presenting information do affect a user's perceptions [Sapir 1956; Whorf 1956; Jain 1973; Belkaoui 1980]. However, unlike previous studies [Bruns 1965; Jensen 1966; Doupuch and Ronen 1973], this study does not include the use of human subjects, only statistical analysis. Therefore, the prediction accuracy of EPSp and EPSr may have been significantly different if humans were asked to make the predictions rather than using statistical predictions.

Given the emphasis on the predictive ability of income and recurring income in the accounting literature, and the small amount of empirical work to date, there are many research topics that have yet to be addressed. For example, a statistical technique that utilizes a shorter data base may be more appropriate than exponential smoothing because long data base periods (i.e., 12 years) require making heroic assumptions regarding the permanency of the underlying process. An extension of the RW with drift model, a multiple regression model than incorporates other economic variables, may better explain or predict cash flows. The data base period of this study may be unrepresentative of the behavior of cash flow variables. Between 1978 and 1982, the GNP changed radically, oil prices increased phenomenally, and disclosure requirements of reserve recognition and changing price (FASB 33) data may have caused the variables to behave erratically. Thus, conducting a similar study using a different data base period may also reveal a significant difference in the predictability of recurring and net income. It is conceivable that research into the above suggested areas could highlight new data combinations that could lead to a redevelopment of fundamental statement analysis.

NOTE

1.   Cash flow variables, as defined in this study, include cash flows from operations and cash flow after investment but before financing [see Bowen et al. 1986, pp. 715-716].

REFERENCES

Accounting Principles Board of the American Institute of Certified Public Accountants, "Reporting the Results of Operations—Reporting the Effects of Disposal of a Segment of a Business, and Extraordinary, Unusual and Infrequently Occurring events and Transactions," *Opinions of the Accounting Principles Board* [AICPA, 1973].

Accounting Trends and Techniques [AICPA, 1985].

Albrecht, S. W., L. L. Lookabill and J. C. McKeown, "The Time-Series Properties of Annual Earnings," *Journal of Accounting* 2 [Autumn 1977], pp. 226-244.

American Institute of Accountants Committee on Accounting Procedure, "Presentation of Income and Earned Surplus—Accounting Research Bulletin No. 35," *Journal of Accountancy* 86 [December 1948], pp. 461-462.

Ball, R., and P. Brown, "Portfolio Theory and Accounting," *Journal of Accounting Research* 7(2) [Autumn 1969], pp. 300-323.

Ball, R. and R. Watts, "Some Time-Series Properties of Accounting Income," *The Journal of Finance* 27(3) [June 1972], pp. 663-681.

Beaver, W. H., "The Time Series Behavior of Earnings," *Empirical Research in Accounting: Selected Studies* [1970], pp. 62-107.

Beaver, W., R. Lambert and D. Morse, "The Information Content of Security Prices," *Journal of Accounting and Economics* [1980], pp. 3-28.

Belkaoui, A., "The Impact of Socio-Economic Accounting Statements on the Investment Decision: An Empirical Study," *Accounting Organization and Society* [1980], pp. 263-283.

Bowen, R.M., "The Incremental Information Content of Accrual Versus Cash Flows," *Accounting Review* [1987], pp. 723-747.

Bowen, R.M., D. Burgstahler, and L. A. Daley, "Evidence on the Relationships Between Various Earnings Measures of Cash Flow," *Accounting Review* [October 1986], pp. 713-725.

Bowerman, B. L. and R. T. O'Connell, *Forecasting and Time Series* [Duxbury Press, 1979].

Brandon, C., J. E. Jarrett and S. D. Khumawala, "Comparing Forecast Accuracy for Exponential Smoothing Models of Earnings-Per-Share Data for Financial Decision Making," *Decision Sciences* [1986], pp. 186-194.

Brooks, L. D. and D. A. Buckmaster, "Further Evidence of the Time Series Properties of Accounting Income," *The Journal of Finance* 30(5) [December 1976], pp. 1359-1373.

Brown, L. D., R. L. Hagerman, P. A. Griffin and M. E. Zmijewski, "Security Analyst Superiority Relative to Univariate Time-Series Models in Forecasting Quarterly Earnings," *Journal of Accounting and Economics* [1987], pp. 61-87.

Brown, R. G., *Smoothing, Forecasting and Prediction of Discrete Time Series* [Prentice-Hall, 1963].

Bruns, W., Jr., "Inventory Valuation and Management Decisions," *The Accounting Review* [April 1965], pp. 345-357.

Casey, J. S., *Exponential Smoothing: An Overview for the Contemporary Forecaster* [University of Texas at Austin, 1979].

Collins, D. W., S. P. Kothari, and J. D. Rayburn, "Firm Size and the Information Content of Prices with Respect to Earnings," *Journal of Accounting and Economics* [July 1987], pp. 111-138.

Cragg, J. G. and B. G. Malkiel, "The Consensus and Accuracy of Some Predictions of the Growth of Corporate Earnings," *Journal of Finance* [1968], pp. 67-84.

Dopuch, N. and J. Ronen, "The Effects of Alternative Inventory Valuation Methods—An Experimental Study," *Journal of Accounting Research* [Autumn 1973], pp. 191-211.

Elton, E. J. and M. J. Gruber, "Earning Estimates and the Accuracy of Expectational Data," *Management Science* [April 1972], pp. b409-b424.

Elton, E. J., M. J. Gruber, and M. Gultekin, "Expectations and Share Prices," *Management Science* [September 1981], pp. 975-987.

Financial Accounting Standards Board, *Statement of Financial Accounting Concepts No. 1* [FASB, 1978].

Financial Accounting Standards Board, "Reporting Earnings," *FASB Discussion Memorandum* [July 1979].

Financial Accounting Standards Board, *Statement of Financial Accounting Concepts No. 5* [FASB, 1984].

Financial Accounting Standards Board, "Proposed Statement of Financial Accounting Standards: Statement of Cash Flows," *Financial Accounting Series Exposure Draft* [July 31, 1986].

Foster, H. H., "Quarterly Accounting Data: Time Series Properties and Predictive-Ability Results," *Accounting Review* [January 1977], pp. 1-21.

Francis, J., *Investments Analysis and Management* [McGraw-Hill, 1980].

Fried, D. and D. Givoly, "Financial Analysts' Forecasts of Earnings—A Better Surrogate for Market Expectations," *Journal of Accounting and Economics* [1982], pp. 85-107.

Gibbons, J. D., *Nonparametric Methods for Quantitative Analysis* [Holt, Rinehart, Winston, 1976].

Gilman, S., *Accounting Concepts of Profit* [Ronald Press, 1939].

Gombola and Ketz, "A Note on Cash Flow and Classfication Patterns of Financial Ratios," *Accounting Review* [January 1983], pp. 105-114.

Gonedes, N. J., "Risk, Information, and the Effects of Special Accounting Items on Capital Market Equilibrium," *Journal of Accounting Research* [Autumn 1975], pp. 220-252.

Gordon, M. J., B. N. Horwitz and P. T. Meyers, "Accounting Measurement and Normal Growth of the Firm," *Research in Accounting Measurement* [1966], pp. 89-137.

Granger, C. W. J. and P. Newbold, *Forecasting Economic Time Series* [Academic Press, 1977].

Groff, G. K., "Empirical Comparison of Models for Short-Range Forecasting," *Management Science* [1973], pp. 19, 22-31.

Hendriksen, E. S., *Accounting Theory,* 4th ed. [Irwin, 1982].

Hendriksen, E. and B. Budge, *Contemporary Accounting Theory* [Dickenson, 1974].

Hoskin, R. E., J. S. Hughes and W. E. Ricks, "Evidence on the Incremental Information Content of Additional Firm Disclosures Made Concurrently with Earnings," *Journal of Accounting Research Supplement* [1986], pp. 1-36.

Imhoff, E. A. and P. V. Pare, "Analysis and Comparison of Earnings Forecast Agents," *Journal of Accounting Research* [Autumn 1982], pp. 429-439.

Jain, J. N., "Alternative Methods of Accounting and Decision Making: A Psycho-Linguistical Analysis," *Accounting Review* [January 1973], pp. 95-104.

Jensen, R., "An Experimental Design for the Study of Effects of Accounting Variations in Decision Making," *Journal of Accounting Research* [Autumn 1966], pp. 224-238.

Johnson, T. E. and T. G. Schmitt, "Effectiveness of Earnings Per Share Forecasts," *Financial Management* [1974], pp. 64-72.

Johnston, J., *Econometric Methods* [McGraw-Hill, 1960].

Judge, G., R. Hill, W. Griffiths, H. Lütkepohl and Tsoung-Chao Lee, *Introduction to the Theory and Practice of Econometrics* [Wiley, 1982].

Largay, J. and C. Stickney, "Cash Flows, Ratio Analysis and the W. T. Grant Company Bankruptcy," *Financial Analysts Journal* [July-August 1980], pp. 51-54.

Lev, B. and J. A. Ohlson, "Market-Based Empirical Research in Accounting: A Review, Interpretation, and Extension," *Journal of Accounting Research Supplement* [1982], pp. 249-322.

Lipe, R. C., "The Information Contained in the Components of Earnings," *Journal of Accounting Research Supplement* [1986], pp. 37-68.

Lorek, K. S., "A Perspective on Time Series Research in Accounting: Some Methodological Considerations," *Working paper of Accounting Research Convocation* [University of Alabama, 1982].

Makridakis, S. and S. C. Wheelwright, *Interactive Forecasting* [Holden-Day, 1978].

Mattessich, R., *Accounting and Analytical Methods* [Irwin, 1964].

Mautz, R. K., "Emphasis on Reporting, Not Calculation, Could Settle Income Statement Controversy," *Readings in Accounting Theory* [Houghton Mifflin, 1966].

Mims, R., "Uneasy Move Toward Multiple Earnings Statement," (Commentary/Accounting) *Business Week* [May 15, 1979], pp. 124-128.

Mortimer, T., "Reporting Earnings: A New Approach," *Financial Analysts Journal* [November-December 1979], p. 68.

Muth, J. F., "Optimal Properties of Exponentially Weighted Forecasts," *American Statistical Association Journal* [1960], pp. 299-306.

Paton, W. A., *Accounting Theory* [Ronald Press, 1922].

Paton, W. A. and A. C. Littleton, *An Introduction to Corporate Accounting Standards* [American Accounting Association (AAA), 1940].

Penman, S. H., "The Predictive Content of Earnings Forecasts and Dividends," *Journal of Finance* [September 1983], pp. 1181-1199.

"Public Hearings on Reporting Earnings Projects," *SEC Accounting Report* (60 [January 1980], p. 67.

Rayburn, J., "The Association of Operating Cash Flow and Accurals with Security Returns," *Journal of Accounting Research Supplement* [1986], pp. 112-137.

Sapir, E., *Selected Writing of Edward Sapir,* D. G. Mandelbaum (ed.) [University of California Press, 1956].

Standard and Poor's COMPUSTAT Services, Inc., *Industrial COMPUSTAT* [Investors Management Services, Inc., 1982].

JENICE P. STEWART

Strauss, N. N. and A. T. Arcady, "A New Focus on the 'Bottom Line' and Its Components," *The Journal of Accountancy* [May 1981], pp. 66-77.

Study Group on the Objectives of Financial Statements, *Objectives of Financial Statements* [AICPA, 1973].

Watts, R., Appendix A to "The Information Content of Dividends," unpublished paper, Graduate School of Business, University of Chicago [October 1970].

Watts, R. L. and R. W. Leftwich, "The Time Series of Annual Accounting Earnings," *Journal of Accounting Research* 15(2) [Autumn 1977], pp. 253-271.

Whorf, B. L., *Language, Thought and Reality* [Wiley, 1956].

Wilson, P. G., "The Relative Information Content of Accurals and Cash Flows: Combined Evidence at the Earnings Announcement and Annual Report Release Date," *Journal of Accounting Research Supplement* [1986], pp. 165-203.

A COMPARATIVE ANALYSIS OF ERROR METRICS APPLIED TO ANALYSTS' FORECASTS OF EARNINGS

Ruth Ann McEwen

ABSTRACT

Previous research efforts have employed various forecast error metrics to compare forecast accuracy of financial analysts with the accuracy of forecasts generated from mechanical models. Little theoretical or empirical support has been offered to justify the choice of the error metrics and none of these studies has provided evidence that alternative error metrics would produce consistent results. This study utilizes a nonparametric approach to test the consistency of alternative error metrics. The results cast doubt on the conclusions of previous studies.

Advances in Accounting, Volume 7, pages 113-126.

INTRODUCTION

The accuracy of analysts' forecasts of earnings and the properties of forecast errors have been the subject of numerous research efforts. For example, Collins and Hopwood [1980], among others, have provided evidence that analysts' forecast accuracy is superior to the accuracy of forecasts generated from mechanical models. Schreuder and Klaassen [1984] found that analysts provided forecasts that were not significantly different from those furnished by management. Brown et al. [1985] investigated the informational content of analysts' accuracy and of forecast revisions, and Comiskey et al. [1986] documented the contemporaneous relationship between analysts' forecast accuracy and capital market risk.

Each of these studies defined analysts' accuracy in terms of forecast error metrics. Various metrics were used for empirical analyses, yet little theoretical or empirical support was offered to justify the metric that was selected. Moreover, none of the studies presented statistical evidence that alternative error metrics would provide consistent results.

This paper reports the results of tests designed to determine whether use of alternative error metrics may have affected the results and conclusions of previous research efforts. Employing a paradigm common to many prior studies, this study compares the accuracy of analysts' forecasts to forecasts generated by three naive, mechanical models. The agent with the highest level of accuracy as represented by the lowest forecast error is considered to be the favored (superior) agent. Unique to this study is an analysis of the consistency of the favored agent designation across eight alternative error metrics. The central question is whether model or analyst superiority is consistent across all eight metrics.

The results indicate that alternative error metrics are not consistent. Error metric definition may affect the results of a comparative study in which analysts' forecasts are compared to those generated by mechanical models.

RESEARCH ISSUES

Givoly and Lakonishok [1984] suggested that in a rational market, analysts' forecasts should be superior to relatively inexpensive naive, mechanical models. Previous empirical studies have generally supported these conclusions. Earlier studies, such as Barefield and Comiskey [1975], provided evidence that analysts slightly outperformed mechanical models, although more recent studies, such as Collins and Hopwood [1980] and Bhaskar and Morris [1984], suggest that analysts are the superior forecasters.

These studies, in addition to other studies such as Richards et al. [1977] and Brown and Rozeff [1980], inferred analyst superiority, yet no tests were performed to ensure that analysts were favored across a variety of error metric forms. In those studies in which more than one metric was employed, no effort was made to justify the metric used for statistical analysis.

The research objective of each of these studies was to determine which forecasting agent was superior by comparing measures of accuracy. Barefield and Comiskey [1975] and Brandon and Jarrett [1977] stated that the choice of error metric employed in comparative analyses should be determined by the theoretical, functional association between forecast error and user loss.

Brandon and Jarrett suggested that the measure of absolute accuracy should reflect the consequences associated with forecasting errors that result from predictions that are not equal to their realizations. Barefield and Comiskey also noted this relationship, but both studies relied on error metrics that had been used in prior studies. Summarizing the problems inherent in defining a user loss function, Barefield and Comiskey stated:

> Since little is known about the nature of the loss function associated with earnings forecast errors, the mean absolute error has been selected due to its simplicity and also to its use in previous studies of earnings forecast errors. [1975, p. 243]

In the aggregate, the loss function related to earnings forecast errors cannot be observed. However, DeGroot [1970] provides an assessment of loss functions related to prediction of any real parameter (in the current setting, the real parameter is earnings) and suggests that loss functions may be defined by the general linear case, in which the penalty associated with error is proportional to the magnitude of error, and by the quadratic case, in which the penalty associated with error is more than proportional to the magnitude of the error.

Without explicit knowledge of the related user loss function, the appropriate metric for use in a comparative analysis cannot be determined. Thus, prior studies have relied on a variety of alternative metrics that correspond to both general linear and general nonlinear loss functions. Only one previous study considered the consistency of alternative metric forms to assess comparative accuracy as an important issue. Brandon and Jarrett [1977] provided an analysis of the effects of five alternative metrics forms on a sample of 40 firms. Although no statistical tests were employed, their results suggest that alternative metrics yield different conclusions. A summary of the metrics employed in these previous efforts is provided in Table 1.

The current study tests the effects of alternative metric forms on the results of these and other studies. Employing nonparametric statistical tests, this study provides evidence that choice of error metric form can affect the outcome of a comparative analysis of analysts' forecast accuracy with the accuracy of forecasts generated from mechanical models.

Table 1.   Summary of Metrics Employed in Previous Research Studies

Year	Authors	Metrics Employed[a]
1975	Barefield and Comiskey	$\lvert F-A \rvert / F$
1977	Brandon and Jarrett	$(F-A)$ $\lvert F-A \rvert$ $(F-A)/A$ $\lvert F-A \rvert / \lvert A \rvert$ $(F-A)^2$
1977	Richards, Benjamin, and Strawser	$\lvert F-A \rvert / A$ $(F-A)/A$
1978	Brown and Rozeff	$\lvert F-A \rvert / \lvert A \rvert$
1980	Collins and Hopwood	$\lvert A-F \rvert / \lvert A \rvert$
1984	Bhaskar and Morris	$(F-A)/F$

[a] F = the forecast of earnings; A = the actual earnings achieved, and all errors are equally weighted across time.

RESEARCH METHODOLOGY

The central research question is whether model or analyst superiority is consistent across all eight metrics. That is to say, if analysts' forecasts are deemed to be superior to those generated from mechanical models when the first error metric (E1) is used in statistical tests, then analysts should also be deemed superior using the other seven metrics (E2 through E8). In alternative form, the hypothesis is stated as:

HYPOTHESIS 1.   At least one of the eight error metrics will produce a different favored agent from the other seven metrics.

ERROR METRIC FORMS

As indicated in Table 1, two geneal forms of error have been employed in previous research efforts. These forms correspond to the general linear case, for example $(F-A)$, and the general nonlinear, quadratic case, for example $(F-A)^2$. However, the metrics provided in Table 1, which are not constrained in sign, are not appropriate for a comparative analysis of forecasting agents for linear and nonlinear cases. Additionally, Foster [1986, p. 267] suggests that the general forms should be deflated by either F or A to reduce scale effects.

The linear metrics that are used in this study were selected because of their use in previous studies (E1) or were adapted to conform to Foster's suggestion (E2 and E3). The linear forms are defined as:

$$E1 = |F{-}A|$$
$$E2 = |F{-}A|/|A|$$
$$E3 = |F{-}A|/|F|$$

where F is the 12-month forecast provided by the analyst, or generated from the mechanical models, A is the actual earnings achieved, and all forms are an equally weighted average error across time. Averages are used to mitigate measurement error and because they were used in previous studies. (Use of the absolute value operator will be discussed in subsequent paragraphs.)

Nonlinear forms include the general quadratic metric employed by Brandon and Jarrett [1977] and additional expressions of quadratic error that are expressed relative to F or A. Nonlinear forms are defined as:

$$E4 = (F{-}A)^2$$
$$E5 = (F{-}A)^2/|A|$$
$$E6 = (F{-}A)^2/|F|$$
$$E7 = [(F{-}A)/A]^2$$
$$E8 = [(F{-}A)/F]^2$$

These definitions of error address the theoretical issues noted by Barefield and Comiskey [1975] and Brandon and Jarrett [1977]. In addition, use of the absolute value operator addresses issues raised by Brown, Foster, and Noreen [1985].

Brown et al. identified linear and nonlinear forms of error and provided an analysis of error metrics. The authors noted interpretational difficulties associated with the effects of error metric definitions that allow denominators to be negative and with the effects of sample outliers.

Brown et al. suggest that negative denominators may affect interpretation of overestimates and underestimates of earnings. For example, when the error metric is defined as the forecast of earnings less the actual earnings achieved, expressed relative to actual earnings achieved—e.g., (Forecast − Actual)/ Actual—positive error metrics ordinarily represent overestimates, whereas negative metrics ordinarily represent underestimates. However, in the event that an actual earnings is negative, these interpretations may not be valid.

Brown et al. [1985] state that this problem may be addressed by constraining the denominators to be positive. However, if only the denominators are constrained to be positive, the linear forms of error may still hold negative signs (representing underestimates), whereas forms of nonlinear (quadratic) expression will hold positive signs for both over- and underestimates. This situation complicates a comparative analysis of linear and nonlinear, quadratic forms. In response to these criticisms, all error metrics are constrained to be positive by using the absolute value operator in both the numerator and denominator.

Outliers may be the result of factors that are specific to a single analyst, or may result from errors in the data base. Brown et al. [1985] suggest that truncating the sample removes the effects of outliers and may provide an assessment of analyst superiority with greater external validity. Of greater interest to this study is the effect on consistency of truncating the sample. If a partitioning scheme is developed that removes only the extreme analysts' errors (those errors that are greater than 100%), then truncation provides a setting in which analysts should generally be favored across all metrics. In this setting, if the models are deemed to be superior for any metric, then metric choice alone may have affected the outcome.

MECHANICAL MODELS

Brown et al. [1985] provides the following models that commonly have been employed in previous studies of comparative accuracy. To ensure consistent forecast horizons, analysts' 12-month forecasts are compared with 12-month forecasts generated by (1) a zero growth model (M1), (2) a naive growth model (M2), and (3) a model that assumes that earnings in year $t+1$ are expected to exceed earnings in the year t by the same percentage as earnings in year t exceeded earnings in year $t-1$ (M3). These models are expressed mathematically as

(M1): $EPS_{t+1} = EPS_t$

(M2): $EPS_{t+1} = EPS_t + [EPS_t - EPS_{t-1}]$

(M3): $EPS_{t+1} = EPS_t + \{[(EPS_t - EPS_{t-1})/EPS_{t-1}] (EPS_t)]\}$

where EPS_{t+1} (Earnings Per Share) is the forecast of earnings and EPS_t and EPS_{t-1} are the actual EPS values reported by the firm.

The Friedman test [Conover 1980], a nonparametric test of differences in means, is used to determine in an overall analysis whether significant differences exist across forecast agents (analysts, M1, M2, and M3) for each metric. The results of these comparisons provide a basis for the assertion that if significant differences exist, then one of the four agents may be deemed to be superior.

The Friedman test is also used in a pairwise setting to determine which agent is superior. In a pairwise analysis, the Friedman test approximates the nonparametric sign test [Conover 1980, p. 299]. The pairwise form of the Friedman test has three possible outcomes: (1) there is no significant difference in the forecast accuracy of the agents, thus, neither agent is favored; (2) there is a significant difference in the forecast accuracy of the agents, and analysts are favored; and (3) there is a significant difference in the forecast accuracy of the agents, and the mechanical model is favored. The Friedman test is used because of its simplicity and because it can be used for both overall and pairwise tests.

The Friedman test is conducted using the following procedures. (1) The mean forecast error is computed across the forecast horizon for each firm. (2) Ranks are assigned, with the rank of 1 assigned to the best forecasting agent, the rank of 2 assigned to the next best, and so on. (3) The mean rank across all firms is computed for each forecasting agent. (4) These mean ranks are compared on an overall basis across forecast agents to determine if significant differences exist and are compared on a pairwise basis between each model and the analysts to determine which agent is superior. After the superiority of forecast agents has been established for each metric, all eight metrics are compared for consistency.

THE SAMPLE

The sample consists of all firms with complete data on the Institutional Brokers Estimate Service (I/B/E/S, Lynch, Jones & Ryan) tape for the years 1979 to 1983. The I/B/E/S tape includes analysts' earnings forecasts for approximately 3400 publicly traded corporations representing 2500 analysts from 131 brokerage and research institutions. Firms for which analysts were forecasting fully diluted EPS were excluded from the sample to ensure that comparable earnings forecasts (primary EPS) were tested. A total of 766 firms met these criteria.

In order to provide a setting in which analysts should generally be favored, a truncated sample also was tested. The truncated sample consisted of all firms in which analyst error, defined by error metric E2 (the error metric most commonly employed in previous studies), was less than 100%. Extreme analyst errors were thus excluded from the truncated sample. A total of 510 firms met this requirement.

RESULTS

A summary set of descriptive statistics of error metrics applied to financial analysts' forecasts of earnings is provided in Table 2. An analysis of metric mean values, ranges, coefficients of variation, and values for skewness provides insights into the underlying distribution of analysts' forecasts. Properties of the distribution of the error metrics calculated for financial analysts' forecasts are dependent on constraints that forced all error metrics

Table 2. Error Metric Descriptive Statistics: Analysts' Forecasts[a]

Metric Form	Metric Mean	Maximum Value	CV%	Skewness
All Firms ($n = 766$)				
$\|F-A\|$	0.86	9.8	115	3.3
$\|F-A\|/\|A\|$	88%	24.3%	255	6.2
$\|F-A\|/\|F\|$	59%	130.1%	802	26.7
$(F-A)^2$	3.07	301.1	445	15.5
$(F-A)^2/\|A\|$	219%	145.0%	381	10.7
$(F-A)^2/\|F\|$	238%	886.4%	1360	26.9
$[(F-A)/A]^2$	61%	983.4%	872	13.3
$[(F-A)/F]^2$	180%	1013.6%	995	27.6
Truncated Sample ($n = 510$)				
$\|F-A\|$	0.39	0.98	59	0.5
$\|F-A\|/\|A\|$	22%	95%	82	1.7
$\|F-A\|/\|F\|$	17%	84%	69	2.0
$(F-A)^2$	0.33	16.67	109	1.5
$(F-A)^2/\|A\|$	18%	178%	134	2.8
$(F-A)^2/\|F\|$	12%	140%	115	3.5
$[(F-A)/A]^2$	14%	98%	136	4.6
$[(F-A)/F]^2$	10%	85%	168	6.5

[a] F = the consensus mean forecast generated by financial analysts, A = the actual EPS reported for each firm, CV% = the coefficient of variation (standard deviation/mean), and metric mean = the mean metric value in which all forms were computed on a yearly basis, then averaged across the time period from 1979 to 1983.

to yield positive values. The minimum value for each metric is, by definition, equal to zero. Maximum values are unconstrained in size but are constrained in sign.

Summary statistics for the entire sample suggest analysts forecast errors contain a high degree of variability and that the distribution of each error metric is skewed. Values for skewness imply that outliers are driving the distribution. In a symmetrical distribution, skewness is equal to zero. This axiom is not violated in the circumstance in which error metrics are constrained to be positive. Positive values for skewness indicate that the median observation is less than the mean observation; thus, outliers have shifted the mean toward the right tail of the distribution.

As expected, a comparison of skewness values between the entire sample and the truncated sample provides evidence that the effects of outliers have been reduced (skewness values are lower for the truncated sample). This result suggests that the truncated sample provides a setting in which analysts should generally be favored.

Table 3 provides the results of overall tests of differences in means across forecast agents. In every instance, differences are significant at an α of at least

Table 3.   Overall Friedman Comparisons of Analysts
with Mechanical Models[a]

Metric Form	Mean Rank for Each Agent				Significance Level
	ANA	M1	M2	M3	
	All Firms ($n = 766$)				
$E1=\|F-A\|$	2.57	2.00	2.55	2.88	0.000
$E2=\|F-A\|/\|A\|$	2.66	2.00	2.53	2.80	0.000
$E3=\|F-A\|/\|F\|$	2.11	2.20	2.78	2.91	0.000
$E4=(F-A)^2$	2.61	1.94	2.60	2.85	0.000
$E5=(F-A)^2/\|A\|$	2.68	1.97	2.54	2.81	0.000
$E6=(F-A)^2/\|F\|$	2.30	2.06	2.73	2.91	0.000
$E7=[(F-A)/A]^2$	2.73	2.01	2.49	2.76	0.000
$E8=[(F-A)/F]^2$	2.07	2.22	2.81	2.91	0.000
	Truncated Sample ($n = 510$)				
$E1=\|F-A\|$	2.33	2.15	2.50	3.01	0.001
$E2=\|F-A\|/\|A\|$	2.37	2.12	2.53	2.98	0.000
$E3=\|F-A\|/\|F\|$	2.15	2.34	2.70	2.81	0.000
$E4=(F-A)^2$	2.36	2.14	2.52	2.98	0.000
$E5=(F-A)^2/\|A\|$	2.42	2.11	2.50	2.97	0.000
$E6=(F-A)^2/\|F\|$	2.23	2.25	2.66	2.87	0.000
$E7=[(F-A)/A]^2$	2.46	2.08	2.50	2.96	0.000
$E8=[(F-A)/F]^2$	2.14	2.35	2.73	2.78	0.000

[a] Differences are considered to be significant at an α of 0.05.

0.001. Therefore, significant differences exist across forecast agents and a pairwise comparison of the accuracy of each model with the accuracy of analysts can be used to determine which agent is the superior forecaster.

Table 4 provides the results of pairwise comparisons of analysts with the mechanical models for the entire sample. Tests of all three models reject the null of consistency in determination of a favored agent (consistency occurs only if all eight metrics provide the same favored agent). For example, in a comparison of analysts with M1, the model is deemed to be the superior agent using forms E1, E2, E4, E5, or E7. If metric forms E3 or E8 are used, analysts are deemed to be superior. No significant difference exists between analysts and M1 using metric E6.

In a pairwise comparison of analysts with M2, no significant differences are noted with metrics E1, E2, and E4. Tests of the superior agent using forms E3, E6, and E8 would favor analysts, whereas M2 is deemed to be superior using metrics E5 and E7.

Comparison of analysts with M3 also indicate inconsistency. If tests of superiority were conducted using E1, E3, E6, and E8, then analysts would be deemed to be superior. Model 3 would be deemed to be superior using metric E7. No significant differences would be noted using metrics E2, E4, and E5.

Table 4.   Friedman Comparisons of Analysts with
Mechanical Models: All Firms[a]
($n = 766$)

Metric Form	Mean Rank for Each Agent				Significance Level	Favored Agent
	ANA	M1	M2	M3		
Pairwise Comparison of Analysts with Model 1						
$\|F-A\|$	1.61	1.39			0.000	M1
$\|F-A\|/\|A\|$	1.64	1.36			0.000	M1
$\|F-A\|/\|F\|$	1.42	1.58			0.000	ANA
$(F-A)^2$	1.63	1.37			0.000	M1
$(F-A)^2/\|A\|$	1.64	1.36			0.000	M1
$(F-A)^2/\|F\|$	1.52	1.48			0.193	Not Sig
$[(F-A)/A]^2$	1.65	1.35			0.000	M1
$[(F-A)/F]^2$	1.42	1.58			0.000	ANA
Pairwise Comparison of Analysts with Model 2						
$\|F-A\|$	1.50		1.50		0.885	Not Sig
$\|F-A\|/\|A\|$	1.52		1.48		0.278	Not Sig
$\|F-A\|/\|F\|$	1.36		1.64		0.000	ANA
$(F-A)^2$	1.50		1.50		0.942	Not Sig
$(F-A)^2/\|A\|$	1.54		1.46		0.049	M2
$(F-A)^2/\|F\|$	1.39		1.61		0.000	ANA
$[(F-A)/A]^2$	1.55		1.45		0.005	M2
$[(F-A)/F]^2$	1.31		1.69		0.000	ANA
Pairwise Comparison of Analysts with Model 3						
$\|F-A\|$	1.46			1.54	0.036	ANA
$\|F-A\|/\|A\|$	1.50			1.50	0.828	Not Sig
$\|F-A\|/\|F\|$	1.32			1.68	0.000	ANA
$(F-A)^2$	1.48			1.52	0.278	Not Sig
$(F-A)^2/\|A\|$	1.51			1.49	0.773	Not Sig
$(F-A)^2/\|F\|$	1.38			1.62	0.000	ANA
$[(F-A)/A]^2$	1.54			1.46	0.049	M3
$[(F-A)/F]^2$	1.31			1.69	0.000	ANA

[a] ANA = analysts; Not Sig indicates no significant difference at α equal to 0.050.

The results provided in Table 4 indicate that in tests of comparative accuracy between analysts and mechanical models, the choice of an error metric affects the outcome of the analysis. The results provided in Table 5 confirm this finding in a setting in which analysis should generally be favored.

The truncated sample was defined in a manner such that analysts' errors that exceeded 100% were excluded from the analysis. In this setting, analysts should generally be deemed to be superior when compared to any of the three models. Yet, in a comparison with M1, six of the eight metrics yield results in which there is no significant difference between forecast agents (E1, E2, E4,

Table 5.   Friedman Comparisons of Analysts with
Mechanical Models: Truncated Sample[a]
$(n = 510)$

Metric Form	Mean Rank for Each Agent				Significance Level	Favored Agent
	ANA	M1	M2	M3		
Pairwise Comparison of Analysts with Model 1						
$\lvert F-A \rvert$	1.50	1.50			1.000	Not Sig
$\lvert F-A \rvert / \lvert A \rvert$	1.51	1.49			0.576	Not Sig
$\lvert F-A \rvert / \lvert F \rvert$	1.39	1.61			0.000	ANA
$(F-A)^2$	1.50	1.50			0.926	Not Sig
$(F-A)^2 / \lvert A \rvert$	1.52	1.48			0.041	M1
$(F-A)^2 / \lvert F \rvert$	1.46	1.54			0.062	Not Sig
$[(F-A)/A]^2$	1.53	1.47			0.032	M1
$[(F-A)/F]^2$	1.39	1.61			0.000	ANA
Pairwise Comparison of Analysts with Model 2						
$\lvert F-A \rvert$	1.44		1.56		0.009	ANA
$\lvert F-A \rvert / \lvert A \rvert$	1.44		1.56		0.012	ANA
$\lvert F-A \rvert / \lvert F \rvert$	1.39		1.61		0.000	ANA
$(F-A)^2$	1.44		1.56		0.015	ANA
$(F-A)^2 / \lvert A \rvert$	1.47		1.53		0.225	Not Sig
$(F-A)^2 / \lvert F \rvert$	1.40		1.60		0.000	ANA
$[(F-A)/A]^2$	1.48		1.52		0.401	Not Sig
$[(F-A)/F]^2$	1.38		1.62		0.000	ANA
Pairwise Comparison of Analysts with Model 3						
$\lvert F-A \rvert$	1.40			1.60	0.000	ANA
$\lvert F-A \rvert / \lvert A \rvert$	1.41			1.59	0.000	ANA
$\lvert F-A \rvert / \lvert F \rvert$	1.37			1.63	0.000	ANA
$(F-A)^2$	1.41			1.59	0.000	ANA
$(F-A)^2 / \lvert A \rvert$	1.42			1.58	0.001	ANA
$(F-A)^2 / \lvert F \rvert$	1.39			1.61	0.000	ANA
$[(F-A)/A]^2$	1.45			1.55	0.020	ANA
$[(F-A)/F]^2$	1.37			1.63	0.000	ANA

[a] ANA = analysts; Not Sig indicates no significant difference at α equal to 0.050.

and E6) or M1 is deemed to be superior (E5 and E7). Consistency is thus rejected.

Pairwise comparisons with M2 and M3 are more consistent. Analysts are deemed to be superior in six of eight cases when compared to M2 and are deemed to be superior in all cases when compared to M3.

An analysis of the outliers provides an opposing view to the results provided in Table 5. Table 6 presents evidence that in settings in which the mechanical models should be favored, metrics E3, E6, and E8 are especially inappropriate in tests of comparative superiority. This result is not surprising because metrics

Table 6. Friedman Comparisons of Analysts with
Mechanical Models: Outliers[a]
(n = 256)

Metric Form	Mean Rank for Each Agent				Significance Level	Favored Agent
	ANA	M1	M2	M3		
Pairwise Comparison of Analysts with Model 1						
$\|F-A\|$	1.77	1.23			0.000	M1
$\|F-A\|/\|A\|$	1.82	1.18			0.000	M1
$\|F-A\|/\|F\|$	1.47	1.53			0.360	Not Sig
$(F-A)^2$	1.83	1.17			0.000	M1
$(F-A)^2/\|A\|$	1.82	1.18			0.000	M1
$(F-A)^2/\|F\|$	1.62	1.38			0.000	M1
$[(F-A)/A]^2$	1.82	1.18			0.000	M1
$[(F-A)/F]^2$	1.46	1.54			0.137	Not Sig
Pairwise Comparison of Analysts with Model 2						
$\|F-A\|$	1.58		1.42		0.003	M2
$\|F-A\|/\|A\|$	1.64		1.36		0.000	M2
$\|F-A\|/\|F\|$	1.32		1.68		0.000	ANA
$(F-A)^2$	1.59		1.41		0.002	M2
$(F-A)^2/\|A\|$	1.63		1.37		0.000	M2
$(F-A)^2/\|F\|$	1.38		1.62		0.000	ANA
$[(F-A)/A]^2$	1.66		1.34		0.000	M2
$[(F-A)/F]^2$	1.28		1.72		0.000	ANA
Pairwise Comparison of Analysts with Model 3						
$\|F-A\|$	1.56			1.44	0.030	M3
$\|F-A\|/\|A\|$	1.64			1.36	0.000	M3
$\|F-A\|/\|F\|$	1.25			1.75	0.000	ANA
$(F-A)^2$	1.58			1.42	0.004	M3
$(F-A)^2/\|A\|$	1.63			1.37	0.000	M3
$(F-A)^2/\|F\|$	1.38			1.62	0.000	ANA
$[(F-A)/A]^2$	1.67			1.33	0.000	M3
$[(F-A)/F]^2$	1.22			1.78	0.000	ANA

[a] ANA = analysts; Not Sig indicates no significant difference at α equal to 0.050.

expressed relative to the forecast may measure how well earnings are able to meet analysts' expectations, rather than how well analysts are able to forecast earnings.

The results provided in the preceding tables reject the null that all eight metrics consistently define either analysts or models as superior forecasters. Metric selection thus may affect the outcome of comparative analyses of analysts with mechanical models.

These conclusions are subject to the limitations of this study. These limitations include (1) the error metrics employed in this study may not adequately capture the functional relationships between loss and forecast error, (2) the models selected for analysis may not provide the most accurate estimates of earnings, and (3) the findings are dependent on a specific time period and a specific data base.

CONCLUSIONS

Subject to the limitations, the results of this study provide evidence that error metric choice affects the results of a comparative analysis of the forecast accuracy of analysts and mechanical models. Truncating the sample removes the effects of outliers, but even in the truncated sample, the outcome depends on error metric choice. Thus, the conclusions of previous studies in which analysts were compared with mechanical models metrics may be in question.

Other areas of research may be affected by error metric choice. For example, Elton et al. [1984] estimated the determinants of forecast error, but provided no evidence that alternative error metrics produced similar results. As well, studies in which forecast error is viewed as a surrogate for systematic risk, such as Comiskey et al. [1986], may be affected by metric choice. If forecast error is employed as a surrogate for security risk and forecast errors are not interchangeable, then some metrics may be superior to other metrics as risk surrogates.

The implications of these findings suggest the need to identify a metric form that best corresponds to notions of user loss. Until these relationships have been more fully explored, careful consideration must be given to the conclusions of research studies that employ error metrics in analyses.

ACKNOWLEDGMENT

The author gratefully acknowledges the comments and helpful suggestions of two anonymous reviewers.

REFERENCES

Barefield, R. and E. Comiskey, "The Accuracy of Analysts' Forecasts of Earnings Per Share," *Journal of Business Research* [July 1975], pp. 241-252.
Bhaskar, K. and R. Morris, "The Accuracy of Brokers' Profit Forecasts in the UK," *Accounting and Business Research* [Spring 1984], pp. 113-124.
Brandon, C. and J. Jarrett, "Accuracy of Externally Prepared Forecasts," *Review of Business and Economic Research* [Fall 1977], pp. 35-47.
Brown, L. and M. Rozeff, "Analysts Can Forecast Accurately!," *Journal of Portfolio Management* [Spring 1980], pp. 31-34.

Brown, P., G. Foster and E. Noreen, *Security Analyst Multi-Year Earnings Forecasts and the Capital Market*, Studies in Accounting Research #21 [American Accounting Association, 1985].

Collins, W. and W. Hopwood, "A Multivariate Analysis of Annual Earnings Forecasts Generated from Quarterly Forecasts of Financial Analysts' and Univariate Time Series Models," *Journal of Accounting Research* [Autumn 1980], pp. 390-406.

Comiskey, E., C. Mulford and T. Porter, "Forecast Error, Earnings Variability and Systematic Risk," *Journal of Business Finance and Accounting* [Summer 1986], pp. 257-265.

Conover, W., *Practical Nonparametric Statistics* [Wiley, 1980].

DeGroot, M., *Optimal Statistical Decisions* [McGraw-Hill, 1970].

Elton, E., M. Gruber and M. Gultekin, "Professional Expectations: Accuracy and Diagnosis of Errors," *Journal of Financial and Quantitative Analysis* [December 1984], pp. 1-13.

Foster, G. *Financial Statement Analysis* [Prentice-Hall, 1986].

Givoly, D. and J. Lakonishok, "Properties of Analysts' Forecasts of Earnings: A Review and Analysis of the Research," *Journal of Accounting Literature* [Spring 1984], pp. 117-152.

Richards, R., J. Benjamin and R. Strawser, "An Examination of the Accuracy of Earnings Forecasts," *Financial Management* [Fall 1977], pp. 78-86.

Schreuder, H. and J. Klaassen, "Confidential Revenue and Profit Forecasts by Management and Financial Analysts: Evidence from the Netherlands," *The Accounting Review* [January 1984], pp. 64-77.

PART II

EDUCATION

ASSESSING THE FURTHER IMPACT OF COLLEGE-LEVEL ACCOUNTING STUDY ON STUDENT PERFORMANCE IN THE MBA-LEVEL MANAGERIAL ACCOUNTING COURSE

Mehmet Canlar and Man Chand Maloo

ABSTRACT

A recently published study investigated the effect of college-level accounting study on student performance in the first MBA-level financial accounting course. It was found that although students who had been exposed to accounting during their undergraduate years performed significantly better overall than those who had not, the gap between the groups' successive average examination scores narrowed as the semester progressed. Would this performance difference continue into the second-sequence accounting course, which is usually managerial accounting, or would the gap continue to narrow and perhaps close altogether

Advances in Accounting, Volume 7, pages 129-139.
Copyright © 1989 by JAI Press Inc.
All rights of reproduction in any form reserved.
ISBN: 0-89232-960-2

in the second course? This study addresses these questions. Difference-between-means test was administered to compare the examination scores of 89 students, 61 of whom were part of the earlier study sample. Test results indicated there was no significant difference between the performance of those students with and those without college-level accounting in the second-sequence managerial accounting course. Although more replication studies should be conducted, it can be inferred from this finding that the impact of college-level study of accounting on student performance ends with the first financial accounting course.

INTRODUCTION

A recent research study investigated the effects of college-level accounting study on student performance in the graduate-level financial accounting course [Canlar 1986]. The principal findings of that study (referred to hereafter as the original study) indicated that although students with prior exposure to accounting performed significantly better overall than did those with no exposure, the gap between successive average examination scores of the two groups progressively narrowed in the course of the semester. Moreover, the amount of prior exposure was found not to be a factor in their performance.

To determine if the amount of prior exposure to accounting would have an impact, the original study further divided the 48 students with college-level exposure to accounting into two subgroups—one consisting of 20 students who had taken only one course, and the other, 28 students who had taken more than one (the mean course number of this subgroup was 2.48). Mann-Whitney test results indicated no significant difference in performance between these two subgroups at the 0.05 level.

A possible bias resulting from the graduate school policy of the university also was addressed in the original study. The university specified that no MBA-level accounting course would be waived unless a student had received a grade of B or better in a college-level accounting course. Therefore, the group with prior exposure to accounting necessarily consisted of students who had received less than a B in their undergraduate course. As a result, the ability or quality of this group (group E) could be ranked as poor. To assess this possibility, GMAT scores of this group were compared with the second group (group N), again using the Mann-Whitney test. The results indicated no significant difference between the two groups, with a decisive p-value of 0.9099.

Because the results of the original study indicated that the performance gap between the two groups successively narrowed as the end of the first semester approached, the question arose whether the gap would continue to narrow or perhaps close altogether in a second accounting course. A two-course sequence (the first financial and the second managerial accounting) is the norm in graduate school, which was confirmed by a review of 26 catalogs of graduate schools offering an MBA program. Furthermore, Welsch and Anthony [1984, p. x], authors of popular MBA-level introductory accounting textbooks, indicate that many accounting instructors prefer such a format, as does the Shillinglaw and Meyer [1983, p. x] textbook usually used at the graduate level.

The present study of performance in second-level accounting courses was a logical extension of the original study. It also was thought that such a study could provide additional evidence on student performance in an interdisciplinary course and could help evaluate policy for MBA programs at institutions that accept students graduating from 4-year programs with a variety of majors.

Managerial accounting also provided a new setting for the study. In financial accounting, the equation—Assets = Liabilities + Owners' equity—provides a unifying theme, but there is no such unifying structure in managerial accounting in which the use of different information for a variety of purposes is emphasized [Anthony et al. 1985, p. vii]. Moreover, managerial accounting is not restricted either by generally accepted accounting principles or by the needs of external users; rather, it focuses on internal decision making.

Nevertheless, all students taking managerial accounting are presumed to have a "common body of accounting knowledge," implying that no student should have an added accounting study advantage over other students in a course. It remained to be answered whether the unique setting of managerial accounting would make a difference in the performance of graduate students with at least one previous accounting course. How concerned should MBA-level accounting teachers and administrators be with the needs of students in a class in which every student has had at least one course, but some have had more?

The authors were unable to locate any previous study that addressed these questions at the graduate level. The few previous studies in this area dealt with undergraduate students with high school exposure to accounting. They reported conflicting findings. For example, Bergin [1983, p. 27] found no significant difference in examination scores between students who had taken high school accounting or bookkeeping and students who had not. Baldwin and Howe [1982] reported similar findings. Smith [1968], however, found that students with prior accounting performed significantly better in their first college-level accounting course than those with no previous study. Schroeder [1986] found that although there was no significant difference in overall course performance between undergraduate students with no high school accounting exposure and those with 1 year or less, students with *more* than 1 year of accounting at the high school level performed significantly better than those with none. Eskew and Faley [1988] reported that precollege exposure to accounting, among other variables, was significantly related to examination performance.

The limited prior research had reported conflicting findings, and it did not address the previously raised questions directly. The primary objective of this study, then, was to examine the impact, if any, of college accounting exposure on student performance in the MBA-level managerial accounting course. The researchers also thought that they might examine the validity of occasional complaints raised by some students, such as "It is not fair to me to be in the same class with those who seem to know so much more about accounting than I do."

STUDY DESIGN

The data for this study were gathered from 89 students enrolled in two sections of an MBA-level managerial accounting course. Six students dropped the course during the semester. The students were divided into three groups. The first (E) consisted of those who had taken at least one undergraduate accounting course. Of the 33 students in this group, 16 had taken one accounting course, 12 had taken two, and 5 had taken more than two. The content of the courses was not investigated, but it was reasoned that because the first course in accounting is usually financial, the 17 students with more than one course were likely to have had some prior exposure to managerial accounting. The second group (N) had no exposure to undergraduate accounting courses. Sixty-one students in these two groups (E = 33 and N = 28) were part of the sample of 90 students in the graduate financial accounting course who, in the preceding semester, were the subjects of the original study. A third group (O) consisted of 28 students who were not part of the original study but had enrolled in the class from other financial accounting sections. This group's undergraduate accounting exposure was not investigated. Because students in this group were not part of the original study, it was necessary to compare their "quality" with that of groups (E) and (N). GMAT scores were used for this purpose because they are standardized and readily available. A two-tailed difference between means test indicated no significant difference at the 0.05 level with a T value of 1.16 between (E) and (O) groups, and a T value of -1.07 between (N) and (O) groups.

Thus, the three groups were undergraduate-accounting exposed (E = 33), nonundergraduate-accounting exposed (N = 28), and the third group, (O = 28).

Next, examination scores of each group were examined to test the following hypothesis:

HYPOTHESIS 1.   There is no significant difference in the MBA-level managerial accounting examination scores between students who have had undergraduate exposure to accounting and those who have not.

A two-sample, two-tailed difference-between-means test was used to test this hypothesis on a MINITAB package that did not require the population variances to be equal. Furthermore, sample size was adequate to satisfy the normal distribution assumption of the test, and it could be used with two samples of unequal number. A two-tailed test was used because mean test scores of one sample could be either higher or lower than the other and the direction could not be known in advance.

THE SAMPLE

The managerial accounting course in which the sample was enrolled was offered during the 1984 spring semester at Suffolk University. One section of the course had 44 students and the other had 45. Each section met once a week in the evenings on different days for 2 hours and 40 minutes. The majority of the students were part-time, but all were degree candidates. The same instructor/ researcher taught both sections using the Anthony and Welsch [1981] management accounting text and the same course material. Homework assignments and examinations were identical.

One midterm and one final exam, each 2 hours long, made up 70% of the semester grade. No make-up exams were administered. The midterm exam was composed of 60% multiple-choice questions and 40% problems; the final exam contained 65% multiple-choice questions and 35% problems. The two sections were given the same test 1 day apart. Because the classes met on different evenings and the number of questions on the exams was substantial, leakage of test material was a negligible factor. A two-tailed difference between means test indicated no significant difference at the 0.05 level between the test scores of the two sections.

Only the examination scores were used to measure performance, because homework and term papers, assessed less objectively, accounted for 30% of the final course grade.

ANALYSIS AND DISCUSSION

Given the results of the original study—namely, that the gap between average examination scores of the (E) and (N) groups progressively narrowed and the amount of prior exposure did not affect performance—no difference in performance should be expected both between (E) and (N) groups and between students in group (O) and those in the other two groups in managerial accounting. The difference between means test results presented in Tables 1, 2, and 3 confirm this expectation. Table 1 shows that although group (E) students scored higher in both the midterm and the final exam than did those

Table 1. Mean Exam Scores and Difference-between-Means Test Results

	Total Points Available	Group (N) Students with No College-Level Accounting			Group (E) Students with College-Level Accounting			Test Results	
		Number	Mean	Standard Deviation	Number	Mean	Standard Deviation	T Value	Decision
Exam 1	100	28	83.1	11.7	33	86.9	8.2	−1.43	Cannot Reject at 0.05
Final Exam	100	27	81.5	8.8	31	82.0	11.2	−0.20	Cannot Reject at 0.05
Semester Total	70[a]	27[b]	57.9	6.0	31[b]	59.1	6.0	−0.79	Cannot Reject at 0.05

[a] Homework assignments and a term paper constituting the remaining 30% of the semester grade equally.
[b] Three students of these groups (61 − 58) dropped the course during the semester.

Table 2.　Mean Exam Scores and Difference-between-Means Test Results

	Total Points Available	Group (E) Students with College-Level Accounting			Group (O) Unknown Group of Students			Test Results	
		Number	Mean	Standard Deviation	Number	Mean	Standard Deviation	T Value	Decision
Exam 1	100	33	86.9	8.2	28	85.5	9.1	0.62	Cannot Reject at 0.05
Final Exam	100	31	82.0	11.2	25	81.0	10.2	0.35	Cannot Reject at 0.05
Semester Total	70[a]	31[b]	59.1	6.0	25[b]	58.7	5.5	0.24	Cannot Reject at 0.05

[a] Homework assignments and a term paper constituting the remaining 30% of the semester grade equally.
[b] Five students of these groups (61 – 56) dropped the course during the semester.

Table 3. Mean Exam Scores and Difference-between-Means Test Results

	Group (N) Students with No College-Level Accounting				Group (O) Unknown Group of Students			Test Results	
	Total Points Available	Number	Mean	Standard Deviation	Number	Mean	Standard Deviation	T Value	Decision
Exam 1	100	28	83.1	11.7	28	85.5	9.1	−0.86	Cannot Reject at 0.05
Final Exam	100	27	81.5	8.8	25	81.0	10.2	0.18	Cannot Reject at 0.05
Semester Total	70[a]	27[b]	57.9	6.0	25[b]	58.7	5.5	−0.54	Cannot Reject at 0.05

[a] Homework assignments and a term paper constituting the remaining 30% of the semester grade equally.
[b] Four students of these groups (56 − 52) dropped the course during the semester.

in the (N) group, the difference was not statistically significant. The narrowing trend in performance continued with the difference virtually disappearing in the final exam, with a much smaller -0.20 T value.

It is interesting to compare the performance of the (E) and (N) groups with the group (O) students whom the instructor/researcher had not taught in the preceding financial accounting class. Although it is safe to assume that this group included both (E)- and (N)-type students, this comparison could reveal any "instructor effect" on student performance and thus provide additional insight into the study results. A comparison of group (O) student performance with that of group (E), presented in Table 2, shows that although mean scores of group (E) in both exams were somewhat higher than those of group (O), the difference was not significant at the 0.05 level. Once again a narrowing trend in performance is apparent with a smaller T value of 0.35 in the final exam. Although slightly higher scores for group (E) might be attributable to instructor familiarity, these results indicate that students having the same instructor in both classes did not affect their performance significantly in the second class.

A comparison of group (O) with group (N) elicits similar results (Table 3). This time, however, group (O) scores were somewhat higher, perhaps indicating a higher concentration of (E)-type students in the group. Nevertheless, the difference was not statistically significant in either exam or in the overall semester grades.

These findings confirm the results reported in the original study and suggest that, although college-level exposure to accounting affects the overall performance in the first MBA-level accounting course, it loses its effect in the second course. Thus, the null hypothesis could not be rejected for any of the comparisons. These findings are similar to those of Bergin [1983] and Baldwin and Howe [1982] in studies that investigated the effect of high school accounting on performance in the first college-level accounting course. They contradict the findings of the more recent Eskew and Faley [1988] and Schroeder [1986] studies, and the Smith [1968] study. Eskew and Faley found that prior exposure to accounting was positively related to student performance in the first college-level accounting course. Schroeder reported no difference in overall course performance between college students with no prior accounting and those with 1 year or less; but students with more than 1 year of high school accounting earned significantly higher scores on all exams in the first college-level financial accounting course. It should be noted that none of these prior studies was conducted at the graduate level nor did they go beyond the introductory level financial accounting course.

SUMMARY AND CONCLUSIONS

This study was conducted to provide additional evidence of the effect of college-level exposure to accounting on student performance in the MBA-level managerial accounting course. The performance of one group of students with some college-level accounting (E) was compared with the performance of another group of students with no college-level accounting (N). The performance of the two groups was further compared with the performance of a third group composed of students who previously had studied under other instructors (O). Performance was measured by examination scores, and no significant differences were found.

The limitations of the original study also were present in this one. The possible effects of factors such as student demographics, course load, examination type, and class time and size were not taken into account. Moreover, a study of students with a variety of undergraduate majors that compares their performance in graduate accounting courses might provide some interesting findings. For example, which students perform better in graduate accounting courses—those who, as undergraduates, majored in business, engineering, or the arts and sciences?

Keeping in mind the findings and the limitations of the present study and the original one, accounting teachers and MBA program administrators should give further thought to separating students with college-level exposure to accounting from those with no exposure in the first MBA-level accounting course, where there seems to be a significant overall performance difference between the two groups. If they are separated, however, is it fair to give the two groups receiving different levels of training in accounting the same credit? Would this lead to different learning levels and thus unfairness of another kind? It should also be kept in mind that the findings of this study indicated that different performance levels do not continue to the next sequential course of managerial accounting. The effect of college-level exposure apparently ends with the first MBA-level accounting course.

It should not be concluded that the two groups are necessarily homogeneous. Homogeneity, in the strict sense of the word, does not preclude diversity among individuals within groups. Each group, and each individual within a group, has different needs and learning aptitudes because of the variation in backgrounds. Thus, accounting teachers and administrators of MBA programs must concern themselves continually with better and more effective ways of teaching and learning. To address these issues and provide answers to some of the questions raised in this study, more studies should be conducted to add to the literature in graduate accounting education.

REFERENCES

Anthony, R. N. and G. A. Welsch, *Fundamentals of Management Accounting* [Irwin, 1981].
Anthony, R. N., G. A. Welsch and J. S. Reece, *Fundamentals of Management Accounting* [Irwin, 1985].

Baldwin, B. A. and K. J. Howe, "Secondary-Level Study of Accounting and Subsequent Performance in the First College Course," *The Accounting Review* [July 1982], pp. 619-626.

Bergin, J. L., "The Effect of Previous Accounting Study on Student Performance in the First College-Level Financial Accounting Course," *Issues in Accounting Education* [American Accounting Association, 1983], pp. 19-28.

Canlar, M., "College-Level Exposure to Accounting Study and Its Effect on Student Performance in the First MBA-Level Financial Accounting Course," *Issues in Accounting Education* [American Accounting Association, Spring 1986], pp. 13-23.

Eskew, R. K. and R. H. Faley, "Some Determinants of Student Performance in the First College-Level Financial Accounting Course," *The Accounting Review* [January 1988], pp. 137-147.

Schroeder, N. W., "Previous Accounting Education and College-Level Accounting Exam Performance," *Issues in Accounting Education* [Spring 1986], pp. 37-47.

Shillinglaw, G. and P. E. Meyer, *Accounting–A Management Approach,* 7th Ed. [Irwin, 1983].

Smith, J. W., "Articulation of High School Bookkeeping and College Elementary Accounting," unpublished Ph.D. dissertation [University of Oklahoma, 1968].

Welsch, G. A. and R. N. Anthony, *Fundamentals of Financial Accounting* [Irwin, 1984].

PARTICIPATION IN SOFTWARE SELECTION:
EFFECTS ON STUDENTS' MOTIVATION AND PERFORMANCE

Dennis Murray and Hugh Grove

ABSTRACT

Participative decision making frequently has been alleged to have positive effects on individuals' motivation and performance. Empirical tests of these relationships have been mixed. This suggests that a number of moderating variables may influence the impact of participation and that participation's effectiveness may be situation specific. This paper reports the results of a study designed to assess the efficacy of permitting students to participate in the selection of software for use by them in an accounting systems class. The results indicate that participation had a positive effect on students' performance, but not on their motivation.

Advances in Accounting, Volume 7, pages 141-149.
Copyright © 1989 by JAI Press Inc.
All rights of reproduction in any form reserved.
ISBN: 0-89232-960-2

INTRODUCTION

The effect of participative decision making on performance has been studied in a number of situations. For example, Latham and Steel [1983] examined participation in an experimental setting involving a routine task; Brownell [1981, 1982b] investigated the usefulness of participative budgeting and Alloway and Quillaid [1983] examined the effect of participative strategies in management information systems related issues. Overall, only limited support has been found for a positive association between participation and performance. These mixed results suggest that the effectiveness of participation may be influenced by one or more moderating variables. Both Locke and Schweiger [1979] and Brownell [1982a] indicate that a large number of variables may condition the relationship between participation and performance. It is likely, therefore, that the degree of association between participation and performance is situation specific.

The purpose of this study is to examine the effect participative decision making has on students' motivation and performance in a classroom setting. The particular decision in which the students were permitted to participate was the selection of software packages for their use in an accounting systems class. The results should be of interest to accounting educators because participation is a relatively low-cost strategy to improve students' performance.

The paper is organized as follows. The theoretical linkages between participation, motivation, and performance are developed in the next section and serve as a basis for the hypotheses. The second section contains a description of the methodology used in this study. The results are reported in section three; section four summarizes the study and notes its limitations.

THEORETICAL DEVELOPMENT AND HYPOTHESES

Locke and Schweiger [1979] have proposed a model of participation's effect on performance. They posit that participation can influence performance via two intervening mechanisms, one cognitive in nature and the other motivational.

Participation potentially may influence two cognitive factors. The first relates to the upward flow of information. In some situations, particularly unstructured ones, subordinates may possess useful task-specific information of which superiors are unaware. Participation provides an opportunity for this information to be shared. The result is more creative ideas and a better strategy, resulting in improved performance.

Participation can affect a second cognitive factor. The participation process may provide subordinates the opportunity to ask task-relevant questions, thereby increasing their understanding of the job, its requirements, and various alternative solutions. As a result, subordinate performance should be enhanced. In a classroom setting, it is unlikely that either of these cognitive factors would play a role. If the instructor has a reasonable amount of experience using the software for class projects, it would be rare to find uninitiated students who can contribute useful knowledge or insights regarding software capabilities. Second, because the purpose of the classroom experience is to transfer knowledge from the instructor to the students, there should be little to gain along this dimension via the participation process.

The second general way in which participation may affect performance is through motivational factors. Locke and Schweiger [1979] hypothesize that participation results in a greater degree of ego involvement on the part of a subordinate. Upon participating in a decision, an individual develops feelings of ownership and commitment to the successful implementation of the decision. Consequently, the individual will become more motivated and work harder at the task. Based on Lawler's [1973] performance model that indicates that motivation is a determinant of performance, it can be concluded that participation may affect performance via the intervening variable motivation.

We propose that this motivational linkage is likely to be operative in the classroom setting that is used in this study. Software selection is an important and meaningful decision that should induce ego involvement. Additionally, Erez and Arad [1986] recently have suggested that social interaction via group discussion may be necessary to enhance and highlight the decision involvement afforded by participation.

In addition to developing a theoretical model, Locke and Schweiger [1979] have reviewed a large body of empirical work assessing the performance effects of participation. The result of these studies are not all uniform. In many situations participation leads to increased motivation and improved performance, whereas in others it does not. This suggests that a number of factors may moderate the effects of participation. Both Brownell [1982a] and Locke and Schweiger [1979] enumerate a number of personality, situational, and organizational variables that might condition the effects of participation. Given this large array of potential moderating variables and the absence of a well-articulated theory that prioritizes the relative importance of these conditioning influences, the effect of participation on motivation and performance in a particular situation is an empirical issue.

Therefore, the two null hypotheses examined in this study are

HYPOTHESIS 1.   Participation in software selection has no effect on students' motivation.

HYPOTHESIS 2.   Participation in software selection has no effect on students' performance.

METHODOLOGY

Subjects and Setting

Two sections of an undergraduate, senior-level course in accounting information systems, which was taught by one of the authors, were chosen for use in this study. Both sections were offered during the same term. One class met in the morning and the other in the afternoon. Thirteen students were enrolled in the morning class and ten students comprised the afternoon class.

Two significant components of the course entailed the use of computer software packages. One component employed a general ledger package to process transactions and to generate financial statements and other reports. Another portion of the course used a decision support package that assisted the students in recommending whether or not to open a new business. The completion of two major projects, using each of the two packages, was part of the course requirements. Students worked individually on the projects.

Participation

The experimental treatment in this study consisted of permitting students to participate in the selection of the particular general ledger package (or decision support package) to be used by them. The control treatment entailed unilateral assignment of a particular package by the instructor. Each class received each treatment once. Random assignment resulted in the morning class receiving the participation treatment with respect to selection of the general ledger software and the no participation treatment regarding selection of the decision support software. Assignment of treatments was reversed for the afternoon class. In both the general ledger and decision support situations, the package the students selected in the participation condition corresponded to the package selected by the instructor in the no participation condition.

In the participation condition, students were provided with a brief description of either the two alternative general ledger software packages or the two decision software packages. In the morning class, the two general ledger software packages were either a highly structured package or a flexible package in terms of a chart of accounts, inputs, and report design. In the afternoon class, the two decision support software packages were either a spreadsheet package or a simple fourth generation programming language package.

These software packages were described by the instructor, and the students evaluated them based on software selection criteria contained in the accounting information systems textbook used in the classes. The students actively discussed the alternatives and reached a consensus as to which package would be used. Students were not allowed to select packages individually because of logistical and coordination difficulties.

Software selection was chosen as the focal decision for two reasons. First, it provided the students an opportunity to participate in an important and meaningful decision. The package selected would be used extensively by the students and would have a significant impact on the nature and extent of the work devoted to the project and the quality of the finished product. Second, we wanted to choose a dimension of decision making in which instructors would not feel that their prerogative was impaired. For example, the effect of students' participation in determining the grading process (e.g., number of exams and quizzes) or class format (lecture versus problems versus discussion) could have been assessed. However, we felt that relatively few instructors would be inclined to permit their students to influence these decisions.

Motivation

Motivation refers to the force experienced by an individual to engage in a given behavior [Jones 1955] and often is operationalized in terms of the effort an individual expends [e.g., Porter and Lawler 1968; Mitchell 1974]. Vroom [1964] has suggested that the amount of time an individual devotes to a particular task is an appropriate proxy for effort, and this operationalization previously has been employed in accounting [Jiambalvo 1979] and educational [Kennedy et al. 1983] settings. Accordingly, we obtained from each student self reports of the number of hours they devoted to each project. This constituted the motivation measure.

Performance

Performance was measured by the grade awarded the student on each project. Projects were graded on a scale of 0 to 60. Grades were based on the quality of the project; no consideration was given to the students' effort levels previously described. In order to eliminate any bias introduced by the instructor during the grading process, projects from the classes were combined and graded anonymously so that a student project from one class could not be distinguished from that of the other class.

Design and Analysis

A 2×2 Latin Squares design with repeated measures was employed [Winer 1971, p. 717]. The two treatments examined were (1) participation in software selection and (2) no participation in software selection. The software package constituted the column variable, and class section or time was the row variable. The design layout (along with means to be discussed later) appears in Table 1.

Table 1. Design Layout and Cell Means

	Package	
Class	General Ledger	Decision Support

Morning
	Treatment	
	Participation	No Participation
Average Motivation	14.3	24.9
Average Performance	52.5	49.1

Afternoon
	Treatment	
	No Participation	Participation
Average Motivation	11.5	23.2
Average Performance	51.3	51.5

Two assumptions that underlie this design are (1) variance homogeneity and (2) an additive model. The null hypothesis of variance homogeneity was tested and could not be rejected at the 0.05 level. Winer [1971] suggests a test to examine the additivity of the model. This test compares the residual variance to the error variance. Unfortunately, when each factor has only two levels, the number of degrees of freedom necessary for the test is unavailable. This situation, however, is mitigated by three considerations. First, the test is only a partial one and does not provide conclusive evidence of additivity. Second, Winer [1971, p. 718] maintains that the assumption of additivity is frequently tenable when one factor (participation) is a treatment variable and the others (class time and software package) are control variables. Third, the consequence of assuming additivity when, in fact, interactions are present is to reduce the power of the test. Therefore, the significance levels reported are, if anything, conservative.

RESULTS

Hypothesis 1 states that participation will have no effect on motivation. Table 2 contains the results for the test of this hypothesis. The treatment effect of participation was not significant at any reasonable level of significance, although the direction of the difference is as predicted. Averaging over projects and classes, the mean motivation for the participation treatment is 18.75 whereas the mean motivation for the no participation condition is 18.20. The results indicate that participation had no effect on students' motivation and Hypothesis 1 cannot be rejected.

Table 2. ANOVA Results: Motivation

Source of Variation	d.f.	Mean Squares	F Value	p value
Between Subjects				
Class	1	57.42	1.02	0.32
Subjects within Groups	21	56.10		
Within Subjects				
Project	1	1414.12	44.56	0.00
Participation	1	3.86	0.12	0.73
Error	21	31.73		

Table 3. ANOVA Results: Performance

Source of Variation	d.f.	Mean Squares	F Value	p value
Between Subjects				
Class	1	4.39	0.26	0.62
Subjects within Groups	21	16.91		
Within Subjects				
Project	1	31.21	5.62	0.03
Participation	1	34.16	6.15	0.02
Error	21	5.56		

The second null hypothesis posits that participation would have no effect on performance. Table 3 contains the test results of this hypothesis. The participation effect was significant at the 0.02 level. Averaging over projects and classes, the mean performance scores were 51.85 and 50.2 for the participation and no participation conditions, respectively. Because the difference is significant and in the predicted direction, Hypothesis 2 is rejected and it can be concluded that permitting students to participate in software selection had a positive effect on their performance.

CONCLUSIONS AND LIMITATIONS

The results of this study indicate that permitting students to influence the selection of software packages in accounting systems courses has a positive effect on their performance. Although the effect is statistically significant, its size was relatively modest. The average performance under the participation condition was approximately 3.3% greater than under the no participation condition.

The theory relied on in this paper posits that participation will affect performance via the intervening variable motivation. Because our results do not indicate that participation had a positive effect on motivation, this linkage is not supported. Several possible explanations exist for this result. First, our measurement of motivation may be less than optimal. Although hours expended has been used in other studies with successful results, it does suffer from at least two drawbacks. First, it is purely a quantitiative measure that does not incorporate any assessment of the quality of each student's input. Perhaps a richer measure would have yielded significant results. Also, the motivation measures were self-assessments and may suffer from various degrees of inaccuracies. Alternatively, the linkage via motivation may not have accounted for the positive assocation between participation and performance. Brownell and McInnes [1986] recently undertook a path analytic approach to investigate the intervening effect of motivation in a participative budgeting setting. Their results indicate that although a positive association between participation and performance did exist, it was not through the path that included motivation. Additional research in both classroom and work situations is needed to identify the causal links between participation and performance.

Several limitations of this study should be noted. First, the sample consisted of only 23 subjects, which limits the external validity and power of the tests. Second, possible nonadditivity of the model can also reduce the power of the tests (although our results for participation were significant at the 0.02 level). Finally, our manipulation of participation possibly could have been stronger. The students' participation in software selection took place at the beginning of the semester. At this stage of the semester, the students' relatively low level of knowledge may have resulted in them feeling that the quality of their contribution was limited. This could dampen the impact of the experimental treatment and can potentially explain the limited difference in performance scores between the participation versus no participation conditions. Future research in which the experimental manipulation is stronger may show a greater effect of participation on performance.

Overall, the results of this study are encouraging because a positive, and statistically significant, although quantitatively modest, effect of participation on performance was found. Given the very low cost associated with the participation condition, we suggest that instructors of accounting systems classes consider a participative approach to software selection.

REFERENCES

Alloway, R. and J. Quillaid, "User Managers' System Needs," *MIS Quarterly* [June 1983], pp. 27-41.
Brownell, P., "Participation in Budgeting, Locus of Control and Organizational Effectiveness," *The Accounting Review* [October 1981], pp. 844-860.

Brownell, P., "Participation in the Budgeting Process: When it Works and When it Doesn't," *Journal of Accounting Literature* [Spring 1982a], pp. 124-153.

Brownell, P., "A Field Study Examination of Budgetary Participation and Locus of Control," *The Accounting Review* [October 1982b], pp. 766-777.

Brownell, P., and M. McInnes, "Budgetary Participation, Motivation, and Managerial Performance," *The Accounting Review* [October 1986], pp. 587-600.

Erez, M. and R. Arad, "Participative Goal-Setting: Social, Motivational and Cognitive Factors," *Journal of Applied Psychology* [November 1986], pp. 591-597.

Jiambalvo, J., "Performance Evaluation and Directed Job Effort: Model Development and Analysis in a CPA Firm Setting," *Journal of Accounting Research* [Autumn 1979], pp. 436-455.

Jones, M. R., *Nebraska Symposium on Motivation* [University of Nebraska Press, 1955].

Kennedy, C. W., J. A. Fossum, and B. J. White, "An Empirical Comparison of Within-Subjects and Between-Subjects Expectancy Theory Models," *Organizational Behavior and Human Performance* [October 1983], pp. 124-143.

Latham, G. and T. P. Steele, "The Motivational Effect of Participation Versus Goal Setting on Performance," *Academy of Management Journal* [September 1983], pp. 406-417.

Lawler, E. E. III, *Motivation in Work Organizations* [Brooks/Cole, 1973].

Locke, E. A. and D. M. Schweiger, "Participation in Decision-Making: One More Look," in B.M. Staw (ed.), *Research in Organizational Behavior,* Vol. 1 [JAI Press, 1979].

Mitchell, T. R., "Expectancy Models of Job Satisfaction, Occupational Preference and Effort: A Theoretical, Methodological, and Empirical Appraisal," *Psychological Bulletin* [1974], pp. 1053-1077.

Porter, L. W., and E. E. Lawler, III, *Managerial Attitudes and Performance* [Dorsey Press, 1968].

Vroom, V. H., *Work and Motivation* [Wiley, 1964].

Winer, B. J., *Statistical Principles in Experimental Design* [McGraw-Hill, 1971].

PART III

AUDITING

THE EFFECT OF PERCEIVED
EXPERTISE ON AUDITORS'
REVIEW JUDGMENTS

E. Michael Bamber

ABSTRACT

Previous research on how the audit review process affects auditors' judgments has yielded mixed results. One explanation for this is that those studies did not allow for individual differences, such as the expertise of the subordinate whose judgments are reviewed. This study reports the results of an experiment that investigated how the subordinate's perceived "expertise" (measured in terms of experience and personnel performance ratings) affected reviewers' judgments. An audit methodology consideration (sampling approach) was also examined as a contextual variable. Thirty-one audit managers reviewed a hypothetical senior's audit sample sizes, and specified the revisions they would make. The results suggest that the manager's review is sensitive to the senior's expertise. Performance ratings and, in one case, experience affected managers' revisions, whereas sampling approach did not. Managers appeared to employ one of two

Advances in Accounting, Volume 7, pages 153-172.
ISBN: 0-89232-960-2

different judgment strategies. The first strategy was consistent with the familiar anchoring and adjustment heuristic. Other managers, however, did not appear to anchor on any of the information provided in the case study, but instead concluded that significantly smaller sample sizes were warranted. Possible explanations (e.g., firm effects) and implications of these results are explored.

INTRODUCTION

Auditors frequently make decisions based on information provided by others. The audit team's hierarchical structure and division of labor require auditors to direct subordinates to conduct audit procedures, and to subsequently review the subordinate's work and make decisions on audit evidence compiled and possibly analyzed by the subordinate. Hence, review plays a fundamental role in conducting an audit. Nevertheless, review has received little attention in the auditing literature. The research that does exist [e.g., Mock and Turner 1979, 1981; Trotman 1985] provides mixed results in terms of judgment variability and accuracy. It is difficult to explain these mixed results because little is known about the characteristics that influence an auditor's review of, and associated reliance on, a subordinate's work. For example, most research neither considers nor controls for individual differences such as the ability and experience of the auditors whose work is reviewed.

This study provides evidence on whether, in the review process, auditors are sensitive to individual differences between subordinates. Specifically, the paper investigates how the senior's perceived "expertise" affects the manager's review (in particular, reliance on the senior's planned sample sizes). The senior's perceived expertise is operationalized in terms of experience and performance ratings, two auditor characteristics that are salient in practice. In a related vein, this study also provides preliminary evidence on apparent judgment strategies or heuristics managers employ in reviewing the senior's planned sample sizes. Specifically, the study investigates the anchoring and adjustment heuristic [e.g., Joyce and Biddle 1981a, 1981b; Kinney and Uecker 1982] in the review process.

PRIOR RESEARCH AND HYPOTHESIS DEVELOPMENT

In a study of internal control evaluation and audit planning decisions, Mock and Turner [1981] asked audit managers to review the sample size recommendations made by audit seniors. Mock and Turner concluded that the managers' review did not reduce the large variability in seniors' sample size judgments, in spite of the fact that all participants were from the same accounting firm. In contrast, Trotman and Yetton [1985] used an internal control evaluation task and found that review did significantly reduce judgment variance. However, two-person composites[1] and interacting groups of two seniors also reduced judgment variance. Trotman and Yetton concluded that "[a] second opinion, regardless of its form, outperforms individual judgments" [1985, p. 265]. Trotman [1985] reported some differences between composite groups, interacting groups, and manager review that suggested that subjects may have been sensitive to expertise. Although Trotman found that judgments of the expected dollar error in inventory were more accurate and less variable after review, he also found that when managers reviewed the substantive tests proposed by seniors, judgment variability was not reduced and managers significantly increased the number of audit hours proposed by the senior.

Although Trotman recognized that "since the managers knew which seniors made the judgment to be reviewed, they were in a better position to differentiate relative expertise between their judgments and those of the senior" [1985, p. 741], he did not measure or control for the seniors' expertise nor specifically test its effect. Other research studies [Joyce and Biddle 1981b; Bamber 1983] have reported that auditors are sensitive to the reliability of information sources. Hence, this study specifically examines how the senior's perceived expertise affects the manager's review of the senior's planned sample sizes.

Previous audit judgment research suggests that the sample size task is appropriate for examining the effects of individual differences (in seniors' expertise, for example) on manager review judgments. Sample size determination is perceived as a senior level responsibility [Abdolmohammadi and Wright 1987] involving making several preliminary judgments (e.g., reliance on internal control) and combining these judgments to arrive at a sample size. However, seniors' sample size judgments (and, more generally, audit program decisions) tend to exhibit greater variability when compared to other types of judgments, such as internal control evaluations (see Ashton [1983] for a review). Such variability suggests that there is sufficient latitude for seniors' sample sizes to be revised, as a result of the manager's review.

With respect to the manager's review of the senior's work, previous accounting and psychology research[2] suggests that the senior's experience and past performance ratings are two likely determinants of the manager's perception of the senior's expertise and, hence, reliance on the senior. Experience involves familiarity with the tasks at hand. In auditing, experience encompasses both (1) years of experience (as reflected in the hierarchical levels in the audit team, e.g., senior, manager) and (2) industry-related experience and specialization. As discussed earlier, sample size determination is perceived as a senior level responsibility. Although all seniors should have the minimal technical skills to perform the task, the more experienced senior should have demonstrated a fine-tuning of these skills, as a result of determining sample sizes in a variety of settings. Consequently, the manager is expected to place greater reliance on the more experienced senior.

HYPOTHESIS 1. Audit managers will exhibit greater reliance on the more experienced senior.

Performance ratings evaluate the proficiency with which tasks are performed. Accounting firms frequently use personnel performance evaluations on each engagement. These engagement evaluations are then combined to determine the auditor's annual evaluation. Wright [1980] found that engagement evaluations are the primary source of information on which staff auditor salary and promotion decisions are based. Although a manager may not be privy to a senior's personnel file, in the sampled offices, the manager would typically have previously supervised the senior and would have discussed the office's seniors' relative performances with other managers and partners. These discussions would result in a ranking of the office's seniors. The managers' discussions and rankings of seniors would provide them with information on seniors' proficiency. Consequently, the manager should exhibit greater reliance on the senior known to be more highly rated.

HYPOTHESIS 2. Audit managers will exhibit greater reliance on the senior with the higher performance ratings.

The sampling approach the senior uses to generate the sample sizes must also be considered. Because of individual idiosyncrasies or firm policies (subsequently tested for), managers may differ in their preference for statistical versus nonstatistical sampling. However, of particular interest is whether the senior's sampling approach interacts with differences in auditor expertise. Although no effect is hypothesized for the senior with high expertise, the senior's sampling approach may affect managers' revisions for the senior with low expertise. Nonstatistical sampling is typically performed as a less structured approach that does not require formal specification of the auditor's judgment. In contrast, statistical sampling is a form of decision aid that requires the explicit determination of sample size factors, which are then combined to arrive at a sample size. It is expected that the guidance provided by statistical sampling will lead the manager to place greater reliance on the low-expertise senior, when that senior uses statistical (as opposed to nonstatistical) sampling.

HYPOTHESIS 3. Audit managers will exhibit greater reliance on the inexperienced and lower rated senior when that senior employs a statistical sampling approach (as opposed to a nonstatistical approach).

The next section of the paper describes the experimental method, including the context (independent variable) manipulation employed in the study. Subsequent sections describe the results and their implications.

METHOD

Subjects

Consistent with previous research [e.g., Mock and Turner 1979, 1981; Bamber 1983; Trotman 1985] this study examines the senior-manager relationship. The senior is responsible for conducting the audit fieldwork, while the manager is responsible for administering all aspects of the engagement, including supervising and reviewing the work of subordinate audit team members.

Six of the "Big Eight" accounting firms located in a Midwestern city provided 35 audit managers, on an availability basis. Participating managers were personally handed the test instrument, briefed about the nature of the task, and instructed to work alone. The test instrument was then returned by mail. Thirty-one instruments were subsequently received, with one firm providing eight subjects, two firms six subjects, and the remaining firms providing four and three subjects, respectively. The subjects' level of audit experience ranged from 5 to 11 years. The small number of nonrandomly selected subjects from similar sized offices within one geographic location may limit the results' generalizability.

Task

Subjects assumed manager responsibility for an audit that was currently underway. The 16-page case study, modeled on the case of Mock and Turner [1979, 1981], also focused on the confirmation of accounts receivable. Similar to their case, the materials contained a variety of information normally found in an audit, including a description of the client's internal control system, compliance test results, the results of last year's confirmations, and the senior's planned sample sizes for this year's confirmations. Two competing anchors were established for the manager-subjects by distinguishing last year's sample sizes from this year's planned sample sizes. The senior was recommending a reduction in the extent of this year's confirmations, based on improvements in the client's internal control system. Subjects either accepted the senior's planned sample sizes, or provided revised sample sizes.

The accounts receivable were stratified for confirmation purposes, as is commonly done in practice. (The strata are similar to Mock and Turner's.) Table 1 summarizes the strata and gives the senior's planned sample sizes. Accounts that were individually significant, in terms of either dollar amount (stratum D3) or days past due (strata D1 and D2) were separated from the body of accounts receivable (stratum D4). Because the sample sizes of Mock and Turner's subjects were considerably below the anchor provided to them,

Table 1.   Population Characteristics and Recommended Sample Sizes
for the Accounts Receivable Strata

Stratum	Population Amount[a] (Book Value) ($)	Population Size[a] (Number of Accounts)	Senior's Planned Sample Sizes	Last Year's Sample Sizes
D1: Accounts over 90 Days Past Due	10,000	14	0	15
D2: Accounts 45 to 90 Days Past Due	52,319	55	20	54
D3: Accounts over $2500	111,320	40	20	35
D4: Accounts under $2500	1,567,213	1,899	160	345
Total	1,740,852	2,008	200	449

[a] This information was obtained from the client's accounts receivable subsidiary ledger.

the senior's planned total sample size in this study (shown in Table 1) was based on the unanchored mean sample size reported by Mock and Turner [1979]. This was believed to be a more realistic sample size and, as shown in Table 1, provided the subjects with two competing anchors: the senior's planned sample size of 200 versus the actual sample size of 449 used in the previous year's audit.

Independent Variables

As indicated in Hypotheses 1 and 2, the senior's experience and performance rating are hypothesized to affect the manager's perceptions of the senior's expertise and, hence, the manager's reliance on the senior's judgments. The test instrument described the senior at either "low" or "high" levels of experience and performance as follows: (1) little or extensive experience in terms of time as a senior *and* familiarity with client type, and (2) low or high performance ratings in terms of a set of factors including technical skills *and* soundness of judgment. The Appendix reports the specific descriptions used in the experiment. Because the auditing literature does not clearly define "relevant experience," and because performance evaluation is multidimensionnal [Wright 1986], both measures were presented as multidimensional variables. The disadvantage of this approach is that it prevents attribution of significant results to specific performance dimensions.

An audit partner from the national office of one of the participating firms assisted in the development of the descriptions presented in the Appendix.

These descriptions were designed to provide reasonable rather than extreme manipulations. The complete case was pilot-tested with three auditors who were liaisons for their respective firms, and five colleagues with auditing experience. Subjects' debriefing responses on the reasonableness of the case materials are discussed subsequently.

The third independent variable was the sampling approach the senior used to derive the planned sample sizes: statistical versus nonstatistical sampling. As hypothesized earlier, the sampling approach may affect the manager's reliance on the senior through interaction with the senior's expertise (i.e., the manager's reliance on the senior's sample sizes derived via a nonstatistical procedure may be more affected by the senior's perceived expertise, whereas reliance on statistical sample sizes may be less sensitive to perceived expertise). In this study, therefore, it is the interactaction with the other independent variables, rather than the sampling approach itself, that is of primary interest.

The case materials did not include any preliminary parameter judgments (e.g., sampling risk and expected error) that the senior may have made in calculating the sample sizes. This is a limitation of the experiment, in that such information would typically be subject to review (at least under statistical sampling), and it is unclear whether this affected the subjects' sample size judgments. However, it was felt that this limitation was outweighed by several factors: (1) different firms use different sample size parameters, (2) sample size parameters are not necessarily identified under nonstatistical sampling, and (3) the chosen approach forced subjects to focus on reviewing the senior's planned sample sizes (given the particular sampling approach) rather than simply mechanically recomputing the sample sizes.

Experimental Design

The three manipulated independent variables, each with two levels, resulted in eight alternative descriptions of the senior. All eight descriptions were attached to the case study in random order to provide a randomized, repeated measures design. A within-subject design employs subjects more efficiently than a between-subjects design. Given the relative scarcity of audit manager subjects, efficiency was an important practical consideration. Although the manager-subjects were aware of the manipulated variables (because of the repeated measures within a single client), this was not considered a serious problem. The potential concern is that subjects' knowledge of the manipulated variables might induce "demand effects" [Pany and Reckers 1987]. However, as will be discussed later, the hypothesized results did not materialize across all classifications of independent variables. It is therefore unlikely that the significant results were simply caused by demand effects. This is consistent with the view that this study's experiment should be relatively less subject to demand effects, because it employed experienced subjects performing a familiar and routine task (compared to the relatively controversial topic of auditor independence examined by Pany and Reckers).

Dependent Variables

The primary dependent variable is one commonly used in audit judgment research—auditors' sample size judgments [e.g., Mock and Turner 1981; Tabor 1983; Bamber and Snowball 1988]. In this study, the audit managers provided four sample size judgments: one for each of the four accounts receivable strata. An additional factor investigated was the extent to which subjects' sample size judgments were affected by (1) the results of the compliance tests conducted by the senior, and (2) the senior's proposed sample sizes. These self-report responses (on an anchored seven-point scale) were included to investigate whether managers' perceptions were differentially sensitive to senior's expertise in two different tasks: (1) the evaluation of internal control and the related compliance tests performed under the senior's supervision, and (2) sample size determination.[3] Although such perceptions should be interpreted with some caution, the self-report responses should be a reasonable task for audit managers, because research suggests that auditors have moderate self-insight across a broad array of tasks [Ashton 1983].

RESULTS

As discussed, the case used in this study was based on the case of Mock and Turner [1979, 1981] and involved a similar improvement in internal control (weak to strong). In order to check the reasonableness of the subjects' responses, the overall mean sample sizes are first compared to Mock and Turner's results. Results are then presented on the effect of the senior's expertise and sampling approach on manager-subjects' sample size revisions. These results provide the basis for the subsequent examination of managers' judgment strategies for revising the senior's sample sizes.

Table 2 compares the relevant results of Mock and Turner with those of this study.[4] In addition to finding that subjects reduced planned sample sizes in response to improved internal control, Mock and Turner's results are consistent with an anchoring and adjustment strategy: subjects who received a planned sample size of 439 specified a mean sample size of 303, whereas a second group of subjects who did not receive this information specified a mean sample of 205. The unanchored mean sample size provided this study's rationale for the senior's planned sample size of 200. This study's subjects' mean sample size of 187 is not significantly different ($p > 0.2$) from the senior's planned sample size of 200, nor from Mock and Turner's unanchored subjects' mean sample size of 205.

Table 2.   Comparison of Mean Sample Sizes with
Mock and Turner's [1979] Results

	Sample Sizes		
	Prior Year Sample Size	Planned Sample Size	Actual Mean (Standard Deviation) for This Year
Mock and Turner Subjects provided an anchor (n = 31)	439	439	303 (104)
Subjects not provided an anchor (n = 43)	439	NP	205 (107)
Current study (n = 31)	449	200	187 (74)

NP = Not Provided.

Expertise

The study's first two hypotheses postulate that audit managers are sensitive to the senior's perceived expertise, as measured by experience (Hypothesis 1) and performance ratings (Hypothesis 2). The ANOVA results presented in Table 3 provide only limited evidence for increased reliance on the more experienced senior (Hypothesis 1), but clear evidence for increased reliance on the highly rated senior (Hypothesis 2). Table 3 indicates that subjects' revisions of the senior's planned sample sizes were affected by the senior's performance rating. The greater reliance on the higher rated senior translated, on average, into significantly smaller sample sizes for all strata ($p < 0.05$). Although inspection of the data indicated that sample sizes were also smaller for the more experienced senior, experience was statistically significant ($p < 0.01$) only for the accounts receivable stratum comprising accounts over \$2500 (the largest individual accounts). This result suggests that audit managers may be more sensitive to the senior's experience level when judgments are required on large accounts.

Sampling Approach

The third hypothesis suggested that the sampling approach would interact with the senior's expertise. However, Table 3 shows that neither sampling approach nor its interaction with other independent variables was associated with a significant change in subjects' sample sizes. As suggested earlier, it is possible that a sampling approach effect on managers' sample size revisions might be confounded by differences in firm policies and practices. To test for a firm effect, a one-way ANOVA was run on subjects' mean sample size for each accounts receivable stratum. Table 4 presents, by firm, subjects' mean sample sizes and associated standard deviations.

Table 3. ANOVA Results for the Effects of Experience, Performance Rating, and Sampling Approach on Subjects' Sample Sizes [a]

Effect	Sample Size for Accounts				Total Sample Size
	Over 90 Days Past Due (D1)	45-90 Days Past Due (D2)	Over $2500 (D3)	Under $2500 (D4)	
A: Experience (A1: Extensive, A2: Little)	0.132	0.241	0.009 A1 < A2	0.850	0.214
B: Performance Rating (B1: High, B2: Low)	0.006 B1<B2	0.035 B1<B2	0.0002 B1<B2	0.006 B1<B2	0.002 B1<B2
C: Sampling Approach (C1: Statistical, C2: Nonstatistical)	0.270	0.381	0.199	0.317	0.569

[a] The figures reported in the table are the p values of the ANOVA tests for main effects. The direction of significant treatment level differences are reported under the p values. No interactions were significant.

Table 4.   Firm Means (Standard Deviations) of Subjects' Sample Sizes

	Mean Sample Sizes for Accounts				
Sampling Orientation	Over 90 Days Past Due (D1)	45-90 Days Past Due[a] (D2)	Over $2500 (D3)	Under $2500[b] (D4)	Total Sample Size[b]
Statistical					
Firm 1 ($n = 8$)	2.2 (2.1)	7.9 (8.2)	13.6 (17.2)	80.5 (40.9)	116.1 (60.1)
Firm 2 ($n = 4$)	5.9 (6.1)	19.7 (2.6)	25.0 (4.2)	138.8 (29.5)	189.3 (21.6)
Intermediate					
Firm 3 ($n = 6$)	7.7 (5.2)	19.3 (9.0)	25.8 (11.1)	124.8 (57.9)	177.6 (66.3)
Firm 4 ($n = 4$)	3.8 (4.8)	9.8 (11.4)	25.0 (14.7)	177.2 (69.9)	215.8 (75.9)
Firm 5 ($n = 3$)	4.7 (8.0)	20.8 (4.9)	28.3 (10.4)	170.0 (17.3)	223.8 (40.0)
Nonstatistical					
Firm 6 ($n = 6$)	4.6 (3.8)	23.5 (9.4)	26.0 (2.8)	199.6 (57.6)	253.8 (60.3)
Overall Mean	4.7 (4.7)	16.4 (9.9)	23.1 (12.0)	142.8 (63.4)	187.4 (74.3)
Senior's Recommendations	0	20	20	160	200

[a,b] One-way ANOVA significance levels of 0.05 and 0.01, respectively. Because the ANOVA homogeneity of variance assumption was not satisfied, Welch's F text [Milliken and Johnson 1984] was also employed—the resulting significance levels were equivalent to those reported above.

The analysis did provide evidence of a firm effect. For example, Table 4 shows that there were significant differences between firms' total sample sizes ($p < 0.01$) and between firms' sample sizes for the D4 ($p < 0.01$) and D2 ($p < 0.05$) strata. It is also interesting that these differences remained when firms were grouped according to their sampling policies, as recently described by Cushing and Loebbecke [1986]. Fims one and two in Table 4 may be described (in terms of firm policies and practices) as statistically oriented, and firm six as nonstatistically oriented. The other firms fit into Kinney's intermediate category.[5] Using this three-level factor in one-way ANOVAs resulted in a significant effect for the D4 stratum ($F = 4.91, p < 0.02$). Inspection of the firm means in Table 4 indicates that the smaller sample sizes of the statistically oriented firms (particularly firm one) underlie this result.[6]

Self-Report Responses

Results based on the self-report responses provide additional evidence on the three hypotheses. Table 5 shows that, on average, subjects reported giving greater weight ($p < 0.001$) to both the compliance tests and sample sizes when the senior's experience level (Hypothesis 1) and performance rating (Hypothesis 2) were higher. However, detailed inspection of treatment means revealed that subjects reported giving significantly more weight ($t = 4.8, p < 0.001$) to the compliance test results (mean of 5.1) than to the senior's planned sample sizes (mean of 3.8). The weight given the senior's sample sizes was heavily influenced by performance ratings (treatment means of 2.7 versus 4.9 for the low versus high rated senior, respectively). Moreover, the significant interaction between experience and performance rating ($p < 0.001$) indicates that experience had a greater effect for the highly rated senior's sample sizes (treatment means of 4.3 versus 5.4 for the inexperienced versus experienced senior) compared to that of the poorly rated senior (2.5 versus 2.9). In sum, the limited effect of the senior's experience on the manager's sample size revisions appears to reflect (1) the minimal consideration given to the poorly rated senior's sample sizes (regardless of the senior's experience level), and (2) the perception that all seniors (even if inexperienced) conduct reliable compliance tests.

Unlike the sample size judgments, the self-report weights provide some support for Hypothesis 3.[7] As hypothesized, the significant interaction between sampling approach and experience ($p < 0.047$) indicated that managers reported placing more weight on the inexperienced senior's sample sizes when statistical sampling was utilized (treatment means of 3.2 for nonstatistical sampling versus 3.6 for statistical sampling: $F = 11.06, p < 0.01$). However, managers did not report placing significantly different weights on the experienced senior's sample sizes based on nonstatistical versus statistical sampling (treatment means of 4.1 and 4.2, respectively: $F = 0.47, p > 0.49$).

Table 5.   ANOVA Results for the Effects of Experience, Performance Rating, and Sampling Approach on Subjects' Self-Report Weights[a]

Effect		Self-Reported Weight on [b]	
		Compliance Test Results	Planned Sample Sizes
A:	Experience	0.0001	0.0001
	(A1: Extensive, A2: Little)	A1 > A2	A1 > A2
B:	Performance Rating	0.0001	0.0001
	(B1: High, B2: Low)	B1 > B2	B1 > B2
C:	Sampling Approach	0.312	0.028
	(C1: Statistical, C2: Nonstatistical)	C1 > C2	
A × B:	Experience by Performance Rating	0.277	0.001
A × C:	Experience by Sampling Approach	0.774	0.047
B × C:	Performance Rating by Sampling Approach	0.752	0.776
A × B × C:	Experience by Performance Rating by Sampling Approach	0.478	0.444

[a] The figures reported in the table are the *p* values of the ANOVA tests. The direction of significant main effects is reported under the *p* values.

[b] Subjects responded on 7-point scales, with a score of seven representing maximum reliance.

Judgment Strategies

It was initially suggested that subjects would anchor on the senior's planned sample sizes, and then make adjustments based on the senior's perceived expertise. The results reported earlier (see Table 3) show that, on average, subjects' responses were consistent with such a strategy. However, the firm means presented in Table 4 imply that some subjects provided sample sizes considerably above and below those proposed by the senior. Such revisions in the senior's sample sizes when the senior was highly rated and experienced are not consistent with the proposed anchoring and adjustment strategy.

Examination of the data at the individual subject level indicated two clearly distinct subject groupings. One group's sample sizes were substantially lower than those of the senior, whereas the other subjects' sample sizes were equal to or above those of the senior.[8] For example, Figure 1 plots the "below" and "above" groups' mean sample sizes for stratum D4 (accounts less than $2500) over the performance rating treatment levels. Figure 1 suggests that the significant effect for performance rating reported in Table 3 may have been driven by the "above" subjects. The "below" subjects' response to the low performance rating was only a relatively slight increase in the extent of sampling. Plots of the other strata were entirely consistent with this pattern.

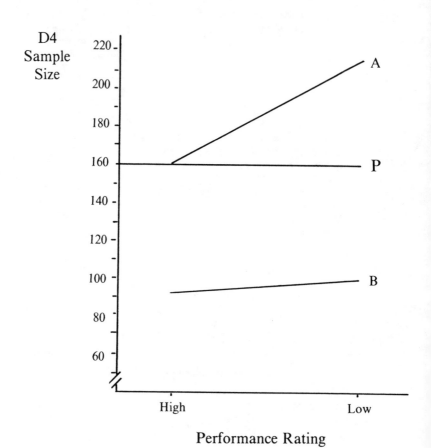

A: "Above" group ($n = 14$); B: "Below" group ($n = 16$); P: Senior's planned sample size.

Figure 1.   Performance Rating Treatment Means for the
"Above" and "Below" Groups.

To test for differences between the "above" and "below" subjects, the
ANOVA analysis reported in Table 3 was replicated on the "above" and
"below" groups separately (not shown). The independent variables (experience,
performance rating, and sampling approach) were not significant at the 0.1
level for the "below" subjects (with the single exception of performance rating
on the sample size for stratum D3, which was significant at the 0.08 level).
For the "above" subjects, in contrast, performance rating was significant for

all strata (D1: $p < 0.045$; D2: $p < 0.06$; D3: $p < 0.001$; D4: $p < 0.011$), and experience was significant for strata D1 ($p < 0.091$), D2 ($p < 0.089$), and D3 ($p < 0.025$). These results suggest that, consistent with the interpretation of Figure 1, subjects in the two groups tended to use different judgment strategies.

The explanation of the "below" subjects' judgment strategies appears to be related to audit methodology. Ten of the 12 managers in the statistically oriented firms were in the "below group." They comprise 10 of the 16 subjects making up this group in Figure 1. Only two subjects in the "above" group are from these statistically oriented firms. The small sample size per firm makes it difficult to generalize this association. However, the significant firm effect reported earlier suggests that, for some subjects, the senior's planned sample sizes (and possibly the previous year's sample sizes) were not representative of the sample sizes typically employed in their firm. Consequently, these subjects made substantial downward adjustments to the senior's sample sizes, and their revised sample sizes were relatively insensitive to the independent variables' manipulation.[9]

LIMITATIONS, CONCLUSIONS, AND IMPLICATIONS

The conclusions and implications are subject to a number of limitations. As noted earlier, the small number of subjects limits generalizability. Furthermore, response bias may have been introduced through the use of a mail administration, repeated measures, or self-report responses (which, because of the repeated-measures design, came before some sample size decisions). Subjects' responses to a short debriefing questionnaire suggested other possible limitations. Two subjects asked for more information on the senior's performance rating (e.g., had he passed the CPA exam on the first attempt). Two subjects would have liked to know the senior's sample size parameters; the reason for their omission was discussed earlier. In terms of subjects' response options, one subject indicated that he would have initially communicated with the previous audit manager, whereas two other subjects noted that in practice their level of supervision would have been higher for the less experienced and lower rated senior. In spite of these comments, subjects' overall responses indicated they were generally favorably disposed to the task. In particular, 21 of the managers said the information provided was sufficient. (Five did not respond and the comments of the other five have been noted.) Also, 27 responded that the task was understandable, with the other four not responding.

With so little known about the characteristics that influence an auditor's review process (and the associated reliance on a subordinate), the primary purpose of the paper was to examine how the senior's expertise affected the manager's reliance on the senior's work. The mangers examined the results of the compliance tests performed under the senior, and the senior's planned sample sizes for the confirmation of accounts receivable. These are typical tasks from both the senior's and manager's perspectives.

The results suggest that managers differentiated between subordinates' expertise. Expertise was operationalized in terms of the senior's experience and performance rating. The senior's performance rating significantly affected the managers' sample size judgments for all accounts receivable strata, whereas experience had a significant effect on only one stratum. These results suggest that experience is an insufficient surrogate for "expertise." In particular, the self-report responses suggest that subjects believed that even the inexperienced senior could provide reliable compliance test results, whereas the sample sizes proposed by the poorly rated senior were given little consideration, regardless of the senior's experience level. Hence, although experience may be a necessary condition, it is apparently not sufficient for expertise. That is, expertise requires that years of experience be coupled with a high level of proficiency.

A secondary purpose of the paper was to provide preliminary evidence on the judgment strategies managers employed in reviewing the senior's planned sample sizes.[10] The study's results provide two insights into their judgment strategies. First, the behavior of approximately half the subjects (i.e., the "above" group) was consistent with an anchoring and adjustment strategy. That is, these managers' sample sizes approximated those planned by the senior for each of the four strata when the senior possessed high expertise, and they were revised upwards when the senior's expertise declined. However, the other managers (i.e., the "below" group) did not seem to anchor on the senior's sample sizes. The difference between these two groups appears to be related to the firms' audit methodologies, particularly sampling approach. Specifically, subjects from the statistically oriented firms tended not to anchor on the senior's sample sizes. Perhaps they resorted to their "normal" sample sizes.

The second insight into managers' judgment strategies relates to the significant interaction between experience and sampling approach. Subjects' self-report responses indicated that they placed greater weight on the inexperienced senior's planned sample sizes when statistical sampling was used. This suggests that managers believe that a more formalized decision-making approach provides greater guidance to audit staff.

Although this study examined only sampling approach, Cushing and Loebbecke's [1986] audit methodology construct is multidimensional. Consequently, it is difficult to draw conclusions about the significant differences found across firms' mean sample sizes. For example, in a recent study, Bamber and Snowball [1988] found that *across firms,* the statistically oriented firms, on average, specified smaller sample sizes than the nonstatistically oriented firms. *Within firms,* however, the nonstatistically oriented auditors tended to specify smaller sample sizes than the statistically oriented auditors. Consequently, the relation between sampling approach and ample size judgments is not straightforward. Further research is needed to xplain the differences in extent of sampling across and within firms, and to lentify other effects of sampling approach on audit judgment (e.g., the endency toward formalization of procedures in terms of extensive ocumentation and the use of decision aids).

Future research should also examine the role of individual differences in nultiauditor judgments involving other audit tasks. This research should onsider two types of tasks: (1) tasks such as internal control evaluation and ubstantive testing decisions in which detailed workpaper documentation acilitates reconstruction of subordinates' decision steps, and (2) tasks such as nateriality and audit risk judgments that are less subject to formalization and n which qualitative factors appear to play a greater role. Finally, research can xamine program planning judgments; interdependence between the nature, xtent, and timing decisions is particularly relevant to the review process.

APPENDIX: MANIPULATION OF INDEPENDENT VARIABLES

Experience: *Little*—Tacket has been a senior for only about a year. Erwin is his first wholesaling client.

Extensive—Tacket has been a senior for four years. He has had extensive commercial experience with both small and large clients, including wholesalers.

Evaluation: *Low*—Tacket has received only mediocre ratings in the firm's formalized performance evaluations. Although he is regarded as competent in administrative and personnel matters, his technical skill, his care in carrying out audit work, and the soundness of his audit judgments are considered barely acceptable. Your own appraisal of the quality of his work supports these ratings.

High—Tacket has received excellent ratings in the firm's formalized performance evaluations. He is regarded as competent in supervising field work, adept at dealing with audit and client personnel, qualified in technical matters, careful in his audit work, and sound in his audit judgments. Your own appraisal of the quality of his work supports these ratings.

Sampling Approach: *Judgmental*—In a memo, Tacket explains that he arrived at the sample sizes he has recommended by adjusting last year's sample sizes to recognize the improvement he judged had taken place in the client's internal controls.

Statistical—In a memo, Tacket explains that he derived the sample sizes he has recommended from sample size tables, having regard for the risk levels he judged acceptable.

ACKNOWLEDGMENTS

The author is grateful for comments received from anonymous reviewers, and from participants at the presentation of a previous draft at the American Accounting Associations' National Convention in Reno, Nevada.

NOTES

1.   A composite group's score is simply the mean of two or more individuals' scores.
2.   Landy and Farr [1980] review the psychology literature.
3.   This additional analysis was viewed as exploratory and, hence, no formal hypotheses were developed. Nevertheless, it was expected that sample size determination was the more complex of the two tasks, and would be more sensitive to the independent variable manipulations.
4.   Given this study's reasonably small number of subjects from one city, finding results similar to Mock and Turner's strengthens the results' generalizability. The two studies differ in that (1) Mock and Turner's subjects were from one firm compared to this study's six firms, and (2) the two studies provided different anchors (see Table 2).
5.   Thanks are due to a reviewer for suggesting the firm-effect analysis. It should also be emphasized that sampling approaches are only one of many firm differences identified by Cushing and Loebbecke [1986]. Consequently, the reported sample size differences between firms may be the result of other factors, such as differences in materiality or audit risk preferences. Firm confidentiality requirements prevent identifying the participating firms by name.
6.   Similar results appeared at the individual subject level. A multidimensional scaling program, MDPREF, converted the weights subjects reported giving to the senior's sample sizes into sampling approach preferences. (For a discussion of multidimensional scaling techniques, see Schiffman et al. [1981].) The MDPREF application assumes that a higher weight implies a greater preference. Subjects' preferences for statistical versus nonstatistical sampling were negatively correlated with their mean total samples sizes ($r = -0.389$, $p < 0.041$) and with their mean sample sizes for the D3 and D4 strata (D3: $r = -0.408$, $p < 0.035$; D4: $r = -0.347$, $p < 0.077$). That is, managers preferring statistical sampling specified lower sample sizes, on average.
7.   A possible reason for the lack of support for Hypothesis 3 in terms of subjects' sample sizes was that the hypothesized effect was dominated by the large firm differences in the extent of sampling. However, the self-report responses were not influenced by differences in the extent of sampling.

8. For the reported results, subjects were assigned to groups based on their sample sizes for each stratum. The alternative was to use a single classification based on subjects' total sample sizes; however, this would ignore differences in firm policies for specific strata. Only a few subjects' classifications were affected by this choice, and the reported statistical results are essentially equivalent under either classification scheme.

9. Obviously, there are other possible explanations for differences between subjects. One explanation is variations in the way managers set materiality levels for the various strata. This could not be tested. Another possible explanation that could be tested was an experience effect. However, subjects' years of experience were not associated with their sample size judgments. As audit managers, all subjects apparently had sufficient experience for the experimental task.

10. Although the typical audit manager has experience with both statistical and nonstatistical sampling [Akresh 1980], it is nevertheless possible that, for example, statistical-oriented managers may have had some difficulty reviewing a senior's nonstatistical-based sample sizes, and vice versa.

REFERENCES

Abdolmohammadi, M. and A. Wright, "An Examination of the Effects of Experience and Task Complexity on Audit Judgments," *The Accounting Review* [January 1987], pp. 1-13.

Akresh, A., "Statistical Sampling in Public Accounting," *CPA Journal* [July 1980], pp. 20-26.

Ashton, R. H., *Research in Audit Decision Making: Rationale, Evidence and Implications* [The Canadian Certified General Accountants' Research Foundation, 1983].

Bamber, E. M., "Expert Judgment in the Audit Team: A Source Reliability Approach," *Journal of Accounting Research* [Fall 1983], pp. 396-412.

Bamber, E. M. and D. Snowball, "An Experimental Study of the Effects of Audit Structure in Uncertain Task Environments," *The Accounting Review* [July 1988], pp. 490-504.

Cushing, B. E. and J. K. Loebbecke, *Comparison of Audit Methodologies of Large Accounting Firms* [American Accounting Association, 1986].

Joyce, E. J. and G. C. Biddle, "Anchoring and Adjustment in Probabilistic Inference in Auditing," *Journal of Accounting Research* [Spring 1981a], pp. 120-145.

Joyce, E. J. and G. C. Biddle. "Are Auditors' Judgments Sufficiently Regressive?," *Journal of Accounting Research* [Autumn 1981b], pp. 323-349.

Kinney, W. F., Jr., "Audit Technology and Preferences for Auditng Standards," *Journal of Accounting and Economics* [March 1986], pp. 73-89.

Kinney, W. F., Jr., and W. C. Uecker, "Mitigating the Consequences of Anchoring in Auditor Judgments," *The Accounting Review* [January 1982], pp. 55-69.

Landy, F. J. and J. L. Farr, "Performance Rating." *Psychological Bulletin* [January 1980], pp. 72-107.

Milliken, G. A. and D. E. Johnson, *Analysis of Messy Data* [Van Nostrand Reinhold, 1984].

Mock, T. J. and J. L. Turner, "The Effect of Changes in Internal Controls on Audit Programs," in T. J. Burns (ed.), *Behavioral Experiments in Accounting II* [Ohio State University Press, 1979].

Mock, T. J. and J. L. Turner, *Internal Accounting Control Evaluation and Auditor Judgment*, Auditing Research Monograph No. 3 [American Institute of Certified Public Accountants, 1981].

Pany, K. and P. M. J. Reckers, "Within- Vs. Between-Subject Experimental Designs: A Study of Demand Effects," *Auditing: A Journal of Practice and Theory* [Fall 1987], pp. 39-53.

Schiffman, S. S., M. L. Reynolds and F. W. Young, *Introduction to Multidimensional Scaling* [Academic Press, 1981].

Tabor, R. H., "Internal Control Evaluations and Audit Program Revisions: Some Additional Evidence," *Journal of Accounting Research* [Spring 1983], pp. 348-354.

Trotman, K. T., "The Review Process and the Accuracy of Auditor Judgments," *Journal of Accounting Research* [Autumn 1985], pp. 740-752.

Trotman, K. T. and P. W. Yetton, "The Effect of the Review Process on Auditor Judgments," *Journal of Accounting Research* [Spring 1985], pp. 256-267.

Wright, A., "Performance Appraisal of Staff Auditors," *The CPA Journal* [November 1980], pp. 37-43.

Wright, A., Performance Evaluation of Staff Auditors: A Behaviorally Anchored Rating Scale," *Auditing: A Journal of Practice and Theory* [Spring 1986], pp. 95-108.

THE EFFECT OF THE LENGTH OF PREDICTION INTERVAL ON PREDICTION ERROR OF REGRESSION MODELS USED IN ANALYTICAL REVIEW

Arlette C. Wilson and G. William Glezen

ABSTRACT

Auditors use regression analysis as a prediction tool in performing analytical reviews. A monthly balance is predicted and compared to the recorded amount to determine the reasonableness of the account balance. A base period (generally 36 months) is used to construct the model. This model is used to predict the account balances of the subsequent 12 months (audit period). This study investigates the potential benefit, if any, to be derived by auditors by reestimating the regression model each month. That is, a new data base consisting of the old data plus the current month's actual amount is used to reestimate the regression

Advances in Accounting, Volume 7, pages 173-186.

parameters. This technique will create 12 regression models with each model predicting only one subsequent month. The results of this research provide empirical evidence that the additional data input improves the point estimate. However, auditor decisions on whether to investigate a given month for errors by using upper limits and materiality did not appear to be affected by the use of the monthly model rather than the annual model.

INTRODUCTION

Analytical review procedures are the study and comparison of relationships among data. When analytical review procedures identify fluctuations that are not expected or the absence of fluctuations that are expected, the auditor should investigate them if he or she believes that they are indicative of matters that have a significant effect on the examination. Statement on Auditing Standards No. 23, *Analytical Review Procedures* [AICPA 1978], provides guidance to auditors when they apply analytical review procedures. The issuance of the *Proposed Statement on Auditing Standards–Analytical Procedures* [AICPA 1987], has placed greater emphasis on analytical review techniques as an integral part of substantive testing of financial statements. If more evidence is provided by analytical procedures, less evidence is necessary from tests of details to establish an audit conclusion.

The basis for analytical review can range from subjective assessment of the reasonableness of account balances based on past information to the application of various statistical methods. One statistical model discussed in accounting literature and existing to some extent in practice is regression analysis. The use of statistical models in analytical review is of particular interest because the objectivity of the results contributes to more consistency in auditors' decisions.

Deloitte Haskins & Sells developed STAR (Statistical Techniques for Analytical Review), a computer program that uses regression analysis to predict account balances and that provides a decision rule for determining balances to be investigated.[1] Regression models constructed with STAR normally use base period data of 36 months. The model is used to generate predictions for the subsequent 12 months under audit. An auditor is interested in any technique that could potentially improve these predictions of account balances if the improvement in auditor decisions is cost effective. Additional input into the data base may better represent the process that is being modeled. The purpose of this study is to combine base period information with audit period information to determine if a model constructed with additional information would produce results improving account balance predictions and auditor decisions. This model is developed by reestimating the coefficients of the regression model each month using base period data (36 months) and all monthly data from the audit period prior to the month being predicted.[2] The model is used to predict only one subsequent month before the model is reestimated. That is, there will be 12 models each predicting 1 month. Model 1 would have a data base of 36 months; model 2, a data base of 37; model 3, a data base of 38; and so forth.

An auditor could build one model for the entire prediction period (referred to as the annual model) or build a unique model for each month of the prediction period (referred to as the monthly model). In this paper we present a comparison of the annual model with the monthly model constructed from actual monthly data used in analytical reviews for 15 companies. This comparison permits the determination of the relative predictive ability for point estimates of the two models as well as the relative sensitivity in signaling investigation of errors when they exist and not signaling investigation when they do not exist. The upper precision limit test for determining if a month is investigated (STAR approach) is the method used in this paper for tabulating type I errors (model indicates an investigation when no accounting error is present) and type II errors (model indicates no investigation is needed when an accounting error equal to or greater than a material amount is present) [Kinney and Salamon 1982; Kinney et al. 1986].

DATA

Monthly data actually used in analytical reviews for 15 companies from various industries were obtained from an accounting firm. Data were available for various financial and nonfinancial[3] variables for each of the companies. Table 1 shows the types of companies and the dependent variables for which simple linear regression models were constructed, whereas Table 2 lists all financial and nonfinancial data of each company that may be included as dependent and independent variables in the regression models. There are 48 monthly observations for all variables of each company of which the most recent 12 observations are considered the audit period.

A comparison was made of the mean absolute relative prediction errors of the two methods by using the Wilcoxon matched pairs test. A comparison of the two models was also made between the number of months investigated when no error existed and the number of months not investigated when an error did exist (several patterns of error seedings are discussed below).

A material error was defined as 2% of the actual audit balance of the account [Kinney and Salamon 1982]. Five different conditions were evaluated:

1. No accounting error
2. Error equal to materiality
3. Error equal to 1/2 materiality

Table 1.   Types of Variables for Which Prediction Models
Were Constructed (by Company)

Company	Type	Type of Variable		
		Revenue	Cost of Sales	Major Expense
1	Retail	1	1	1
2	Retail	1	1	1
3	Utility	1	0	1
4	Retail	1	1	2
5	Financial	2	0	0
6	Manufacturing	1	1	1
7	Financial	1	0	1
8	Manufacturing	1	1	1
9	Extractive	1	0	1
10	Brokerage Firm	1	1	1
11	Utility	1	0	1
12	Manufacturing	1	1	1
13	Retail	1	1	1
14	Extractive	1	0	1
15	Retail	1	1	0
Total		16	9	14

Table 2.   Variables Available for Model-Building

Company	Type	Number of Variables in Data Set	Variable Names
1	Retail	6	Net Sales, Cost of Sales, Selling Expense, Service Expense, Patent Expense, Number of Shipments
2	Retail	6	Sales, Purchases, Discounts Earned, Sales Discount, Sales Expense, Freight Expense
3	Utility	4	Operating Revenue, Power Sales, Kilowatt Hours Sold, Operating Expense
4	Retail	7	Sales, Discounts Earned, Finance Charges, Purchases, Store and Warehouse Expense, General and Administrative Expense, Warehouse Shipping
5	Financial	6	Mortgage Loans, Other Loans, Total Loans, Mortgage Interest Income, Other Interest Income, Loan Fees

(*continued*)

Table 2. (Continued)

Company	Type	Number of Variables in Data Set	Variable Names
6	Manufacturing	6	Sales, Cost of Sales, Expenses, Number of Employees, Payroll Benefits, Expense Less Benefits
7	Financial	6	Total Loans, Loan Interest Income, New Loans, Loan Fees, Savings Accounts, Saving Interest Expense
8	Manufacturing	6	Sales, Cost of Sales, Expenses, Number of Employees, Payroll Benefits, Expenses Less Benefits
9	Extractive	5	Sales, Tons Produced and Sold, Tons Purchased and Sold, Purchases and Operating Expense, Tons Produced
10	Brokerage Firm	9	Total Sales, Direct Sales, Stock Sales, Total Cost of Sales, Direct Cost of Sales, Stock Purchases, Purchase Discount, Sales Discount, General and Administrative Expense
11	Utility	4	Total Operating Revenues, Power Sales, Kilowatt Hours Sold, Total Operating Expense
12	Manufacturing	7	Manufacturing Sales, Square Feet Sold, Square Feet Ran, Material Cost, Variable Manufacturing Cost, Cost of Sales, Selling Expense
13	Retail	5	Net Sales, Total Cost of Sales, Selling Expense, Shipping Expense, Patent Expense
14	Extractive	4	Sales, Cost of Sales, Cost and Operating Expense, Barrels per Day
15	Retail Gas	9	No Lead Gallons, No Lead Sales, No Lead Cost of Sales, Regular Gallons, Regular Sales, Regular Cost of Sales, Oil Gallons, Oil Sales, Oil Cost of Sales

4. Error equal to 1/6 materiality
5. Error equal to 1/12 materiality.

For the analysis dealing with overstatements, the error was added to the account balance; for understatements, the error was subtracted from the account balance.

The most easily detected error would be a material error found in one month, whereas the most difficult to detect would be 1/12 of a material error found in each of 12 months. The various degrees of errors were included in the analysis to determine the sensitivity of the annual model and monthly model in detecting these seeded errors.

METHODOLOGY

Stepwise regression was used to determine the independent variable for inclusion in the simple linear regression model.[4] Akresh and Wallace [1982] warned against using stepwise procedures as mechanical devices to select variables without theoretical justification. All of the variables used in this study were deemed appropriate by auditors during actual analytical reviews. Therefore, the stepwise procedures were used to support the variable selections rather than to search for the descriptor variables.

One model was constructed for each revenue, cost of sales, and major expense account available for each company.[5] Various financial and nonfinancial accounts included in the data set for each company were available for inclusion as the independent variable in the regression model. The variable with the highest R^2 was selected as the independent variable. Thirty-six monthly observations were used to establish the regression relationship. This 36-month base period has been found useful in audit practice [Stringer 1975] and in other research on the use of regression [Kinney 1978].

The annual model developed from the 36-month data base was used to predict the account balance for each of the subsequent 12 months in the audit period. The monthly model, which used a 36-month base period, was used to predict the expected balance for the first month of the audit period. Then new coefficients were reestimated for the monthly model using a 37-month base period consisting of the original 36 months plus the actual amount[6] for the first month of the audit period. This reestimated model was used to predict the account balance for the second month of the audit period. Adding the actual value to the data base and reestimating the model coefficients is continued until amounts are predicted for the entire 12-month period. The book values were compared to the respective predicted amounts to determine the residual for each month calculated as follows:

$$\hat{M}_t = Y_t - \hat{Y}_t \quad \text{for overstatements}$$
$$\hat{M}_t = \hat{Y}_t - Y_t \quad \text{for underestimates}$$

where

$\hat{M}_t$ is the estimated residual for month t
Y_t is the book value for month t
$\hat{Y}_t$ is the predicted account balance for month t.

The performance of the two model-building techniques for point predictions was evaluated using the absolute relative prediction error calculated for each predicted month. Mean absolute relative error (MARE) was defined as follows:

$$\text{MARE} = \sum_{t=1}^{n} \frac{|\hat{Y}_t - Y_t|}{Y_t} / n$$

where t represents the month being predicted and n equals the number of months being predicted, which in this study was 12.

MARE measures the severity of forecast error as the absolute value of the difference in prediction and actual amount relative to the actual amount without regard to the direction of the error. The choice of a measure of loss must reflect the seriousness of forecast inaccuracies whether linear or nonlinear, symmetrical or asymmetrical. The MARE was chosen because it is linear and symmetrical, and has been used in previous studies [Copeland and Marioni 1972; Malcolm and Fraser 1977; McDonald 1973; Salamon and Smith 1977]. Furthermore, because the purpose of this paper is to compare forecast methodologies rather than determine absolute accuracy, "the choice of cost function may not be too critical" [Newbold and Granger 1974, p. 137].

The MARE was used to test the hypothesis that the mean absolute relative error of the annual model (X) is equal to or less than the mean absolute relative error of the monthly model (Y).

$$H_0: \quad E(X) \leq E(Y)$$
$$H_1: \quad E(X) > E(Y)$$

The Wilcoxon matched paired signed-ranks were used to test this hypothesis [Siegel 1956].

The STAR approach was used for determining whether investigation for an overstatement or understatement was indicated for a given month.[7] A set of $1-A$ upper precision limits on each $\hat{M}_t$ was calculated via:

$$\text{UPL}_{(1-A)}(m,n) = \hat{M}_t + t_{(1-\sqrt[n]{A}),34} \cdot \hat{\sigma}_{\hat{M}_t} \quad \text{for } n = 1,2,\ldots,\infty$$

where $t_{(1-\sqrt[n]{A}),34}$ is a t value[8] with an α equal to 1 minus the nth root of the type II error risk (incorrect acceptance risk) and 34 degrees of freedom. The allowable risk (A) was set at 0.37 for all tests. This value is consistent with the levels used in practice and in Kinney and Salamon [1982].

An incorrect rejection occurs when the model signals investigation of a month in which no error occurs (condition 1). An incorrect acceptance occurs when the equivalent of a material error is present, but no signal for investigation occurs. A material error could be $1/12$ of materiality in each of 12 months, $1/6$ of materiality in each of 6 months, $1/2$ of materiality in each of 2 months, or materiality in 1 month.

The error, whether equal to materiality or a fraction of materiality, is considered individually for each month to determine if the annual or monthly model will signal investigation. The approach taken in Kinney and Salamon [1982] was to randomly seed the errors in the number of months that would total to materiality. That is, an error equal to materiality would be randomly seeded in only 1 month, whereas an error equal to $1/6$ materiality would be randomly seeded in 6 months. Depending on the months in which the errors were seeded, the results may have differed. For example, if the error had been added to a month in which the model had predicted a higher amount than that recorded in the books, the adding of the error to the book amount would have made the book amount closer to the predicted amount and less likely for investigation than if the error had never been added. On the other hand, if the error had been added to an account balance that the model had underpredicted, the adding of the error would create a wider difference, and the balance would be more likely to be investigated. This potential effect is controlled by seeding the error into each month and deciding whether to investigate on an individual basis.[9] The month by month comparison would help identify the sensitivity of the models in detecting errors no matter which months they occur in, assuming they occur in enough months to equal materiality.

The hypothesis of no difference was tested at the $\alpha = 0.05$ level of significance using the parametric paired differences approach to determine if a difference exists between the number of months investigated by each model.

$$\mathbf{H_0}: \quad D = 0$$
$$\mathbf{H_1}: \quad D \neq 0$$

The t_{test} value of $(\bar{d} - 0)/S_{\bar{d}}$ (is compared to $t_{0.05,38}$, and, if t_{test} is larger, the null hypothesis is rejected and the difference between the two approaches is great enough to be considered significant.

In addition, an investigation was made to determine the effect, if any, on the monthly model if undiscovered errors remained in various months of the audit period. These undiscovered errors would affect the amount of the estimated parameters of the monthly model because audit period months were included in the model construction.

To investigate any potential effect, one-sixth of a material error was seeded randomly into each of 6 months of the audit period using a random numbers generation.[10] The monthly models were then reconstructed using the 36-month base period data and the audit period data with errors. The number of incorrect rejections and incorrect acceptances was tabulated for the monthly model and corresponding annual model as follows:

> *Incorrect rejection.* A month that was signaled for investigation that contained no error was considered an incorrect rejection. There was a total possible of six incorrect rejection errors per model.
>
> *Incorrect acceptance.* A month that was not signaled for investigation that contained an error was considered an incorrect acceptance. There were a total possible of six incorrect acceptance errors per model.

To determine if there was any difference between the annual and monthly models when errors remained in the months used to construct the monthly model, a comparison was made between the number of incorrect rejections and incorrect acceptances of the respective models.

The hypothesis of no difference in number of incorrect rejections and no difference in number of incorrect acceptances were tested at the $\alpha = 0.05$ level of significance using the paired differences approach.

$$\mathbf{H_0}: \quad D = 0$$

$$\mathbf{H_1}: \quad D \neq 0$$

RESULTS

Table 3 presents a comparison of the differences in mean absolute relative prediction error of the two types of models and the results of the Wilcoxon test. The results indicate that the prediction error of the annual models is consistently larger than that of the monthly models. Only 9 of the 39 annual models produced mean relative prediction errors smaller than those of the corresponding monthly models, and the majority of these differences were not large. Apparently, the additional data in the monthly model improve the prediction capability of the regression model. The real issue, however, is whether the difference in predictive ability is significant enough to improve audit usefulness.

Table 4 summarizes the results for the signaling of investigation of individual months when different error conditions exist in the data. There are a total of 39 models and each model predicts 12 months. Therefore each audit period error condition deals with a total of 468 months. When months are investigated under the No Error condition this is considered an incorrect rejection, and when a month is not investigated when an error does exist, this is considered an incorrect acceptance. Notice that very few months are investigated when no error exists, which is a reasonable result. When an error is equal to materiality

ARLETTE C. WILSON and G. WILLIAM GLEZEN

Table 3.   Comparison of Differences in Mean Absolute Relative Prediction
            Error of Annual and Monthly Models

Model	Annual Model (X)	Monthly Model (Y)	Differences (D)	Rank
1	0.026299	0.025661	0.000638	8
2	0.038971	0.033550	0.005421	17
3	0.062372	0.116810	−0.054344	34[a]
4	0.162372	0.171344	−0.008972	23[a]
5	0.152743	0.134635	0.018108	29
6	0.336224	0.246283	0.089941	35
7	0.196863	0.162550	0.034313	33
8	0.109717	0.108727	0.000990	10
9	0.123106	0.111171	0.011935	25
10	0.243909	0.251132	−0.007223	19[a]
11	0.079756	0.083583	−0.003827	13[a]
12	0.225750	0.201331	0.024419	31
13	0.043533	0.033168	0.010365	24
14	0.210036	0.065266	0.144770	37
15	0.004659	0.004552	0.000107	5
16	0.004664	0.004568	0.000096	4
17	0.060115	0.041158	0.018957	30
18	0.053121	0.039459	0.013662	26
19	0.109510	0.082435	0.027075	32
20	0.003932	0.003897	0.000035	1
21	0.003972	0.003920	0.000052	2
22	0.056287	0.054792	0.001495	11
23	0.061495	0.054881	0.006614	18
24	0.128629	0.112490	0.016139	28
25	0.022535	0.018402	0.004133	15
26	0.020940	0.018642	0.002298	12
27	0.050001	0.050781	−0.000780	9[a]
28	0.004901	0.004781	0.000120	6
29	0.335965	0.187108	0.148857	38
30	0.028459	0.028548	−0.000090	3[a]
31	0.022957	0.015072	0.007885	21
32	0.066869	0.059131	0.007739	20
33	0.051778	0.059987	−0.008209	22[a]
34	0.045861	0.042030	0.003831	14
35	0.068069	0.054141	0.013928	27
36	0.017074	0.012608	0.004467	16
37	0.002738	0.002560	0.000178	7
38	0.183148	0.301149	−0.118000	36[a]
39	0.123166	0.275659	−0.152493	39[a]

[a] Negative

$$T = \sum_{i=1}^{39} R_i = 582 \text{ where } R_i = \text{Rank if } X > Y \text{ or } 0 \text{ if } X < Y.$$

Critical value: $W_{0.05} = \dfrac{39(40)}{4} + 1.64\sqrt{\dfrac{39(40)(79)}{24}} = 390 + 118 = 508.$

Because the test statistic (582) > the critical value (508), reject H_0.

Table 4. Results for Signaling Investigation: Models Constructed
with Error-Free Data

Audit Period Error Condition	Model	Overstatement Number of Months Investigated[a]	Understatement Number of Months Investigated[a]
No Error	Annual	76	32
	Monthly	59	32
Error = Materiality	Annual	435	406
	Monthly	432	415
Error = 1/2 × Materiality	Annual	350	308
	Monthly	369	315
Error = 1/6 × Materiality	Annual	216	145
	Monthly	194	137
Error = 1/12 × Materiality	Annual	115	63
	Monthly	96	51

[a] Number of models, 39; number of months, 468.

almost all the months are signaled for investigation and, as expected, the number of months signaled decreases as the size of the error becomes smaller. In most of the error conditions, the same months were signaled for investigation for both the annual and the monthly models. (Even though the monthly model produced signaling of more or fewer months than the annual model for given error conditions, these differences are small enough to be considered insignificant.) None of the differences was large enough to reject the null hypothesis of no difference between the two models.[11] Thus, although the point estimate from the monthly model appears to be consistently better, the improved accuracy was not significant enough to affect the auditor's decision of whether to investigate an individual month for an error.

Table 5 summarizes the incorrect rejection and incorrect acceptance decisions when errors remained in the audit period data used for monthly model construction. Many of the same months were signaled for investigation by both models. Differences that did exist were not significant. The respective calculated t values for the difference in number of incorrect rejections and difference in number of incorrect acceptances were 0.0005 and 0.4528. These calculated t values are considerably smaller than the $t_{0.05,38}$ needed to reject the null hypothesis, indicating that any difference that appears to exist is so small that it may be atttributable to chance variation alone. Auditor decisions do not appear to be affected by the existence of undiscovered errors in the

Table 5. Results for Incorrect Rejections and Incorrect Acceptances:
Models Constructed with Undiscovered Errors in Audit Period

	Annual Model	Monthly Model
Number of Incorrect Rejections[a]	42	36
Number of Incorrect Acceptances[b]	140	162

[a] Number of possible incorrect rejections: 39 models × 6 = 234.
[b] Number of possible incorrect acceptances: 39 models × 6 = 234.

audit period data. If the errors considered undiscovered had been larger than those considered in this study, the results may have differed. However, the larger the error the more likely it would not remain undiscovered.

This lack of difference in performance of the two models may be a result of having only gradual changes in the model structure that are not significant over the 12-month period and therefore have little impact on the prediction results. Larger changes in model structure may have produced different results. The monthly model would better adapt to these changes and probably provided better predictions than the annual model. However, the auditor should be aware that a fairly large change in the audit period that occurs in increasing stages throughout the audit period may lead to the model adapting to the change so that the effect is obscured. Because these changes may be of interest to auditors even though they may not be caused by errors, the monthly model should not be used to the exclusion of other analytical procedures.

CONCLUSIONS

Given the general availability of regression programs and the ease of their use, auditors may wish to build multiple models for analytical reviews rather than use one annual model. Although multiple models in this study produced consistently better point estimates of account balances, the improved accuracy did not significantly affect the decision to investigate an individual month for an error. However, data sets with rapidly changing patterns that significantly affect the model structure may produce better estimates of account balances with the added use of audit period information.

ACKNOWLEDGMENTS

The authors appreciate the helpful comments of Clarence Fries, two anonymous reviewers, and an associate editor.

NOTES

1. Other accounting firms have indicated some use of regression analysis, but the STAR program is the only one for which detail model building methodology is widely available. See Stringer and Stewart [1986].

2. McKeown and Lorek [1978] demonstrate that model updating may be accomplished through adaptive techniques, reestimation, or reidentification. Based on a study of quarterly earnings, they suggest that reestimation be used because adaptive techniques result in significantly less accurate predictions and because reidentification is a more costly procedure.

3. Nonfinancial data are those quantitative amounts that are not recorded as account balances, but that have a relationship to account balances, for example, barrels per day, number of shipments, tons produced.

4. While multiple regression models are available, discussions with operating office personnel of the accounting firm indicated that simple regression was most commonly used.

5. The models are not transformed for violation of regression assumptions. In theory the presence of violations such as autocorrelation and heteroscedasticity may affect the calculated confidence intervals. However, research by Wilson and Glezen [1987] indicates that the presence of regression assumption violations may not affect auditor decisions when using the Deloitte, Haskins & Sells STAR approach.

6. Because the 48 monthly observations acquired from the CPA firm have been audited, the actual amounts added to the base period to construct the monthly models are assumed to be error free; however, to the extent errors were corrected in months other than when they occurred, the results of this study could be affected. In practice auditors should recognize the integrated nature of the audit process including the impact on income statement amounts of errors found when applying audit procedures to balance sheet accounts.

7. Explanation can be found in Kinney and Salomon [1982].

8. Technically for the monthly model approach, the t value should have degrees of freedom of 34, 35, 36, . . . 46. The difference in values from that of 34 is immaterial.

9. An error equal to materiality was seeded in month one and a decision of whether to investigate was made using the montly model and then the annual model. The error was then removed from month one so that the data base to construct the subsequent model would not be affected by inclusion of the error. Then an error equal to materiality was seeded in month two and a decision of whether to investigate was made again using both models. The error was removed from month two. This procedure was continued until a comparison was made between the two models of their ability to signal the error if it had occurred in any of the audit period months.

This procedure was repeated with seedings equal to 1/2, 1/6, and 1/12 of materiality to determine the sensitivity of the two models as the error became smaller.

10. One-twelfth of a material error would be the most difficult to detect whereas a material error in 1 month would be the easiest to detect. One-sixth of a material error in each of 6 months was chosen for this investigation because it was not the most difficult of the error patterns to detect, and yet the errors occurred in several months thus affecting the parameter estimation of several of the monthly models.

11. The Wilcoxon matched pair signed-ranks were also performed so that the parametric assumptions could be relaxed. The same decision resulted.

REFERENCES

Akresh, A. D. and W. A. Wallace, "The Application of Regression Analysis for Limited Review and Audit Planning," *Symposium on Auditing Research IV* [University of Illinois, 1982], pp. 67-162.

American Institute of Certified Public Accountants, Inc., *Statement on Auditing Standards No. 23-Analytical Review Procedures* [AICPA, 1978].

American Institute of Certified Public Accountants, Inc., *Proposed Statement on Auditing Standards-Analytical Procedures* [AICPA, 1987].

Copeland, R. M. and R. Marioni, "Executives' Forecasts of Naive Models," *Journal of Business* 15 [October 1972], pp. 497-512.

Kinney, W. R., "ARIMA and Regression in Analytical Review: An Empirical Test," *The Accounting Review* [January 1978], pp. 48-60.

Kinney, W. R. and G. L. Salamon, "Regression Analysis in Auditing: A Comparison of Alternative Investigation Rules," *Journal of Accounting Research* [Autumn 1982], pp. 350-366.

Kinney, W. R., G. L. Salamon, and W. C. Uecker, *Computer Assisted Analytical Review Systems* [American Accounting Association, 1986], pp. 51-54.

Malcolm, R. R. and D. R. Fraser, "Further Evidence: A Comparison Among Analysts," *Journal of Economics and Business* 29 [Summer/Spring 1977], pp. 193-197.

McDonald, L., "An Empirical Examination of the Reliability of Published Predictions of Future Earnings," *Accounting Review* 48 [July 1973], pp. 502-510.

McKeown, J. C. and K. S. Lorek, "A Comparative Analysis of the Predictive Ability of Adaptive Forecasting, Re-estimation, and Re-identification Using Box-Jenkins Time Series Analysis in Quarterly Earnings Data," *Decision Sciences* [October 1978].

Newbold, P. and C. W. J. Granger, "Experience with Forecasting Univariate Time Series and the Combination of Forecasts," *Journal of Royal Statistical Society Series A* 137(2) [1974], pp. 131-165.

Salamon, G. L. and E. Smith, "Additional Evidence in the Time Series Properties of Reported Earnings per Share," *Journal fo Finance* 31 [December 1977], pp. 1795-1801.

Seigel, S., *Nonparametric Statistics for the Behavioral Sciences* [McGraw-Hill, 1956].

Stringer, K. W., "A Statistical Technique for Analytical Review," *Journal of Accounting Research-Supplement* [1975], pp. 1-9.

Stringer, K. W. and T. R. Stewart, *Statistical Techniques for Analytical Review in Auditing* [Wiley, 1986].

Wilson, A. and G. W. Glezen, "Use of Regression in Audits of Financial Statements: An Empirical Investigation of Effect of Assumption Violations on Audit Decision," Bureau of Business and Economic Research, Working Paper 87-905 [University of Arkansas, 1987].

FACTORS AFFECTING MATERIALITY JUDGMENTS:

A COMPARISON OF "BIG EIGHT" ACCOUNTING FIRMS' MATERIALITY VIEWS WITH THE RESULTS OF EMPIRICAL RESEARCH

Alan H. Friedberg, Jerry R. Strawser, and Judith H. Cassidy

ABSTRACT

To gain insight into the guidance provided to practicing auditors making materiality judgments, this research surveys the audit manuals of "Big Eight" accounting firms. Consistent with previous materiality research, the relationship of a misstatement to net income and the effect of a misstatement on earnings trend were consistently mentioned by the firms as affecting quantitative and qualitative materiality, respectively. However, for the most part, the quantitative and qualitative guidance provided by the firms differed substantially. The results of this research suggest the need for more explicit authoritative guidance relating to auditors' materiality judgments.

Advances in Accounting, Volume 7, pages 187-201.
Copyright © 1989 by JAI Press Inc.
All rights of reproduction in any form reserved.
ISBN: 0-89232-960-2

INTRODUCTION

During an auditor's examination of an entity's financial statements, materiality judgments influence both the planning of substantive testing procedures and the evaluation of audit evidence. *Statement on Auditing Standards No. 47* (SAS 47) [AICPA 1986] requires that the auditor consider both qualitative and quantitative factors in making these judgments. Estimates of materiality levels are necessary during the planning stages of an audit, since the auditor is required to design audit procedures "to detect errors that he believes could be large enough . . . to be quantitatively material to the financial statements" [AICPA 1986 (AU 312.13)]. In addition, the auditor must consider materiality levels when evaluating misstatements identified by his substantive testing procedures.

In spite of the importance of materiality in the audit process, SAS 47 provides little guidance to the auditor for implementing procedures to search for material errors and evaluate misstatements discovered during the examination. Likewise, previous research concerned with auditors' materiality perceptions has added only marginal insight into the understanding of this issue. To gain insight into the guidance provided to practicing auditors in making materiality judgments, this study surveyed the audit manuals of the "Big Eight" accounting firms. The guidance provided in these manuals was then compared to the results of previous empirical research related to materiality.

DATA COLLECTION AND METHODOLOGY

Data for this research were gathered by examining relevant sections of audit manuals obtained from "Big Eight" accounting firms.[1] This method of gathering information about the audit approaches of accounting firms is similar to that used by Cushing and Loebbecke [1986]. Of the eight firms contacted, six supplied the requested materials; one rejected the request; and one failed to respond.[2] The cooperation of each firm was conditional on the authors' assurances that they would be identified only as "Big Eight" firm. The six cooperating firms are referred to throughout the paper as firms A through F to ensure their anonymity.

The information provided by these firms was examined to determine the specific quantitative and qualitative factors that may be used to (1) establish materiality levels during the planning phase of the examination and (2) evaluate the materiality of an identified misstatement. Comparing the factors mentioned by the firms provides some measure of the extent of interfirm consensus regarding the guidelines provided to auditors making materiality judgments.[3]

Although the process of identifying factors mentioned by each firm's literature was relatively objective, some interpretation was necessary in classifying and organizing the factors. The reliability of the conclusions drawn from this examination was enhanced by the method used to examine the firms' manuals. First, each researcher independently examined the entire set of information and recorded the specific materiality factors identified by each firm. The recorded factors were referenced to the appropriate section of the firm's audit manual for subsequent verification, if necessary. Any differences between the factors identified by the researchers were resolved to the agreement of all three authors by referring to the appropriate firm's audit manual. For example, the failure of one researcher to identify a materiality factor noted by the other researchers and mentioned in one firm's literature was corrected on review of the appropriate section of the audit manual. This method of resolving differences is similar to that used by Cushing and Loebbecke [1986].

Another method of determining the degree of consensus between firms is identifying the relative importance of the various factors mentioned by each firm. The relative importance among quantitative materiality factors (QNFs) within a firm was measured by computing the frequency with which each QNF was referenced in that firm's discussion of quantitative materiality. This frequency measure was not determined by simply counting the number of times a materiality factor was mentioned, since this procedure would be subject to the vagaries of journalistic style. Instead, an effort was made to compute the frequency with which a QNF topic was broached, and each reference or cross-reference was counted individually.[4] For example, if a QNF was mentioned four times in one section, either by name or pronoun, it was counted as a single reference. However, if it was mentioned again in a subsequent section, it was counted as another reference.

All results presented in this paper are drawn from the information provided by the cooperating firms. Although the excerpts received from the cooperating firms may serve a variety of functions within the firm, it is logical to assume that the information supplied represents the firms' official positions on the subject of materiality.[5] Because the audit manuals represent a primary source for internal training and/or reference, examination of this information provides insight into the materiality practices of the cooperating firms. The results of this examination are summarized in the following sections of this paper.

QUANTITATIVE MATERIALITY FACTORS (QNFs)

Quantitative materiality factors (QNFs) relate to the absolute dollar size of a misstatement. According to SAS 47, the auditor should utilize QNFs at two points during the audit examination. First, QNFs are used in a preliminary role during the planning phase of the audit. These factors are used in this phase to design audit procedures that will detect errors greater than or equal to a specified amount. For example, if materiality during the planning phase is judged to be 10% of net income, and net income is $1,000,000, the auditor should design procedures that allow him to detect errors that, individually or in the aggregate, exceed $100,000. Although SAS 47 notes that qualitative factors do influence materiality judgments, these factors have a limited role in the planning process, because "it is ordinarily not practical to design procedures to detect [qualitative errors]" [AICPA 1986 (AU 312.13)].

The second use of QNFs is during the auditor's evaluation of misstatements discovered during the audit examination. In this application, QNFs relate to the absolute dollar size of a misstatement and the relationship of this misstatement to a particular base. For example, a misstatement error that overstates net income by $10,000 is more likely to be considered material by the auditor when uncorrected net income is $100,000 rather than $500,000. This misstatement has a higher probability of being material in the former case, because it is 10% of uncorrected net income, than in the latter case, in which it is only 2%. It should be noted that the auditor also weights qualitative materiality considerations when evaluating misstatements identified by his substantive tests.

Previous Research Related to QNFs

The importance of QNFs in the audit process has been confirmed through several previous research efforts. A review of this research is provided by Holstrum and Messier [1982]. Much of this research has attempted to determine the relative importance of various QNFs on the auditors' evaluation of misstatements. Boatsman and Robertson [1974], Moriarity and Barron [1976, 1979], Woolsey [1954a, 1954b], Krogstad et al. [1984], Firth [1980], and Messier [1983] examined the effect of a misstatement on several bases (QNFs). The consensus of this research was that the percentage effect of a misstatement on a company's net income was the most important factor in determining the perceived materiality of that misstatement. Table 1 summarizes this research and includes (1) the QNFs examined and (2) the QNFs that had the highest perceived importance in the auditor' materiality judgments.

Table 1 highlights the importance of the relationship between the dollar amount of a misstatement and current net income on perceptions of materiality. As shown in Table 1, the potential effect of an item on current net income was selected for examination in *every* study. In these studies, this effect was found to be the most important determinant of perceived materiality.

Table 1.   Previous Research Examining Quantitative Materiality

Study	QNFs Examined	Important QNFs
Woolsey [1954a]	Current Net Income Average Net Income Absolute Dollar Amount Fixed Assets Total Equity	Current Net Income Absolute Dollar Amount
Woolsey [1954b]	Open-Ended Questionnaire	Current Net Income Working Capital
Boatsman and Robertson [1974]	Current Net Income Total Revenue Total Expense Working Capital Absolute Size	Current Net Income
Moriarity and Barron [1976]	Current Net Income Total Assets Debt-to-Equity Ratio	Current Net Income
Moriarity and Barron [1979]	Current Net Income Total Assets	Current Net Income Total Assets
Firth [1980]	Current Net Income Net Assets Total Assets Market Capitalization Sales Current Assets	Current Net Income Net Assets
Messier [1983]	Current Net Income Total Assets Total Inventories Current Ratio	Current Net Income
Krogstad et al. [1984]	Current Net Income Current Ratio	Current Net Income

As a means of evaluating actual materiality judgments, Frishkoff [1970], Morris et al. [1984], and Chewning et al. [1987] examined audit reports issued during years when companies experienced a change in accounting principle. This examination allowed these researchers to evaluate actual materiality judgments made by auditors, because current professional standards require the auditor to modify his opinion as to consistency when an accounting change has a material effect on the financial statements [AICPA 1986 (AU 420.05)]. Therefore, if the report is not qualified, it can be assumed that the effect of the change on the company's financial statements is not considered material. Both the results of these studies and of those utilizing questionnaires agree that the relationship of an item to net income has an important effect on the decision of the auditor to qualify his report.

QNF Guidance Provided to Auditors

As demonstrated by the QNFs examined in previous research, most auditors' materiality judgments are made by considering the ratio of a misstatement to a selected QNF. The information received from the responding "Big Eight" firms implies that this is frequently the procedure practiced in the audit environment. The six "Big Eight" firms indicated that a total of 27 different QNFs may be appropriate in establishing materiality levels in the auditing process.[6] These QNFs are categorized and listed in Table 2.

Table 2. Quantitative Considerations in Establishing Materiality

Income-Based QNFs
#1. Net Income before Taxes
#2. Total Revenues
#3. Total Sales
#4. Gross Margin
#5. Income from Continuing Operations
#6. Forecasted Sales
#7. Change in Income from Continuing Operations
#8. Reasonable Rate of Return on Current Sales
#9. Association among Related Items on the Income Statement
#10. Effect on Earnings per Share

Balance Sheet-Based QNFS
#11. Total Assets
#12. Shareholders' Equity
#13. Total Liabilities
#14. Current Assets
#15. Liquid Assets
#16. Working Capital
#17. Monetary Items
#18. Nonmonetary Items
#19. Tangible Net Worth
#20. Change in Net Assets
#21. Industry Return on Assets

Income and/or Balance Sheet-Based QNFs
#22. Account Total
#23. Category Total
#24. Classification Total
#25. Lower of Total Assets or Net Income
#26. "Size"
#27. Percentage of Change in Financial Statement Item(s) or Relationship(s)

Table 3. Commonly Mentioned QNFs and Total QNFs by Firm

QNF Number[a]		Firm						Total
		A	B	C	D	E	F	
Income-	#1	X	X	X	—	X	X	5
Based	#2	X	X	—	—	X	X	4
	#5	—	—	—	—	X	X	2
Balance	#11	X	X	X	—	—	—	3
Sheet	#12	X	X	X	—	X	X	5
Based	#13	—	X	X	—	—	—	2
	#14	—	X	—	—	X	—	2
Most frequently mentioned QNF		#1	#1, #11	[b]	#26, #25	#5	#1	
Total number of Income-Based QNFs		2	2	5	1	6	3	
Total number of Balance Sheet-Based QNFs		2	4	7	1	2	1	
Total number of Items Mentioned[c]		4	6	17	2	8	7	

[a] See Table 2 for a description of each QNF.
[b] Although no item was mentioned more than once, this firm indicated that income statement items were more critical in the determination of materiality.
[c] This total may not equal total income-based items and total balance sheet-based items, because firms may specify other QNFs (income and/or balance sheet-based QNFs). See Table 2 for classification of QNFs adopted in this study.

Compared to the QNFs examined in previous research (see Table 1), Table 2 indicates that a much greater number of quantitative factors are mentioned by the firms as possible QNFs.[7] However, many of these QNFs appear to be firm specific, as they are not mentioned consistently in the material supplied by other cooperating firms.

Two methods of analysis were performed to indicate the guidance provided for assessing quantitative materiality. These analyses (1) compared the QNFs mentioned by the six firms and (2) computed the number of references to each QNF. Table 3 provides a summary of the QNFs included in the audit manuals on a firm-by-firm basis.

Comparison of QNFs Mentioned by Firms

Although Table 2 indicated that a large number of QNFs may be considered by auditors, a much smaller number were mentioned consistently across the sample of firms. As shown in Table 3, only three income-based items (#1, Net Income before Taxes; #2, Total Revenues; and #5, Income from Continuing

Operations) and four balance sheet-based items (#11, Total Assets; #12, Shareholders' Equity; #13, Total Liabilities; and #14, Current Assets) were included by more than one "Big Eight" firm as a quantitative base for determining materiality. This finding suggests that a relatively small number of QNFs were consistently applied by auditors affiliated with different firms.

Of these seven items, only four were included by more than two firms. The most frequently mentioned bases across firms were #1 (Net Income before Taxes) and #12 (Shareholders' Equity). Both of these bases were included by five of the six firms. The importance of net income before taxes does not seem unusual, given the importance of the net income base noted in previous research. Interestingly, few previous studies had specifically examined the effect of shareholders' equity on perceptions of materiality.

Comparison of the Relative Importance of QNFs

The number of references to a particular QNFs was computed to measure its relative importance within each firm. As anticipated, based on the previous analysis and the results of previous research, our examination found that Net Income was a frequently mentioned item. Three firms (firms A, E, and F) referred to a net income-based QNF (#1, Net Income before Taxes or #5, Income from Continuing Operations) most frequently, whereas a fourth firm (firm B) referred to Net Income before Taxes (#1) and Total Assets (#111) with equal frequency. Although firm C did not mention any QNF more than once, this firm specifically indicated that income statement items were the most critical determinants of materiality. The final firm (firm D) mentioned only two items as possible QNFs: "Size" (#26) and the Lower of Total Assets or Net Income (#25). These findings once again are consistent with the previous research summarized earlier in this section.[8]

QUALITATIVE MATERIALITY FACTORS (QLFs)

As noted earlier, in addition to quantitative materiality factors, the auditor should also base materiality judgments on qualitative materiality factors [AICPA 1986 (AU 312.06)]. Unlike QNFs, qualitative materiality involves auditor consideration of nonmonetary aspects of errors, such as the nature of an item, special circumstances surrounding an item, and the uncertainty within which an item is evaluated. In support of this consideration, the Financial Accounting Standards Board (FASB) notes that "items too small to be thought material if they result from routine transactions may be considered material if they arise in abnormal circumstances" [FASB 1980, paragraph 123]. Examples of qualitative materiality considerations include errors resulting from illegal acts, errors indicative of a failing business environment, and errors that, when corrected, would result in violations of restrictive covenants.

Previous Research Related to QLFs

Although most previous research efforts have focused primarily on the quantitative aspects of materiality, four studies [Boatsman and Robertson 1974; Moriarity and Barron 1979; Messier 1983; Krogstad et al. 1984] examined the effect of one or more QLF(s) on the perceived materiality of an item. The results of these studies indicated that the effect of QLFs on the auditor's materiality judgments was secondary to that of QNFs. As discussed earlier, a QNF (the effect of a misstatement on net income) was the most important determinant of perceived materiality. However, Moriarity and Barron [1979], Messier [1983], and Krogstad et al. [1984] found a QLF (the effect of an item on an established earnings trend) to be the second most important factor.

A fifth study [Jennings et al. 1987] examined the effect of several qualitative materiality factors on the perceived materiality of that item. The materiality thresholds provided for the four cases indicated that the auditors considered both qualitative and quantitative factors in their judgments. This is consistent with SAS 47 [AICPA 1986]. In agreement with Krogstad et al. [1984], these researchers found a large variance in the subjects' materiality thresholds. This large variance indicates that little consensus may exist concerning the effect of the QLF on materiality.

In summary, previous research related to QLFs indicates that these factors are considered by auditors in their materiality judgments. However, QLFs are perceived as secondary to QNFs (in particular, the effect of a misstatement on net income). These studies also suggest that auditors exhibit a low degree of consensus in their use of QLFs for materiality judgments.

QLF Guidance Provided to Auditors

An examination of the audit manuals revealed a total of 41 possible QLFs. Of these, only 17 were identified by more than one firm. These QLFs were mentioned by the firms as factors, other than quantitative factors, that should be considered in the evaluation of the materiality of a discovered misstatement. Table 4 lists and classifies the QLFs identified by the firms. A summary of commonly mentioned QLFs on a firm-by-firm basis is provided in Table 5.

Table 5 indicates that a degree of QLF consensus exists among firms. In particular, three classifications of QLFs were consistently mentioned by more than two firms; (1) "Trends," (2) "Sensitivity of the Circumstances," and (3) "Aggregation of Errors." These QLF categories are discussed following Tables 4 and 5.

Table 4.   Qualitative Considerations in Establishing Materiality[a]

Trends

#1. Changes in the Magnitude of Established Trend of Profits or Losses (4)
#2. Changes in the Magnitude of Established Trend of Deficits or "Surpluses" in Retained Earnings (5)
#3. Changes in the Directions of Trends (1)
#4. Misstatement Reverses a Deficit in Equity or Working Capital or an Operating Loss or Net Loss to a Profit (3)

Sensitive Situations

#5. Misstatement Resulting from Illegal Acts (Fraud, Bribes) (4)
#6. Misstatement Resulting from Related Parties (4)
#7. Misstatement Resulting from Conflict of Interest (2)
#8. Misstatement Resulting from Violations of GAAP (3)
#9. Effect of Misstatement on Contracts (Buy-Sell Agreements, Union Contracts, or Violations of Loan Covenants) (6)
#10. Misstatement Resulting from Management of Earnings (Smoothing Behavior) (1)
#11. Effect of Misstatement on Threat of Liquidation (2)
#12. Effect of Misstatement on Management Integrity (2)
#13. Sensitivity of Account Affected by Misstatement (2)

Aggregation of Errors

#14. Precisely Measurable Errors Are Offset by less Easily Measured Errors (3)
#15. Treatment of Prior Period Errors (Reversing of Cumulative Errors) (5)

Environment of Entity

#16. Business Practices and Customs (1)
#17. Industry Practices (1)
#18. Nature of Operations (1)
#19. Financial strength and Resources (2)
#20. Business Purpose (For-Profit or Not-For-Profit) (2)
#21. Public or Private Entity (2)
#22. Organizational Structure (1)
#23. Ownership of Entity (1)
#24. Public Image of Entity (1)
#25. Special Users of Financial Statements (1)
#26. New or Established Firm (1)
#27. Stable or Cyclical Business (1)
#28. Profit, Loss, or Breakeven Situation (1)
#29. Political Situation (1)
#30. Capital Market Conditions (1)
#31. Income Tax Considerations (1)

Relationship to Normal Operations

#32. Frequency and Usual Nature of Misstatements (2)
#33. Pervasiveness of Misstatement (1)
#34. Expectations as to Usual or Normal Timing and Amount of Misstatements (1)

(continued)

Table 4. (Continued)

Uncertainty

#35. Possible Effect of Future Events on Current or Prior Items (1)
#36. Valuation of Assets (1)
#37. Risk (1)

Other

#38. Errors Due to Intentional or Unintentional Selection or Application of Accounting Principles (1)
#39. Errors Due to Carelessness or Misunderstanding (1)
#40. Timing of Dollar Values (Present Value) (1)
#41. Nearness of Item to Cash (1)

---

[a] The number of firms mentioning each item is indicated in parentheses.

Table 5. Commonly Mentioned QLFs and Total QLFs by Firm

	Firm					
	A	B	C	D	E	F
Trends						
#1	X	—	—	X	X	X
#2	X	X	X	—	X	X
#4	X	—	—	X	X	—
Sensitive Situations						
#5	X	X	X	—	X	—
#6	X	X	X	—	X	—
#7	—	X	—	—	X	—
#8	X	—	X	—	X	—
#9	X	X	X	X	X	X
#11	—	—	—	—	X	X
#12	X	X	—	—	—	—
#13	X	—	X	—	—	—
Aggregation of Errors						
#14	X	—	X	—	X	—
#15	X	X	—	X	X	X
Environment						
#19	X	—	X	—	—	—
#20	—	—	X	—	—	X
#21	—	—	X	—	—	X
Relationship to Normal Operations						
#32	—	—	X	—	X	—
Total Number of QLFs						
Mentioned by Firm	12	7	32	4	15	7

Three of the QLFs in the "Trend" group (#1, #2, and #3) reflect a concern with the effects of changes in the direction of trends between accounting periods. The remaining QLF in this category, #4, deals with reversals of the year-end status of net income or equity accounts within an accounting period rather than between accounting periods. For example, a misstatement that changes a small profit to a loss could be considered material under #4, even though the amount of the misstatement is quantitatively immaterial. Three of these QLFs (#1, #2, and #4) were mentioned by over half of the firms. The importance of the effect of a misstatement on an established trend is consistent with the findings of previous studies [Krogstad et al. 1984; Moriarity and Barron 1979; Messier 1983].

Sensitive situations were mentioned by a large number of firms. Some sensitive situations are the result of the nature of the transaction giving rise to a misstatement. In particular, transactions associated with illegal acts (#5), transactions among related parties (#6), transactions involving conflicts of interest (#7), transactions recorded in violation of GAAP (#8), and transactions that result in managed earnings ("smoothing behavior") (#10) are all sensitive, and therefore potentially material, because of the people and circumstances surrounding the event. Other situations are sensitive because they signal a future threat. The possibility that a misstatement will lead to contract violations (#9) and liquidity problems (#11) is a threat to the client's ability to maintain going-concern status. Management integrity (#12) and sensitivity of the account (#13) are internal control vulnerabilities. All but one of these sensitive situations were mentioned by more than one firm and four (#5, #6, #8, and #9) were mentioned by at least half of the firms. Contract violations (#9) were cited by all six firms as being potentially material.

There are two QLFs in the Aggregation of Errors category. The first QLF in this category is the practice of offsetting objective and subjective errors (#14). Netting the effects of (1) a misstatement caused by a faulty inventory count with (2) a misstatement based on disagreement between the auditor and client over the valuation of accounts receivable is an example of this aggregation issue. The second QLF, the treatment of prior period errors (#15), was the most frequently mentioned factor in the Aggregation of Errors category.

An examination of the QLFs discussed by each firm shows considerable diversity. As indicated in Table 5, the QLF guidance offered by firms varies substantially. The number of QLFs mentioned by each firm ranged from four (firm D) to 32 (firm C). Interestingly, this is consistent with the variance in QNF guidance provided (see Table 3). In other words, firms that provide extensive QLF guidance also provided extensive QNF guidance.

CONCLUSIONS

This paper presents the results of an examination of selections from the audit manuals of six "Big Eight" accounting firms. The sections examined were those concerned with the firms' guidelines about the role of various factors in the auditors' materiality judgments. Consistent with the results of prior research, the relationship of a misstatement to net income (QNF) and the effect of a misstatement on earnings trends (QLF) are frequently mentioned in the firm-specific literature as factors that should be considered by the auditor in his materality judgments.

The results of this research suggest the need for more explicit authoritative guidance relating to auditors' materiality judgments.[9] In spite of the relatively uniform importance of the two factors previously mentioned, the quantitative and qualitative guidelines provided by the firms differ substantially. As shown in Tables 3 and 5, the number of QNFs and QLFs identified by the firms varies greatly. The differences noted in the materiality views of the six firms reflect the lack of in-depth, operational guidance offered by the authoritative literature. In addition, this diversity indicates that different factors are considered by the various firms in establishing materiality levels during the audit examination.

ACKNOWLEDGMENTS

The authors would like to acknowledge the helpful comments of Noel D. Addy, Kenneth N. Orbach, Robert H. Strawser, Wanda A. Wallace, and two anonymous reviewers.

NOTES

1. Because of the exploratory nature of this research, it was decided to limit the number of firms whose materiality literature was examined. "Big Eight" accounting firms were selected for examination because the authors believe that the audit approaches of these firms are the most innovative and well developed. However, these firms are not a representative sample of all accounting firms. The fact that the results of the research are not generalizable to all accounting firms represents a limitation of this study.

2. The firms were contacted through letters addressed to partners in national or regional offices of the firm. The nonresponding firm was contacted by telephone to confirm that the initial letter was received. A second letter was mailed to another partner of the firm. Follow-up calls confirmed the receipt of the second letter. Although this firm did not explicitly refuse cooperation, it was believed that additional efforts to obtain cooperation would not be welcomed. Therefore, further efforts to obtain cooperation from this firm were abandoned.

3. Although this comparison will provide insight into the materiality guidance provided to auditors affiliated with different firms, it will not enable any assertions to be made about the

consensus of materiality judgments within a firm. Most, if not all, firms would be more concerned about the consistency of their own practices than the consistency of their procedures with those of other firms. However, examination of this issue is beyond the scope of the current research. See Schultz and Reckers [1981] for an example of the effects of situational variables on the materiality judgments of auditors within a single firm.

4.   A potential weakness of using this method to determine the relative importance of QNFs within a firm relates to the writing style adopted in the firm's manual. Some firms provided extensive "check lists" of possible QNFs with very little discussion about each item. Other firms had elaborate discussions about some QNFs, but then merely listed other QNFs. However, it seems reasonable to believe that the integration of a particular QNF throughout the firm's discussion of quantitative materiality indicates the importance of that QNF. Therefore, in the absence of any statement acnknowledging the primary importance of a particular QNF, frequency counts were used to measure relative importance.

5.   To determine whether the excerpts provided by the cooperating firms represented their positions on materiality, all six firms were contacted after the materials were received. Each firm responded that the information contained in its audit manual was the primary source of firm training. In addition, these firms indicated that the audit manuals were representative of their practices. Therefore, it appears that the excerpts supplied by the six firms represent their official positions on the subject of materiality and are the primary sources of guidance provided to their auditors. If there are discrepancies between the guidance provided in the audit manuals and actual practice, the generalization of the findings of this research to current practice is inhibited. This lack of generalizability is a limitation of the current study.

6.   In addition to these QNFs, five QNFs were identified for use in audit examinations of nonbusiness entities. These QNFs were (1) Gross Revenues, (2) Endowment Income, (3) Public Contributions, (4) Gross Expenditures, and (5) Program, Administrative, and Fund Raising expenditures. Only two of the six responding firms (firms E and F) mentioned specific QNFs for use in the audit of nonbusiness entities. Because previous research did not address the role of materiality judgments in these types of audit examinations, further analysis of these QNFs was not performed.

It should also be noted that the audit manuals examined in this research were the firm's "general" audit manuals that provide guidelines for the firm's overall audit practices. In addition to this "general" audit manual, many firms also have separate audit manuals for specialized industries. Because this research was concerned with the overall materiality guidance provided to "Big Eight" auditors, the specialized audit manuals were not examined in this study.

7.   As stated earlier, QNFs are used in both the planning and the evaluation stages of the auditor's examination. Of the 27 QNFs listed in Table 2, only 8 were explicitly mentioned by the firms as being used in establishing preliminary materiality levels. These eight QNFs were (1) Net Income Before Taxes (#1), (2) Total Revenues (#2), (3) Income from Continuing Operations (#5), (4) Total Assets (#11), (5) Shareholders' Equity (#12), (6) Current Assets (#14), (7) lower of Total Assets or Net Income (#25), and (8) "Size" (#26). However, it should be noted that these QNFs were also mentioned by the firms as being used in evaluating errors discovered during the audit examination. These "planning stage" QNFs are consistent with those identified in a survey of practicing auditors [Reed et al. 1987].

8.   One issue not addressed in this research is the cause of similarities between the excerpts from the audit manuals and the results of previous research. It would be interesting to know whether these similarities exist because (1) exposure to firm training manuals affected the responses of auditor-subjects in the various research studies, or (2) previous research efforts identified factors affecting materiality judgments that were subsequently incorporated by firms in their audit manuals. However, this issue is beyond the scope of the current research.

9.   A summary of the literature that discussed uniform materiality guidelines is presented by Leslie [1985].

REFERENCES

American Institute of Certified Public Accountants, *Codification of Statements on Auditing Standards Numbers 1 to 49* [AICPA 1986].

Boatsman, J. R. and J. Robertson, "Policy Capturing on Selected Materiality Judgments," *The Accounting Review* [April 1974], pp. 342-352.

Chewning, E. G., K. J. Pany and S. Wheeler, "Materiality Judgments involving Accounting Principle Changes: Some Evidence on Materiality Thresholds," Working paper, Arizona State University [1987].

Cushing, B. E. and J. K. Loebbecke, *Comparison of Audit Methodologies of Large Accounting Firms*, SAR #26 [American Accounting Association 1986].

Financial Accounting Standards Board, *Qualitative Characteristics of Accounting Information*, Statement of Financial Accounting Concepts No. 2 [FASB, 1980].

Firth, M., "Consensus Views and Judgment Models in Materiality Decisions," *Accounting, Organizations, and Society* [March 1980], pp. 283-295.

Frishkoff, P., "Empirical Investigation of the Concept of Materiality," *Journal of Accounting Research* [Supplement 1970], pp. 116-129.

Holstrum, G. L. and W. F. Messier, Jr., "A Review and Integration of Empirical Research on Materiality," *Auditing: A Journal of Practice and Theory* [Fall 1982], pp. 45-63.

Jennings, M., D. C. Kneer and P. M. J. Reckers, "A Reexamination of the Concept of Materiality: Views of Auditors, Users, and Officers of the Court," *Auditing: A Journal of Practice and Theory* [Spring 1987], pp. 104-115.

Krogstad, J. L., E. T. Ettenson and J. Shanteau, "Context and Experience in Auditors' Materiality Judgments," *Auditing: A Journal of Practice and Theory* [Fall 1984], pp. 54-75.

Leslie, D. A., *Materiality-The Concept and Its Application to Auditing* [The Canadian Institute of Charted Accountants, 1985].

Messier, W. F., "The Effect of Experience and Firm Type on Materiality/Disclosure Judgments," *Journal of Accounting Research* [Autumn 1983], pp. 611-618.

Morris, M. H., W. D. Nichols and J. W. Pattillo, "Capitalization of Interest, Materiality Judgment Divergence and Users' Information Needs," *Journal of Business Finance & Accounting* [Winter 1984], pp. 547-555.

Moriarity, S. R., and F. H. Barron, "Modeling Materiality Judgments of Audit Partners," *Journal of Accounting Research* [Autumn 1976], pp. 320-341.

Moriarity, S. R., and F. H. Barron, "A Judgment-Based Definition of Materiality," *Journal of Accounting Research* [Supplement 1979], pp. 114-135.

Reed, W. J., J. E. Mitchell and A. D. Akresh, "Planning Material and SAS No. 47," *Journal of Accountancy* [December 1987], pp. 72-79.

Schultz, J. J. and P. M. J. Reckers, "The Impact of Group Processing on Selected Audit Disclosure Decisions," *Journal of Accounting Research* [Autumn 1981], pp. 482-501.

Woolsey, S., "Development of Criteria to Guide the Accountant in Judging Materiality," *Journal of Accountancy* [Febrary 1954a], pp. 167-173.

Woolsey, S., "Judging Materiality in Determining Requirements for Full Disclosure," *Journal of Accountancy* [December 1954b], pp. 745-750.

THE RELATIONSHIP OF COMMUNICATION SATISFACTION TO TURNOVER INTENTIONS AND JOB SATISFACTION FOR CERTIFIED PUBLIC ACCOUNTANTS

Terry Gregson and Dennis M. Bline

ABSTRACT

This study examines the relationship among communication satisfaction, job satisfaction, and turnover intentions for public accountants. A questionnaire was sent to a random sample of 889 members of the American Institute of Certified Public Accountants involved in public accounting. Although job satisfaction and turnover intentions of accountants have been investigated previously, accounting researchers have not considered how communiation satisfaction may impact this relationship. The conceptual model proposed in this study combines communication satisfaction, job satisfaction, and turnover intentions with the

Advances in Accounting, Volume 7, pages 203-222.
Copyright © 1989 by JAI Press Inc.
All rights of reproduction in any form reserved.
ISBN: 0-89232-960-2

goal of increasing job satisfaction and decreasing turnover intentions for employees of public accounting firms. The items comprising the job satisfaction and communication satisfaction sections of the questionnaire were factor analyzed resulting in five job satisfaction and eight communication satisfaction dimensions. General linear models were used to estimate the relationships among the variables. Job satisfaction and communication satisfaction were observed to be related to turnover intentions and communication satisfaction was observed to be related to job satisfaction. Public accounting firms may be able to increase job satisfaction and decrease turnover intentions by altering the appropriate communication dimensions.

INTRODUCTION

The relationships between accountants and their organizations have received increasing attention in recent years, particularly in the areas of job satisfaction and employee turnover intentions. Ross and Bomeli [1971, p. 384] stated that accountants' "job satisfaction may indeed be a very important end in itself ... and certainly is most desirable from a behaviorialistic point of view." The need for affiliation [Harrell and Stahl 1984], organizational commitment [Aranya et al. 1982; Meixner and Bline 1987], and organizational/professional conflict [Aranya and Ferris 1984; Harrell et al. 1986; Meixner and Bline 1987] have all been observed to be related to job satisfaction. Job satisfaction of accountants has also been observed to be negatively related to employee turnover intentions [Benke and Rhode 1984].

This study analyzed the relationships among communication satisfaction (a variable that has not previously been investigated with respect to accountants), job satisfaction, and employee turnover intentions in a sample of CPAs. It is anticipated that the identification of these relationships may lead to increased job satisfaction and decreased turnover for accountants affiliated with CPA firms. The way a CPA perceives the communication within a CPA firm would be easier for the firm to alter than the way a CPA perceives such items as need for affiliation, organizational commitment, or organizational/ professional conflict.

The next sections of this paper review the relevant literature and present the conceptual model and hypotheses addressed by this study. The methodology and results are discussed in subsequent sections and the final section presents the conclusions and suggestions for future research.

LITERATURE REVIEW

Communication satisfaction has been defined as "an individual's satisfaction with various aspects of communication in his organization" [Crino and White

1981, pp. 831-832]. Communication satisfaction has been observed to be positively related to job satisfaction in nonaccounting settings [Applbaum and Anatol 1979; Wheeless et al. 1983]. The type of job held by the individual has been observed to have a moderating effect on the relationship of communication satisfaction to job satisfaction [Downs 1977; Falcione et al. 1977; Richmond et al. 1982].

Job satisfaction, which has been defined as an attitude toward a work-related condition, facet, or aspect [Wiener 1982]; has been widely examined among accountants [Sorensen 1967; Ivancevich and Strawser 1969; Strawser et al. 1969; Fetyko 1972; White and Hellriegel 1973; Sorensen and Sorensen 1974; Faircloth and Carrell 1978; Dillard and Ferris 1979; Albrecht et al. 1981; Benke and Argualo 1982; Aranya et al. 1982; Benke and Rhode 1984; Aranya and Ferris 1984; Bullen and Flamholtz 1985; Harrell et al. 1986; Lachman and Aranya 1986]. Although Aranya et al. [1982] and Lachman and Aranya [1986] failed to observe a significant relationship between job satisfaction and organizational turnover intentions, most studies have observed an inverse relationship between job satisfaction and turnover intentions for professional employees of public accounting firms [Fetyko 1972; White and Hellriegel 1973; Sorensen and Sorensen 1974; Faircloth and Carrell 1978; Dillard and Ferris 1979; Benke and Argualo 1982; Benke and Rhode 1984; Bullen and Flamholtz 1985; Harrell et al. 1986].

Excessive turnover in public accounting is viewed as a serious problem [Istvan and Wollman 1976; Pearson 1977]. Benke and Argualo [1982, p. 7] stated that "the high turnover rate is a problem for CPA firms—an expensive one . . . the present high level of turnover is not desirable. There is a need to optimize this [organizational turnover] level." Although numerous practitioner-oriented accounting journals frequently publish articles suggesting ways to reduce turnover among accountants [Pearson 1977; Yorks 1978; Rachlin 1981; Giacomino 1982; Goldstein 1982; Half 1982; Doll 1983; Bellus 1984; Davidson 1985], little has been done to empirically investigate variables that are under the control of the firm and are related to organizational turnover intentions.

CONCEPTUAL MODEL AND HYPOTHESES

The relationship between job satisfaction and organizational turnover intentions for accountants has been reported extensively in the literature. Although the relationship between communication satisfaction and job satisfaction has been investigated for some groups, this relationship has not been investigated with respect to accountants. Figure 1 provides a conceptual model for the relationship between communication satisfaction, job satisfaction, and organizational turnover intentions among accountants affiliated with public accounting firms.

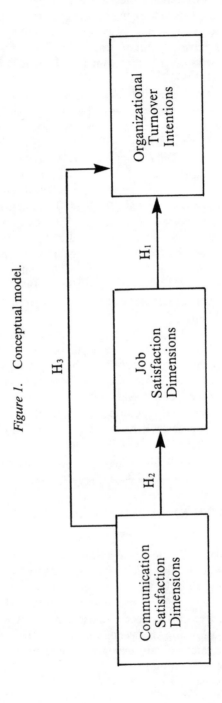

Figure 1. Conceptual model.

As illustrated in Figure 1, job satisfaction is viewed as an antecedent of organizational turnover intentions and communication satisfaction is viewed as an antecedent of job satisfaction and organizational turnover intentions. Previous literature supports the premise that a negative relationship exists between job satisfaction and organizational turnover intentions for accountants (see previous section). Because people can be assumed to be utility maximizers, employees unhappy with their jobs can be assumed to desire to increase their job satisfaction. The conceptual model is premised on the notion that employees less satisfied with their job will be more likely to seek alternative employment opportunities. The desire to increase job satisfaction is predicted to lead to an inverse relationship between job satisfaction and organizational turnover intentions, hence Hypothesis 1.

HYPOTHESIS 1. Job satisfaction is negatively related to the organizational turnover intentions of certified public accountants.

As with job satisfaction, employees are assumed to be utility maximizers with respect to communication satisfaction. Employees with a low level of communication satisfaction may perceive the possibility of increasing their communication satisfaction by seeking alternative employment opportunities. As an employee's communication satisfaction decreases, they are assumed to have more incentive to find work elsewhere. The desire to increase communication satisfaction is predicted to lead to an inverse relationship between communication satisfaction and organizational turnover intentions, hence Hypothesis 2.

HYPOTHESIS 2. Communication satisfaction is negatively related to the organizational turnover intentions of certified public accountants.

In his two-factor theory of satisfaction, Herzberg [1966] originally identified 10 factors of job satisfaction, one of which was communication. The original 10 factors were later collapsed into motivation and maintenance factors. By including communication as one of the original 10 satisfaction factors, Herzberg implied a relationship between communication satisfaction and job satisfaction. Based on the premise that job satisfaction is concerned with factors related to work conditions and that communication can be considered a work-related condition, the conceptual model proposes that communication satisfaction will partially explain the variability in job satisfaction, hence Hypothesis 3:

HYPOTHESIS 3. Communication satisfaction is positively related to the job satisfaction of certified public accountants.

RESEARCH METHOD

Sample

A random sample comprising the list of potential participants was obtained from the current American Institute of Certified Public Accountants membership roster of individuals affiliated with CPA firms. Questionnaires were mailed to 889 CPAs and 311 (35%) usable questionnaires were returned.

The sample selected consisted of a cross-section of the accounting profession. Approximately 79% of the sampled CPAs were males. Seventy percent were affiliated with nonnational as compared to national firms. The audit and tax areas of the firm were each represented by approximately 39% of the respondents and 22% were from the consulting area.

Instrument

The questionnaire used in this study was composed of three parts. One of the parts was a modified version of the Downs and Hazen [1977] communication satisfaction questionnaire. The wording of the 40 items that comprised the Downs and Hazen communication satisfaction questionnaire was modified to reflect the unique environment of the accounting profession. Each of the communication satisfaction items was scored on a Likert-type scale from one (very dissatisfied) to five (very satisfied).

Another part of the questionnaire used a modified version of the job descriptive index (JDI) developed by Smith et al. [1969]. The JDI measures job satisfaction on five dimensions: work, supervision, pay, promotions, and co-workers. The JDI was originally designed as a 72-item adjective checklist. The 72 adjective type items were modified to 30 Likert-type questions to reduce the size of the questionnaire and make it consistent with the communication satisfaction portion of the questionnaire. Johnson et al. [1982] found little difference between the Likert-type questions and the yes/no? format for the JDI. Each of the job satisfaction items was scored on a Likert-type scale from one (very dissatisfied) to five (very satisfied).

The last part of the questionnaire consisted of items designed to measure personal and job characteristics of the respondents. Turnover intention and personal/job characteristics were assessed by asking specifically designed questions. The personal/job characteristics examined were sex, age, education, type of firm (national versus nonnational), tenure with the firm, area of specialization, and most recent peformance evaluation. Turnover intention was measured by using a single question that asked subjects to assess the likelihood of staying with their current employer for the foreseeable future. A single dimension of turnover intention was used because intent to turnover has been observed to be a concept that precedes actual turnover [Mobley et al. 1978; Miller et al. 1979] and the use of a single dimension kept the instrument to a reasonable length. Arnold et al. [1985] observed a positive correlation of 0.34 (significance level <0.001) between expressed intent to turnover and actual turnover for their sample of Canadian accountants. Expressed intention to stay or leave has been used frequently to measure turnover in an accounting context [Sorensen and Sorensen 1974; Dillard and Ferris 1979; Dillard 1980; Aranya and Ferris 1984; Benke and Rhode 1984; Harrell and Stahl 1984; Meixner and Bline 1987].

Data Analysis

Factor analysis was performed on the job satisfaction and communication satisfaction items to reduce the number of variables into a more manageable number of subsets called dimensions [Kerlinger 1979]. Naming the set of items that comprise a dimension is a subjective process and the names given may vary depending on the researcher's perception of the concept represented by the dimensions. Internal reliability of each dimension was assessed by Cronbach's [1951] α.[1]

The data were analyzed by using general linear models to examine the relationships proposed in the hypotheses. Hypotheses 1 and 2 were tested simultaneously to examine the impact of job satisfaction and communication satisfaction on organizational turnover intentions. The independent variables in the model included the dimensions of job satisfaction and communication satisfaction and the seven personal/job characteristic variables (sex, age, education, type of firm—national versus nonnational—tenure with the firm, area of specialization, and most recent performance evaluation).[2] Hypothesis 3 examined the impact of communication satisfaction on the dimensions of job satisfaction that were significant in the test of Hypothesis 1 while controlling for the personal/job characteristic variables not significant in tests of Hypotheses 1 and 2. An examination of the relationships between the communication satisfaction dimensions and the job satisfaction dimensions unrelated to turnover intentions is not undertaken because it would not increase the understanding of the relationships between communication satisfaction, job satisfaction, and turnover intentions. A significance level (α) of 0.05 was used to test all hypotheses.[3]

RESULTS

The 30 job satisfaction and 40 communication satisfaction items were initially factor analyzed together[4] and tended to load with items from their respective scales. The only dimension that included items from both communication

Table 1. Varimax Factor Loadings Communication Satisfaction Items

	Factor Loadings							
	1	2	3	4	5	6	7	8
Performance Feedback								
1. Evaluation of My Performance.	0.81							
2. Information about My Progress at My Firm.	0.80							
3. Recognition of My Achievements.	0.77							
4. The Ability of the Feedback I Receive to Improve My Performance.	0.72							
5. Information About How I Am Doing in My Firm in Comparison to Others.	0.72							
6. Information About What Is Expected of Me at My Firm.	0.66							
Firmwide Communication								
7. The Amount of Communication That Occurs within My Firm.		0.78						
8. My Firm's Overall Attitude to Communication.		0.72						
9. The Amount of Communication I Receive from My Firm.		0.67						
10. The Ability of the People in My Firm to Communicate with Each Other.		0.63						
11. The Flexibility of Communication Practices within My Firm.		0.57						
12. The Motivational Aspect of the Firm's Communication.	0.45	0.56						
13. Meetings within My Firm.		0.52		0.43				
14. The Handling of Conflicts within My Firm.		0.43						
15. Extent to Which the Firm's Communication Makes Me Identify with the Firm or Feel a Vital Part of the Firm.	0.47	0.43						
16. The Firm's Publications.		0.37						
Subordinates Communication:								
17. The Initiation of Communication by My Subordinates to Me.			0.78					
18. Extent to Which My Subordinates Anticipate My Needs for Information.			0.77					
19. The Ability of My Subordinates to Respond to Communication from Me.			0.66					
20. The Receptiveness of My Subordinates to Evaluation, Suggestions, and Criticisms.			0.65					

Internal Communication

#	Item							
21.	Information About Tax and Accounting Changes That Affect My Work.	0.39				0.69		
22.	Information About My Benefits and Pay.	0.43	0.45			0.60		
23.	Information About My Firm's Policies and Goals.					0.52		
24.	Information About Personnel Policies at My Firm.					0.50		
25.	Information About Policy Changes in My Organization.					0.45		
26.	Information About Policies and Goals of My Division/Area of Specialty.					0.37		
	Supervisor							
27.	The Trust My Supervisors Have in Me.			0.70				
28.	The Amount of Supervision Given Me.			0.60				
29.	Extent to Which My Supervisors Listen and Pay Attention to Me.			0.56				
30.	The Guidance of My Supervisors in Solving Work-Related Problems.		0.39	0.53				
31.	My Supervisors' Knowledge and understanding of the Problems I Face.			0.52				
32.	The Openness of My Supervisors to New Ideas.		0.42	0.40				
33.	Clarity and Conciseness of Memos I Receive from My Firm.		0.37	0.38	0.39			
	Firm External							
34.	Information about My Firm's Profits and Financial Standing.				0.80			
35.	Information about Accomplishments and/or Failures of the Firm.				0.71			
	Horizontal							
36.	Communication with Other Employees at My Same Level.						0.72	
37.	Extent to Which the People I Work with Are Compatible to Me.						0.58	
	Informal							
38.	The Grapevine within My Firm.							0.76
39.	The Accuracy of Informal Communication within My Firm.		0.52					0.50
40.	Extent to Which I Receive on Time from My Clients and Firm the Information I Need to Do My Work.					0.38		0.40

satisfaction and job satisfaction consisted of "It is easy to make enemies of my co-workers" (job satisfaction) and "The grapevine within my firm" (communication satisfaction). Not too surprisingly, the respondents associated the grapevine with making enemies at their firm. The resulting output led to the determination that job satisfaction and communication satisfaction are viewed separately by the respondents; therefore, these items were factor analyzed separately.

The job satisfaction items loaded similarly to the way they did for Smith et al. [1969] resulting in the same five dimensions (work, supervision, pay, promotions, and co-workers).[5] When a minimum eigenvalue of one cut-off criterion was used for the 40 communication satisfaction items, eight dimensions were obtained.[6] Table 1 shows the factor loadings of 0.37 or above for each of the 40 communication satisfaction items. Table 1 also illustrates that some items loaded on more than one dimension. These items were grouped in a manner that would make interpretability and naming of the dimensions more meaningful.

Table 1 implies that the respondents considered that there were eight communication satisfaction dimensions, viewed as measures representing the respondents' satisfaction with

1. Feedback communication (items 1-6)—communication that respondents received concerning how well they do on their job.
2. Firmwide communication (items 7-16)—communication that occurred across the entire firm.
3. Subordinate communication (items 17-20)—communication that occurred with subordinates.
4. Internal firm communication (items 21-26)—communication that concerned the respondents work environment.
5. Supervisor communication (items 27-33)—communication that occurred with supervisors.
6. External firm communication (items 34-35)—communication received from the firm concerning information about the firm's outside environment.
7. Horizontal communication (items 36-37)—communication that occurred with others at their own hierarchical level.
8. Informal communication (items 38-40)—communication that occurred at the personal level.

The means for the dimensions of job satisfaction and communication satisfaction are presented in Table 2. The mean job satisfaction scores (higher scores indicating more satisfaction) ranged from 4.0 (work and co-workers dimensions) to 3.6 (pay and supervision dimensions), whereas communication satisfaction scores ranged from 3.8 (horizontal communication) to 3.2 (external firm communication).

Table 2.   Mean for the Dimensions of Job Satisfaction
and Communication Satisfaction

Satisfaction Dimensions	Number of Items in Scale	Mean of Dimension Items
Jobs		
Work	6	4.0
Pay	6	3.6
Promotions	6	3.8
Supervision	6	3.6
Co-workers	6	4.0
Communication		
Feedback	6	3.4
Firmwide	10	3.3
Subordinate	4	3.5
Supervisor	7	3.6
Internal	6	3.6
External	2	3.2
Horizontal	2	3.8
Informal	3	3.3

Table 3.   Cronbach α for the Dimensions of Job Satisfaction
and Communication Satisfaction

Dimensions of Communication Satisfaction	α	Dimension of Job Satisfaction	α
Feedback	0.91	Work	0.84
Firmwide	0.92	Pay	0.85
Subordinate	0.82	Promotions	0.90
Internal	0.83	Supervision	0.86
Supervisor	0.83	Co-workers	0.84
External	0.84		
Horzontal	0.72		
Informal	0.78		

Table 3 contains the Cronbach α for the dimensions of job satisfaction and communication satisfaction. The Cronbach α for the communication satisfaction dimensions ranged from 0.72 (horizontal communication) to 0.92 (firmwide communication). The Cronbach α for job satisfaction ranged from 0.84 (work and co-workers dimensions) to 0.90 (promotions dimension).

Tests of Hypotheses 1 Through 3

The general linear model output presented in Table 4 indicates that several variables (two personal/job characteristics, two job satisfaction dimensions, and one communication satisfaction dimension) were significantly related to organizational turnover intentions. With regard to the two personal/job

Table 4.   Test of Hypotheses 1 and 2[a]

Source	d.f.	Sum of Squares	Mean Square
Model	21	230.912	10.996
Error	261	202.812	0.777
Total	282	433.724	

F Value	PR > F	R^2	
14.15	0.0001	0.532	

Source	d.f.	Estimate	T Value	PR > T
Sex[b]	1	−0.119	−0.83	0.407
Age	1	−0.070	−0.91	0.363
Education[c]	1	0.023	0.17	0.865
Firm Type[d]	1	0.297	2.24	0.026[f]
Tenure-Employer	1	−0.079	−1.80	0.072
Area[e]				
(Audit)	2	−0.224	−1.46	0.147
(Tax)		−0.147	−0.96	0.339
Performance	1	−0.326	−3.68	0.000[g]
Work Satisfaction	1	−0.076	−4.00	0.000[g]
Pay Satisfaction	1	−0.021	−1.31	0.192
Promotion Satisfaction	1	−0.054	−3.14	0.002[g]
Supervision Satisfaction	1	−0.025	−1.46	0.144
Co-workers Satisfaction	1	0.001	0.02	0.981
Feedback Communication	1	−0.021	−1.16	0.248
Firmwide Communication	1	−0.037	−2.45	0.015[f]
Subordinate				
Communication	1	0.053	1.70	0.091
Internal Communication	1	−0.004	−0.16	0.874
Supervisor Communication	1	−0.005	−0.21	0.834
External Communication	1	0.004	0.10	0.921
Horizontal Communication	1	−0.031	−0.58	0.565
Informal Communication	1	0.022	0.62	0.539

[a] Dependent variable: intent to leave the organization.
[b] Female = 0, male = 1.
[c] Nonbachelors = 0, bachelors = 1.
[d] Nonnational firm = 0, national firm = 1.
[e] Audit and tax areas as compared to the consulting area.
[f] Significant at the 0.05 level.
[g] Significant at the 0.01 level.

characteristic variables, the most recent performance evaluation ($\alpha < 0.01$) and the firm type (national versus nonnational) were significant ($\alpha = 0.03$). The worse the performance evaluation, the more likely it is that the person will leave the organization. It was also observed that national public accounting firm employees were more likely to leave their firms than were members of nonnational public accounting firm employees.

Two job satisfaction dimensions (work and promotion) were each significant ($\alpha < 0.01$). Each of these dimensions was negatively associated with organizational turnover intentions. The greater the level of satisfaction, the less likely the employee will leave the organization. This observation supports Hypothesis 1—job satisfaction is negatively related to the turnover intentions of certified public accountants.

One communication satisfaction dimension (firmwide) was significantly related to organizational turnover intentions ($\alpha = 0.02$). The greater the firmwide communication satisfaction, the less likely the employee will leave the organization. This observation supports Hypothesis 2—communication satisfaction is negatively related to the turnover intentions of certified public accountants.

The dependent variables for the test of Hypothesis 3 were the significant job satisfaction dimensions (work and promotion) observed in the test of Hypothesis 1. The general linear model presented in Table 5 indicated that several variables (two personal/job characteristics, and two communication satisfaction dimensions) were significantly related to the work dimension of job satisfaction. With regard to the personal/job characteristic variables, age ($\alpha < 0.01$) and sex ($\alpha = 0.02$) were significantly related to the work dimension of job satisfaction. Similar to the results of Benke and Rhode [1980] and Adler and Aranya [1984], older employees were more satisfied with their work than were their younger counterparts. It was also observed that female employees were more satisfied with the work dimension of job satisfaction than were male employees. Prior accounting studies have observed conflicting findings between sex and job satisfaction. Albrecht et al. [1981] failed to observe a relationship between sex and job satisfaction whereas Maupin [1981] observed that men were more satisfied than women with regard to the work dimension of job satisfaction.

The two communication satisfaction dimensions related to the work dimension of job satisfaction were feedback and supervisor communication ($\alpha < 0.01$), both positively related to the work dimension of job satisfaction. In each of these instances, as the levels of communication satisfaction increased the level of the work dimension of job satisfaction increased.

The general linear model output presented in Table 6 indicates that several variables (one personal/job characteristic and five communication satisfaction dimensions) were significantlty related to the promotion dimension of job satisfaction. The personal/job characteristic (sex) was significant ($\alpha = 0.03$). Male employees were observed to be more satisfied with their promotion opportunities than female employees.

Table 5.　Test of Hypotheses 3—Work Satisfaction Dimension[a]

Source	d.f.	Sum of Squares	Mean Square
Model	13	1227.006	94.385
Error	294	2675.991	9.102
Total	307	3902.997	

F Value	PR > F	R^2	
10.37	0.0001	0.314	

Source	d.f.	Estimate	T Value	PR > T
Sex[b]	1	−1.069	−2.38	0.018[f]
Age	1	0.734	3.16	0.002[g]
Education[c]	1	0.179	0.42	0.678
Tenure-Employer	1	−0.067	−0.49	0.626
Area[e]				
(Audit)	2	−0.680	−1.38	0.167
(Tax)		−0.602	−1.25	0.211
Feedback Communication	1	0.143	2.72	0.007[g]
Subordinate				
Communication	1	−0.007	−0.07	0.941
Internal Communication	1	0.035	0.49	0.625
Supervisor Communication	1	0.220	3.23	0.001[g]
External Communication	1	0.067	0.59	0.557
Horizontal Communication	1	0.198	1.17	0.243
Informal Communication	1	0.074	0.64	0.521

[a] Dependent variable: work dimension of job satisfaction.
[b] Female = 0, male = 1.
[c] Nonbachelors = 0, bachelors = 1.
[d] Nonnational firm = 0, national firm = 1.
[e] Audit and tax areas as compared to the consulting area.
[f] Significant at the 0.05 level.
[g] Significant at the 0.01 level.

With regard to the dimensions of communication satisfaction that were related to the promotion dimensions of job satisfaction, two dimensions (feedback and internal) were significant at $\alpha < 0.01$, one dimension (supervisor) was significant at $\alpha = 0.02$, and two dimensions (external and informal) were significant at $\alpha < 0.05$. Each of the communication satisfaction dimensions was positively related to the promotion dimension of job satisfaction. The greater the level of communication satisfaction (feedback, internal, supervisor, external, and informal), the greater the level of the promotion dimension of job satisfaction. Hypothesis 3—communication satisfaction is related to the job satisfaction of certified public accountants—is supported by Tables 5 and 6.

Table 6.   Test of Hypotheses 3—Promotion Satisfaction Dimension[a]

Source	d.f.	Sum of Squares	Mean Square
Model	13	3707.614	285.201
Error	294	3860.269	13.130
Total	307	7567.883	

F Value	$PR > F$	R^2
21.72	0.0001	0.490

Source	d.f.	Estimate	T Value	$PR > T$
Sex[b]	1	1.210	2.25	0.025[f]
Age	1	−0.203	−0.73	0.468
Education[c]	1	−0.678	−1.31	0.190
Tenure-Employer	1	−0.001	−0.00	0.997
Area[e]				
(Audit)	2	0.229	0.39	0.698
(Tax)		−0.943	−1.64	0.103
Feedback Communication	1	0.294	4.66	0.000[g]
Subordinate				
Communication	1	−0.205	−1.73	0.085
Internal Communication	1	0.270	3.14	0.002[g]
Supervisor Communication	1	0.196	2.41	0.017[f]
External Communication	1	0.271	1.98	0.049[f]
Horizontal Communication	1	0.019	0.09	0.927
Informal Communication	1	0.281	2.04	0.043[f]

[a] Dependent variable: work promotion of job satisfaction.
[b] Female = 0, male = 1.
[c] Nonbachelors = 0, bachelors = 1.
[d] Nonnational firm = 0, national firm = 1.
[e] Audit and tax areas as compared to the consulting area.
[f] Significant at the 0.05 level.
[g] Significant at the 0.01 level.

In accordance with the conceptual model presented in Figure 1, Figure 2 illustrates the relationships observed among organizational turnover intentions, job satisfaction, and communication satisfaction for the CPAs surveyed. Two dimensions of job satisfaction (work and promotion) and one dimension of communication satisfaction (firmwide) were observed to be related to organizational turnover intentions. Two dimensions of communication satisfaction (feedback and supervisor) were observed to be related to the work dimension of job satisfaction. Five dimensions of communication satisfaction (feedback, supervisor, internal, external, and informal) were observed to be related to the promotion dimension of job satisfaction.

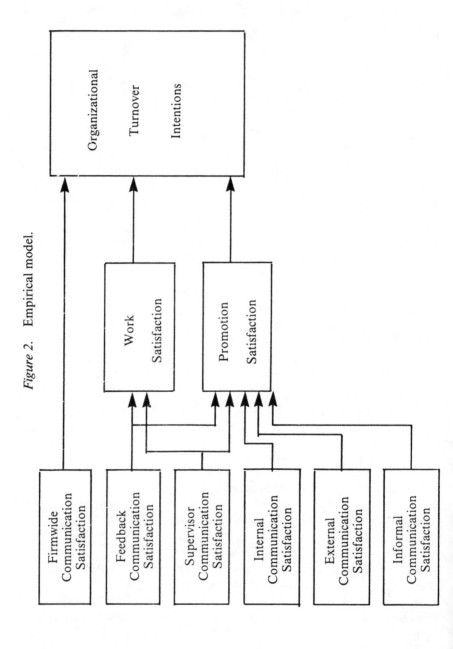

Figure 2. Empirical model.

CONCLUSIONS

Each of the three items observed to be related to organizational turnover intentions (the work and promotion dimensions of job satisfaction and the firmwide dimension of communication satisfaction) can be viewed as broad measures of how the employee fits in with their organization. These items could be viewed as addressing the way the employee perceives their relationship with the entire firm instead of specific aspects of the firm. An employee may be willing to accept dissatisfaction related to a specific aspect of the firm; however, dissatisfaction in areas that are broad based may be more likely to result in an increase in the employee's intention to leave the firm.

For the two broad dimensions of job satisfaction (work and promotion) that were related to organizational turnover intentions, specific aspects of communication satisfaction were observed to be related. The feedback and supervisor dimensions of communication satisfaction were observed to be related to the work dimension of job satisfaction and are each downward communications that address the issue of how well the employees are accomplishing their jobs. When employees perceive greater levels of downward communication satisfaction regarding their jobs, they may have a higher level of satisfaction regarding their work.

The feedback, internal, supervisor, external, and informal dimensions of communication satisfaction were observed to be related to the promotion dimension of job satisfaction. This observation could imply that communication, in general, is an integral part of the way employees perceive their promotion opportunities. When employees perceive greater levels of communication satisfaction, they may have a higher level of satisfaction regarding the promotion dimension of job satisfaction. An increased level of communication satisfaction by the employee regarding the criteria the firm uses in making promotion decisions may result in an increased level of the promotion dimension of job satisfaction.

Job satisfaction and the variables associated with it have been much studied in the accounting literature. However, the way a CPA perceives the communication that takes place within his/her firm has not been previously investigated. The CPA's perception about communication satisfaction would be easier to influence by the firm than such variables as need affiliation, organizational commitment, and organizational/professional conflict.

The relationships among job satisfaction, communication satisfaction, and organizational turnover intentions for certified public accountants affiliated with CPA firms were examined in this study. Future research is needed to determine how to alter the relevant communication variables. Also, replication of this study on other groups of accountants, such as internal auditors or managerial accountants, may increase the generalizability of the findings.

Variables, in addition to the variables used in this study, could be included in a model to predict the job satisfaction, communication satisfaction, and turnover intentions of accountants. Additional studies should also strive to measure more items, such as organizational turnover intentions, on multidimensional scales. The identification of the relationships between job satisfaction, communication satisfaction, and turnover intentions may lead to increased job satisfaction and decreased turnover for certified public accountants affiliated with CPA firms.

NOTES

1. Cronbach's α is a measure of internal consistency of individual dimensions based on the correlations between the questions that comprise the dimension.
2. A correlation matrix of all variables was prepared and the correlations between the variables was small enough to indicate no serious problem with multicollinearity. The highest correlation coefficient (involving a demographic variable) was between age and tenure in public accounting ($R = 0.52$). This indicates that age and tenure in public accounting explain only 27% of the variability of the other variable. The correlation matrix is not included in this paper because of the size of the table. Readers interested in the output can obtain a copy from the authors.
3. The significance level is the probability of incorrectly concluding that a relationship exists when it does not.
4. The output from the combined factor analysis is not included in this paper because of the length of the table. Readers interested in the output can obtain a copy from the authors.
5. See Gregson [1987] for a complete discussion.
6. An eigenvalue of at least one indicates that the dimension accounts for at least as much variance as a single variable [Hair et al. 1987].

REFERENCES

Adler, S. and N. Aranya, "A Comparison of the Work Needs, Attitudes, and Preferences of Professional Accountants at Different Career Stages," *Journal of Vocational Behavior* 25 [1984], pp. 45-57.
Albrecht, W. S., S. W. Brown and D. R. Field, "Toward Increased Job Satisfaction of Practicing CPAs'," *Journal of Accountancy* [August 1981], pp. 61-66.
Applbaum, R. L. and K. W. E. Anatol, "The Relationships Among Job Satisfaction, Organizational Norms, and Communication Climate Among Employees in an Academic Organization," *Journal of Applied Communication Research* 7 [1979], pp. 83-90.
Aranya, N. and K. R. Ferris, "A Reexamination of Accountants: Organizational Professional Conflict," *The Accounting Review* [January 1984], pp. 1-15.
Aranya, N., R. Lachman and J. Amernic, "Accountants' Job Satisfaction: A Path Analysis," *Accounting, Organizations and Society* 3 [1982], pp. 201-215.
Arnold, H. J., D. C. Feldman and M. Purbhoo, "The Role of Social-Desirability Response Bias in Turnover Research," *Academy of Management Journal* 28 [1985], pp. 955-966.
Bellus, D., "Turnover Prevention: Third Year Staff Accountants," *Journal of Accountancy* 158(2) [1984], pp. 118-122.
Benke, R. L. and C. B. Argualo, "Why Do Professional Employees in CPA Firms Leave?" *The Virginia Accountant* 35(2) [March 1982], pp. 7-10.

Benke, R. L. and J. G. Rhode, "The Job Satisfaction of Higher Level Employees in Large CPA Firms," *Accounting, Organizations and Society* 5 [1980], pp. 187-201.

Benke, R. L. and J. G. Rhode, "Intent to Turnover Among Higher Level Employees in Large CPA Firms," *Advances in Accounting* 1 [1984], pp. 157-174.

Bullen, M. L. and E. G. Flamholtz, "A Theoretical and Empirical Investigation of Job Satisfaction and Intended Turnover in the Large CPA Firm," *Accounting, Organizations and Society* 3 [1985], pp. 287-302.

Crino, M. D. and M. C. White, "Satisfaction in Communication: An Examination of the Downs-Hazen Measure," *Psychological Reports* 49 [1981], pp. 831-838.

Cronbach, L., "Coefficient Alpha and the Internal Structure of Tests," *Psychometrika* [September 1951], pp. 297-334.

Davidson, J. P., "Tips on Spotting and Preventing Job Seeking," *The CPA Journal* 55(7) [1985], pp. 71-73.

Dillard, J. F., "Migration of Public Accountants into the Industrial Sector," *Review of Business and Economic Research* 16 [1980], pp. 69-80.

Dillard, J. F. and K. R. Ferris, "Sources of Professional Staff Turnover in Public Accounting Firms: Some Further Evidence," *Accounting, Organizations and Society* 4(3) [1979], pp. 179-186.

Doll, B. F., "Staff Turnover: How To Manage It," *Journal of Accountancy* 156(6) [1983], pp. 76-82.

Downs, C. W., "The Relationship between Communication and Job Satisfaction," in R. C. Huseman, C. M. Logue and D. L. Freshley (eds.), *Readings in Interpersonal and Organizational Communication,* 3rd Ed. [1977], pp. 363-376.

Downs, C. and M. D. Hazen, "A Factor Analytic Study of Communication Satisfaction," *The Journal of Business Communication* 14(3) [1977], pp. 63-73.

Faircloth, A. and M. Carrell, "Evaluating Personnel Procedures in CPA Firms—A Study," *The Journal of Accountancy* 146(4) [1978], pp. 38-48.

Falcione, R., J. A. Daly and J. C. McCroskey, "Job Satisfaction: A Function of Employee's Communication Apprehension, Self-Esteem, and Perceptions of Their Immediate Supervisors," in B. D. Ruben (ed.), *Communication Yearbook,* Vol. 1 [Transaction Books, 1977], pp. 363-375.

Fetyko, D. F., "Retention of Staff Personnel in Michigan CPA Firms," *The Michigan CPA* 23(6) [1972], pp. 21-25.

Giacomino, D. E., "Toward Managed Attrition in Public Accounting," *The Ohio CPA Journal* 61(3) [1982], pp. 131-135.

Gregson, T., "Factor Analysis of a Multiple-Choice Format for Job Satisfaction," *Psychological Reports* 61 [1987], pp. 747-750.

Goldstein, M., "Management of Staff Retention," *CPA Journal* 52(12) [1982], pp. 12-17.

Hair, J. F., R. E. Anderson and R. L. Tathman, *Multivariate Data Analysis with Readings* [Macmillan 1987].

Half, R., "Keeping The Best—Employee Retention in Public Accounting," *The CPA Journal* 52(8) [1982], pp. 34-38.

Harrell, A., E. Chewning and M. Taylor, "Organizational-Professional Conflict and the Job Satisfaction and Turnover Intentions of Internal Auditors," *Auditing: A Journal of Practice and Theory* 5 [Spring 1986], pp. 109-121.

Harrell, A. M. and M. J. Stahl, "McClelland's Trichotomy of Needs Theory and the Job Satisfaction and Work Performance of CPA Firm Professionals," *Accounting, Organizations and Society* 9 [1984], pp. 241-252.

Herzberg, F., *Work and the Nature of Man* [The World Publishing Company, 1966]

Istvan, D. F. and J. B. Wollman, "Turnover in CPA Firms," The CPA Journal 66(7) [1976], pp. 21-25.

Ivancevich, J. M. and R. H. Strawser, "A Comparative Analysis of the Job Satisfaction of Industrial Managers and Certified Public Accountants," *Academy of Management Journal* [June 1969], pp. 193-203.

Johnson, S. M., P. C. Smith and S. M. Tucker, "Response Format of the Job Descriptive Index: Assessment of Reliability and Validity by the Multitrait-Multimethod Matrix," *Journal of Applied Psychology* 67 [1982], pp. 500-505.

Kerlinger, F. M., *Behavioral Research: A Conceptual Approach* [Hold, Rinehart, & Winston, 1979].

Lachman, R. and N. Aranya, "Job Attitudes and Turnover Intentions Among Professionals in Different Work Settings," *Organization Studies* [1986], pp. 279-293.

Maupin, R. J., "An Analysis of Job Satisfaction and Professional Practice Patterns of Women Certified Public Accountants," unpublished Ph.D. dissertation, University of Arkansas, Fayetteville [1981].

Meixner, W. F. and D. M. Bline, "Professional and Job-Related Attitudes and the Behaviors They Influence Among Governmental Accountants," unpublished Working Paper [1987].

Miller, H. E., R. Katerberg and C. L. Hulin, "Evaluation of the Mobley, Horner, and Hollingsworth Model of Employee Turnover," *Journal of Applied Psychology* 64 [1979], pp. 509-517.

Mobley, W. H., S. O. Horner and A. T. Hollingsworth, "An Evaluation of Precursors of Hospital Employee Turnover," *Journal of Applied Psychology* 63 [1978], pp. 408-414.

Pearson, M.A., "Eight Ways to Increase Staff Turnovers," *Journal of Accountancy* 144(4) [1977], pp. 50-51.

Rachlin, N. S., "Retaining and Motivating Your Professional Staff," *Practical Accountant* 14(11) [1981], pp. 75-79.

Richmond, V. P., J. C. McCroskey and L. M. Davis, "Individual Differences Among Employees, Management Communication Style, and Employee Satisfaction: Replication and Extension," *Human Communication Research* 8 [1982], pp. 170-188.

Ross, T. L. and E. C. Bomeli, "A Comment on Accountants' Job Satisfaction," *Journal of Accounting Research* 9 [1971], pp. 383-388.

Smith, P., L. Kendall and C. Hulin, *The Measurement of Satisfaction in Work and Retirement* [Rand McNally, 1969].

Sorensen, J. E., "Professional and Bureaucratic Organizations in the Public Accounting Firm," *The Accounting Review* [July 1967], pp. 553-565.

Sorensen, J. E. and T. L. Sorensen, "The Conflict of Professionals in Bureaucratic Organizations," *Administrative Science Quarterly* 19 [1974], pp. 98-106.

Strawser, R. H., J. M. Ivancevich and H. L. Lyons, "A Note on the Job Satisfaction of Accountants in Large and Small CPA Firms," *Journal of Accounting Research* [Autumn 1969], pp. 339-345.

Wheeless, V., L. R. Wheeless and R. D. Howard, "An Analysis of the Contribution of Participative Decision Making and Communication with Supervisor as Predictors of Job Satisfaction," *Research in Higher Education* 18 [1983], pp. 135-160.

White, G. E. and D. Hellriegel, "Attitudes of CPAs Related to Professional Turnover," *Journal of Accountancy* 135(6) [June 1973], pp. 86-88.

Wiener, Y., "Commitment and Organizations: A Normative View," *Academy of Management Review* [1982], pp. 418-428.

Yorks, L., "High Staff Turnover: What Causes It and How to Prevent It," *Practical Accountant* 11(7) [1978], pp. 60-62.

STAFF PERFORMANCE EVALUATION BY AUDITORS:

THE EFFECT OF TRAINING ON ACCURACY AND CONSENSUS

Roy W. Regel and Dennis Murray

ABSTRACT

In public accounting firms staff auditors are evaluated on a number of performance dimensions, which, in turn, serve as the basis for an overall or global rating. Previous research has shown that disagreement exists among various hierarchical levels within firms regarding the relative importance of each performance dimension in forming overall ratings. This can result in dysfunctional attitudinal, motivational, and performance consequences. This paper reports the results of a study designed to test the effect of a training procedure intended to enhance firm members' agreement regarding overall employee performance evaluations by increasing the correspondence between performance dimension weights employed by partners and staff members. Agreement (accuracy and consensus) is measured in correlational and other terms. The results show that training is effective in improving staff auditors' accuracy. Consensus results are mixed.

Advances in Accounting, Volume 7, pages 223-239.

INTRODUCTION

A critical resource for a CPA firm is its professional staff. People are the major asset of any service organization, so it is essential to attract and retain the best personnel available. Performance appraisal systems are a key element in the effective use of these vital human resources [Wright 1982; Kida 1984]. These systems are used for retention, promotion, and pay decisions, which are extremely important for the success of CPA firms [Jiambalvo et al. 1983], because (1) if effectively utilized, talented people will move upward in the organization, and (2) if coupled with an appropriate reward structure, top performers will feel satisfied and unwanted turnover will be minimized.

Performance evaluation systems should also provide feedback that motivates subordinates to engage in activities desired by superiors. The evaluation process can affect employees' perceptions of the job dimensions (e.g., planning audit work and reviewing work of assistants) considered important by their superiors [Kida 1984]. By emphasizing certain dimensions in the formation of overall performance evaluations, partners should be able to direct employee effort toward desired activities. A staff member's inaccurate perceptions of the linkage between evaluated performance on a certain dimension(s) and an overall evaluation may not lead to less total effort; rather, effort may be expended on aspects of the task not considered by superiors to be particularly important while more important aspects are slighted. Therefore, incomplete or inaccurate perceptions may lead to lower overall performance levels.

Several previous studies have documented both the existence and consequences of inaccurate perceptions regarding the relative importance of various performance dimensions. Maher et al. [1979] examined the perception accuracy of two groups of CPA firm employees: high performers and low performers. Their results indicate that high performers held more accurate perceptions, that is, they conformed more closely to the views held by partners. This suggests that accurate perceptions lead to improved performance. Jiambalvo [1982] investigated similar issues and found substantial discrepancies between seniors' perceptions and the views of partners with respect to the relative importance of performance dimensions. However, in only one of three offices studies were accurate perceptions associated with high performance. Kida [1984] found that although seniors and managers, on average, agreed on the relative importance of performance dimensions, there was substantial disagreement among individuals, even at the same hierarchical level. He did not relate perception inaccuracies to performance.

Overall, these studies show that inaccurate perceptions of the relative importance of performance dimensions are pervasive in public accounting firms. Additionally, these inaccurate perceptions are frequently translated into poorer performance. It seems, therefore, that a strategy useful for improving the effectiveness of performance evaluation systems and enhancing the performance of employees is to increase the accuracy with which the relative importance of performance dimensions are perceived.

This research examines the performance evaluation process and tests a training procedure designed to enhance firm members' agreement regarding the relative importance of various performance dimensions and hence overall performance evaluations. It also recognizes and takes advantage of a certain characteristic of the performance evaluation process in CPA firms. Employees work for several different nonpartner supervisors during a year. Each supervisor rates the employee on performance dimensions and also develops an overall performance rating.[1] Thus, by forming overall performance ratings, each supervisor implicitly communicates his or her perception of the importance of each dimension in forming these ratings. For the employee to form perceptions about performance dimension importance that correspond to those held by the partners, it is advisable that the supervisor use the weights that partners would have used in forming overall evaluations.

Specifically, this paper investigates whether nonpartner raters can be induced to use the weights desired by partners when forming overall performance evaluations. Without exception, the studies by Maher et al. [1979], Jiambalvo [1981], and Kida [1984] all suggested that merely communicating desired weights may be sufficient to bring firm members into agreement. This paper empirically investigates this issue.

HYPOTHESES

A possible way to train auditors to properly weight performance dimensions when making the overall evaluation decision involves the use of task properties feedback and hypothetical staff profiles. Essentially, task properties feedback provides the subject with statistical information about the task, e.g., the actual relationship between preferred (i.e., partner) overall ratings and performance dimension ratings. This training procedure has not been tested in a CPA firm performance appraisal setting but has been shown to be effective in other settings [e.g., Harrell 1977; Kessler and Ashton 1981]. In summary, the evidence indicates that the communication of desired performance evaluation dimension weights (i.e., task properties feedback) may be an effective means to achieve agreement among firm members.

The first null hypothesis addressed in this study is

HYPOTHESIS$_0$ 1. There is no difference in performance evaluation accuracy between a trained group of auditors and a control group of auditors.

Accuracy refers to agreement between partners and lower level personnel. *Consensus,* or interrater agreement, refers to agreement among personnel of the same group, e.g., staff auditors. Consensus is important because if raters do not exhibit a significant amount of agreement, inconsistent signals will be sent to ratees. This will make it difficult for them to discern any preferred weighting scheme. The second null hypothesis is

HYPOTHESIS$_0$ 2.   There is no difference in performance evaluation consensus between a trained group of auditors and a control group of auditors.

METHODOLOGY

Task

Each subject was presented with the same 33 hypothetical staff auditor profiles (plus three practice profiles). Each profile contained predetermined ratings on six evaluation dimensions (cues) and the subjects were asked to form overall performance evaluations for each profile. An illustrative profile appears in Figure 1.

For the task to be valid, the performance evaluation dimensions (cues) must be relevant to the subjects. Therefore, the performance evaluation form currently used by the staff members' firm as well as the work of previous researchers [Wright 1980, 1982; Jiambalvo et al. 1983; Kida 1984] were examined. Based on these sources, an evaluation form with six dimensions was developed. This form was reviewed by the participating CPA firm's personnel manager to ensure that the six dimensions captured the major aspects of a staff member's performance.

Two factors were considered in determining the number of profiles.

1.   In order to avoid model overfitting, the profile-to-cue ratio generally should be at least five to one [Miller et al. 1975]. In general, the greater the number of profiles, the greater the reliability of the statistical analyses used to obtain the representations of judgment policy [Miller et al. 1975].
2.   Because staff members were to evaluate the profiles in conjunction with a scheduled CPE program during regular office hours, the task had to be assigned so that each session could be completed within 30 to 45 minutes. Based on trial runs, it was estimated that 30 to 40 profiles with four to seven dimensions could be completed in the desired time frame. Results from a pilot study confirmed the reasonableness of these estimates. The final choice of 33 profiles was made in conjunction with the decision regarding the number of cues.

Figure 1. Example of Auditor Profile

Staff Auditor No. 2

Staff Auditor Performance Profile

Rating letter	Description of rating
A	Excellent
B	Very Good
C	Good
D	Satisfactory
E	Unsatisfactory

Dimension	Evaluation
1. Technical Skills—Has thorough knowledge of GAAP and GAAS. Prepares neat, orderly, and conclusive working papers.	A Ⓑ C D E
2. Judgment—Considers alternatives, has original ideas, and raises meritorious questions. Alert to client business, shows ability to develop constructive service comments.	Ⓐ B C D E
3. People Relations—Works well with others, demonstrated ability to deal with other firm members and clients with tact.	A B Ⓒ D E
4. Responsibility and Drive—Demonstrated willingness and ability to accept responsibility. Is a self-starter. Gets things done on time.	Ⓐ B C D E
5. Breadth of Interest—Interested in and reasonably informed on general business and economic matters and in other matters not related to accounting.	Ⓐ B C D E
6. Bearing and Conduct—Dresses and conducts self in a manner that conveys the impression of a competent professional person to client management.	A Ⓑ C D E

Final Evaluation

Indicate, in terms of the rating letters listed above, your evaluation of
overall performance of this person.   A   B   C   D   E

A 5-point scale, ranging from excellent to unsatisfactory, was used to evaluate performance on each dimension as well as overall performance. This type of scale is widely used in actual firms' performance reports [Kida 1984, p. 139] and is identical to the participating firm's scale. Discussions with personnel from the participating firm revealed that although a 5-point scale is used, the lowest rating is almost never given. Therefore, although the participating firms' 5-point scale was retained, the hypothetical ratings were assigned to only the top four categories.

It was desirable that cue intercorrelations be relatively low in order to obtain the partners' relative weights, which were used for training in this study (training is discussed in the following section). Providing a set of "independent" variables should also simplify the subjects' task of interpreting the feedback message. If the cues were nonorthogonal, subjects would need to study cue intercorrelations in order to interpret the feedback. Based on previous work by Deane et al. [1972] and Kessler [1977], a maximum cue intercorrelation level of plus or minus 0.20 was selected as being approximately orthogonal. A random number generator was used to produce cue values meeting this standard. The average correlation between cues was 0.017.

Development of Weights

In the participating firm's local office, three members of management normally make the year-end evaluation of staff members. Two of these people, partner in charge of audit and office managing partner, evaluated the 33 hypothetical profiles. That is, based on the predetermined dimension ratings, they gave an overall rating for each profile. *Together* they provided a single set of completed profiles. This multiple person review procedure is consistent with the firm's regular year-end performance evaluation process, except that that third management member was excluded because he had been involved in the development of the profiles. The results of this expert evaluation served as criterion (i.e., environmental) scores. The use of expert opinion to serve as a criterion has been employed previously in performance appraisal research [Wright 1985] and in other contexts [Goldberg 1970; Dawes 1971].[2] These scores were regressed on the profiles cue set to obtain relative weights [Hoffman 1960] reflecting the importance of each dimension in forming an overall performance evaluation. These weights serve as the basis for the training procedure and they appear in Table 1.

Table 1.   Partners' Relative Weights[a]

Dimension	Relative Importance of Each Dimension
1 Technical Skills	32%
2 Judgment	4%
3 People Relations	46%
4 Responsibility and Drive	16%
5 Breadth of Interest	2%
6 Bearing and Conduct	0%
Total	100%

[a] The multiple r for the partners' regresion = 0.915.

Training

In this study, training (the treatment variable) has two levels: trained and control. The trained group was provided with the weights obtained from the partners' decisions and instructed that they reflected the firm's general policy. The control group received no such instructions. This procedure is recommended by Kida [1984] and is similar to those employed in other studies, e.g., Harrell [1977] and Kessler and Ashton [1981].

Subjects and Data Collection

Forty-nine staff-level auditors from an office of one "Big Eight" accounting firm were the subjects in this study. We chose these auditors as subjects because introducing performance evaluation training at this stage in their career allows for two distinct benefits. First, the staff members sooner become aware of the proper performance dimension weights. Expectations will be clarified, allowing them to better plan, organize, and perform their work. Their efforts should be channeled more precisely toward partners' desired activities. Additionally, training should assist them in avoiding bad evaluation habits when they begin to evaluate other auditors.

The experiment was performed during regularly scheduled continuing professional education programs at the firm's office. Scheduling arrangements at the participating firm required that the work be accomplished on two different days. The first session, held on a Monday afternoon, was with staff members having approximately 2 years of experience. The second session, conducted the following Friday morning, was with staff members having approximately 1 year of experience. Therefore, the effects of three potential sources of variation were confounded in this study: (1) time of day, (2) day of week, and (3) approximate experience level. For expediency, these three items were labeled *experience*. Experience, which was utilized as a blocking variable in this study, has two levels or "blocks": LEV1, representing 1-year staff members performing the task on Friday morning, and LEV2, representing 2-year staff members performing the task on Monday afternoon. Random assignment of staff members to treatment conditions was achieved within the blocks. That is, staff members were randomly assigned to trained and control groups on each day. Each group contained 12 members, except for the LEV2 control group, which contained 13.

Measures

Brunswik's [1952] lens model motivated the selection of many of the measures used in this study. A primary measure of accuracy was correlational achievement or the correlation between the subject's overall ratings (Ys) of the profiles and the partners' ratings (Ye). Correlational achievement can be decomposed as follows [see Tucker 1964]:

$$ra = (G)(Rs)(Re) + C \sqrt{1 - Re^2} \sqrt{1 - Rs^2}$$

where $ra = r_{YeYs}$, $G = r_{\hat{Ye}\hat{Ys}}$, $Rs = r_{Ys\hat{Ys}}$, $Re = r_{Ye\hat{Ye}}$, and $C =$ the correlation between the residual variances of Ye and Ys. Two of these components were also analyzed since this should provide valuable information concerning specific effects of the training procedure.

The matching index, G, is the correlation between the least-squares regression prediction from a model of the environment and a subject's model (sometimes referred to as subject knowledge). G represents an overall measure of the accuracy of performance evaluation dimension weighting because human inconsistency and environmental (partner) unpredictability are eliminated in the regressions. In this study, G is a primary link between performance evaluation dimension weighting and overall evaluation performance. The G component is important because the training procedure implemented in this study is expected to result in an increase in knowledge, i.e., an increase in G values for the trained staff members, thus increasing overall achievement.

The multiple correlation coefficient, Rs, is called the consistency index or response linearity. It indicates the extent of the linear predictability of the subjects' responses. In other words, it is an indication of the extent to which an individual follows his prediction strategy (as represented by his multiple regression equation). Rs is of interest in this study because consistency of rater evaluation of ratees is desirable and because greater consistency leads to greater overall correlational achievement.

The expectation concerning the effects of training on staff members' consistency is uncertain. Some staff members may not have developed very strong beliefs about the relative importance of the performance dimensions on their own. Without training, these individuals might apply a continuously changing set of weights, resulting in low consistency, whereas with training, they may focus on one set of weights and apply them fairly consistently. On the other hand, some individuals may already hold strong beliefs about the relative importance of the performance dimensions. Providing different suggested weights to these persons may serve to confuse them, resulting in decreased consistency. Thus, it is difficult to speculate, a priori, on the directional effect of training on consistency.

Environmental predictability, Re, indicates the extent to which a weighted linear combination of the performance evaluation dimensions can predict the partners' ratings. Since Re does not vary across subjects, it is not analyzed here. Because research evidence has consistently shown that complex nonlinear models provide little, if any, increase in predictive power over that provided by simple linear models [Ashton 1982], C was not analyzed.

Because the loss function of actual decision makers is unknown, a separate analysis was performed for mean squared error (MSE). For each subject, the following measure was calculated:

$$\text{MSE} = \sum_{i=1}^{33} [Ye_i - Ys_i]^2 / 33$$

The inclusion of MSE allows us to determine whether the achievement results are consistent across different performance measures employed.

Two measures of consensus were utilized. Pairwise correlations (PCs) were developed for each pair of subjects within a cell. PCs were calculated by correlating the 33 overall evaluations from each subject pair. The average correlation within a cell reflects the degree of judgmental overlap. A similar process was used to calculate the second consensus measure, pairwise absolute deviation (PAD). For each subject pair within a cell, the absolute difference between the two overall evaluations was summed across the profiles and divided by 33.

Statistical Analysis

A 2×2 analysis of variance with training as the treatment variable and experience level as the blocking variable was used. Each operationalization of accuracy and consensus was separately analyzed.

Because the distribution of correlation coefficients tends to be nonnormal, correlation values were transformed to Fisher's Z values prior to testing. The sampling distribution of Z is approximately normal in moderate-sized samples for almost all ρ values [see Glass and Stanley 1970].

RESULTS

Because F tests are robust with regard to departures from homogeneity of variance (Winer [1971]), the homogeneity of variance assumption was tested at the 0.01 level of significance. The results[3] of these tests indicate that the hypothesis of homogeneity of variance appears tenable for each of the performance measures.

Accuracy

Mean values for accuracy under each condition, with Z tranformations in parentheses, are summarized in Table 2. Also presented in Table 2 are p values[4] from the ANOVA analyses for the training effect. The training by experience interaction was not significant at the 0.05 α level for any of the accuracy measures; thus, examination of the main effects is appropriate.

Table 2.   Mean Accuracy for Each Condition

	Condition			
	Lev1	*Lev2*	*Mean*	*P Value*[a]
Correlational Achievement (*ra*)[b]				
Trained	0.809	0.804	0.807	
	(1.168)	(1.116)	(1.142)	
				0.000
Control	0.689	0.705	0.697	
	(0.869)	(0.894)	(0.882)	
Mean	0.749	0.755	0.751	
	(1.019)	(1.005)	(1.009)	
Matching (*G*)[b]				
Trained	0.911	0.950	0.931	
	(1.684)	(1.946)	(1.815)	
				0.000
Control	0.833	0.868	0.851	
	(1.264)	(1.400)	(1.332)	
Mean	0.872	0.909	0.890	
	(1.474)	(1.673)	(1.570)	
Consistency (*RS*)[b]				
Trained	0.904	0.893	0.899	
	(1.512)	(1.455)	(1.484)	
				0.006
Control	0.872	0.879	0.876	
	(1.350)	(1.388)	(1.369)	
Mean	0.888	0.886	0.887	
	(1.431)	(1.422)	(1.425)	
Mean Squared Error (MSE)				
Trained	0.245	0.364	0.305	
				0.037
Control	0.361	0.389	0.375	
Mean	0.303	0.377	0.340	

[a] There is no significant interaction between training and the blocking variable, LEV.
[b] Z transformation values in parentheses.

The mean *ra* value of the trained group (0.807) is significantly greater than the mean of the control group (0.697). This difference represents an almost 16% increase of the trained group over the control group. We may reject Hypothesis$_0$ 1 at the 0.05 significance level and conclude that training was effective in increasing accuracy, as measured by *ra*.

The two analyzed components of *ra* (*G* and *Rs*) are also significant. The mean *G* value of the trained group (0.931) is significantly greater than the mean of the control group (0.851). On average, the difference represents an increase of 9%. Note that the absolute values of *G* are quite high for both trained and control groups. This indicates that *G* makes a substantial contribution to overall achievement (*ra*).

The mean *Rs* value of the trained group (0.899) is significantly greater than the mean of the control group (0.876). This difference represents an increase of about 2.5% for the trained group over the control group. Although training improved staff members' performance evaluation consistency and is significant at the 0.05 level, the amount of improvement is not very dramatic.

The results for our second accuracy measure show that mean MSE of the trained group (0.305) is significantly less than the mean of the control group (0.375).[5] Recall that MSE is a "negative" measure, thus lower values imply greater accuracy. On average, training decreases MSE and thus improves accuracy by 19%. Again, the rejection of Hypothesis$_0$ 1 is warranted.

Consensus

Our second null hypothesis posited no difference in performance evaluation consensus between trained and untrained staff members. Mean performance values for consensus under each condition, with *Z* transformations in parentheses, are summarized in Table 3.

ANOVA results for PC indicate that the interaction between training and experience is not significant. The mean PC of the trained group (0.766) is greater than the mean of the control group (0.752) at the 0.076 α level. Although the directional difference between the groups is as hypothesized, we are unable to reject Hypothesis$_0$ 2 at the 0.05 α level.

A significant training by experience interaction occurred for PAD. This indicates that usual tests of main effects can be misleading because the effect of training may vary, depending on the experience level. Therefore, tests of simple effects were carried out in order to investigate the different performance patterns. For simple effects of training, *T* tests were conducted at each level of the experience factor. Test results indicate that training had no significant effect ($p = 0.501$) on LEV1 auditors' PAD and a significant negative effect ($p = 0.000$) on LEV2 auditors' PAD. These results are inconsistent with our expectations; a possible explanation is discussed in the next section.

Table 3. Mean Consensus for Each Condition

	Condition			
	Lev1	*Lev2*	*Mean*	*P Value*
Mean Pairwise Correlation (PC)[a]				
Trained	0.752	0.780	0.766	
	(0.994)	(1.063)	(1.029)	
				0.076[b]
Control	0.719	0.779	0.752	
	(0.927)	(1.061)	(0.994)	
Mean	0.736	0.779	0.758	
	(0.961)	(1.062)	(1.013)	
Mean Pairwise Absolute Deviation (PAD)				
Trained	0.344	0.371	0.356	
				0.000[c]
Control	0.332	0.281	0.304	
Mean	0.338	0.322	0.332	

[a] Z transformations in parentheses.
[b] There is no significant interaction between training and the blocking variable, LEV.
[c] This result may be misleading because significant interaction exists between training and the blocking variable, LEV.

LIMITATIONS AND CONCLUSIONS

Limitations

A limitation of this study is the specificity of the situation. Because the subjects were not randomly selected from the population of auditors, the external validity of the study is limited. Note, however, that the study's objective is *not* to identify/develop one evaluation form with one set of weights that should be used in all firms and offices. Rather, the purpose is to investigate whether, given a set of performance dimensions and the desired weighting strategy by firm management, training is effective in bringing about improved performance evaluation accuracy and consensus.

Realism in the study is another limiting factor. Staff members were asked to rate 33 ratees during one session in a room with other raters performing the same task. Although this aspect of the study does not demonstrate good "mundane reality" (i.e., raters in CPA firms do not usually work under those conditions), it is adequate in terms of "experimental reality" (i.e., the staff members understood the task and took it seriously).

Conclusions

The purpose of this research was to ascertain whether a simple, low-cost training procedure could improve firm members' performance evaluation accuracy and consensus. The results indicate that training is effective. Significant positive training effects were found for both correlational (*ra*) and mean squared error accuracy measures. A major contribution to *ra* came from improvement in the staff members' matching indexes (*G*). In terms of the objectives of this research, this result is very important. It demonstrates the effectiveness of training in developing a correspondence between the performance evaluation weights employed by the partners and staff members.

The effect of training on staff members' consensus is less certain. Mean pairwise correlation (PC), a typical consensus measure, showed improvement (trained group = 0.766, control = 0.752) but only at a 0.076 significance level. Comparison of this result with findings of previous accounting researchers reveals that consensus was relatively good for both trained and untrained staff members. Wright [1982] reported an "extremely high" level of consensus among senior accountants (mean PC = 0.85). Jiambalvo et al. [1983] reported mean PC levels of 0.61, 0.64, and 0.49 for accountants in auditing, management services, and tax, respectively. They describe their results as indicating a fairly low level of consensus. Because the mean PC of the control group in this study is high, relative to findings of other researchers, there may not have been much room for improvement.

Results for the pairwise absolute deviation measure of consensus showed interaction between training and experience. Simple effects tests indicated no significant training effects for LEV1 auditors and a significant negative training effect for LEV2 auditors. A possible explanation for these unexpected results is that auditors may make reasonably homogeneous performance evaluation decisions that become even more homogeneous and ingrained with additional experience (the LEV2 control group demonstrated significantly greater consensus than the LEV1 control group). Training may successfully affect some persons' decision making but not everyone's. This may result in *greater* pairwise absolute differences in the trained group when compared to the control group because some trained persons change away from the previous (untrained) homogeneous weights and toward the partner weights, whereas other trained persons do not change. This underscores the advisability of implementing training procedures early in an individual's career.

In summary, the results support suggestions for improved communication regarding the proper weighting of performance evaluation dimensions voiced by earlier researchers. Future research could expand the training process to include a group discussion. With proper group leadership, such discussions may lead to greater accuracy and consensus.

APPENDIX 1:
INSTRUCTIONS *FOR CONTROL GROUP*

With the help of the firm's personnel, I am undertaking a research project designed to assess the performance evaluation process of audit staff members. The results should provide evidence useful to those in the firm who are involved in designing and implementing the performance evaluation system.

You will be presented with a group of 33 audit staff member profiles. You are to assume that you have previously rated the performance of each staff member on each performance dimension as given. Performance dimensions are general categories of job-related behavior (e.g., technical skills, client relations). Your task is to circle the appropriate letter to indicate your evaluation of the *overall performance* of each staff member. Please circle only one letter for each profile.

The 33 profiles included in this project represent only a small sample of all possible staff auditors, and thus may not be representative of auditors in this office.

In order for you to become familiar with the rating task, three profiles are included for "practice." Please respond to the practice profiles before responding to the 33 profiles that follow them.

In order for the research project to be most meaningful, I ask that you not discuss the profiles or the way in which you are making your ratings with anyone else until after completion of the entire project.

Note that none of these pages contains your name. You will remain anonymous.

When you have completed your evaluation of the profiles, please complete the brief questionnaire and return all the materials to me.

Your cooperation in this project is sincerely appreciated.

APPENDIX 2:
INSTRUCTIONS *FOR TRAINED GROUP*

With the help of the firm's personnel, I am undertaking a research project designed to assess the performance evaluation process of audit staff members. The results should provide evidence useful to those in the firm who are involved in designing and implementing the performance evaluation system.

As you know, each staff member at the firm is evaluated on various performance dimensions by a number of different supervisors throughout the year. Performance dimensions are general categories of job-related behavior (e.g., technical skills, client relations). Supervisors also form overall ratings based on ratings of specific dimensions. At year-end, a partner or group of partners ultimately makes promotion and pay raise decisions. Because staff members are evaluated by a number of supervisors during the year and by partners at year-end, it is desirable to have agreement among all persons in the firm regarding the relative importance of each performance dimension in forming overall evaluations. This should result in staff members channeling their efforts toward the most important performance dimensions and developing reasonable expectations regarding promotion and pay raises.

I have performed an analysis between *performance dimension ratings* and *overall ratings* assigned by senior audit personnel at the firm. The results that follow may be considered a valid reflection of the firm's general policy regarding the relative importance of each dimension.

Dimension	Relative Importance of Each Dimension
1. Technical Skills—Has thorough knowledge of GAAP and GAAS. Prepares neat, orderly, and conclusive working papers.	32%
2. Judgment—Considers alternatives, has original ideas and raises meritorious questions. Alert to client business, shows ability to develop constructive service comment.	4%
3. People Relations—Works well with others, demonstrated ability to deal with other firm members and clients with tact.	46%
4. Responsibility and Drive—Demonstrated willingness and ability to accept responsibility. Is a self-starter. Gets things done on time.	16%
5. Breadth of Interest—Interested in and reasonably informed on general business and economic matters and in other matters not related to accounting.	2%
6. Bearing and Conduct—Dresses and conducts self in a manner that conveys the impression of a competent professional person to client management.	0%
Total	100%

You will be presented with a group of 33 audit staff member profiles. You are to assume that you have previously rated the performance of each staff member on each performance dimension as given. Your task is to circle the appropriate letter to indicate your evaluation of the *overall performance* of each staff member. Please circle only one letter for each profile.

The 33 profiles included in this project represent only a small sample of all possible staff auditors, and thus may not be representative of auditors in this office.

In order for you to become familiar with the rating task, three profiles are included for "practice." Please respond to the practice profiles before responding to the 33 profiles that follow them.

In order for the research project to be most meaningful, I ask that you not discuss the profiles or the way in which you are making your ratings with anyone else until after the completion of the entire project.

Note that none of these pages contains your name. You will remain anonymous.

When you have completed your evaluation of the profiles, please complete the brief questionnaire and return all the materials to me.

Your cooperation in this project is sincerely appreciated.

ACKNOWLEDGMENTS

The authors gratefully acknowledge the contributions of Katherine Frazier, Jack Hulst, Charles Judd, Ron Reed, and John Tracy. This research was partially supported by the University of Montana School of Business Administration Faculty Research Fund.

NOTES

1.   For example, seniors rate staff, supervisors rate seniors, and managers rate supervisors. Terminology and the number of hierarchical levels vary by firm.

2.   An alternate perspective is to view both partners and staff members on the right-hand side of the lens model (see Measures Section). The theoretical framework, including correlational achievement, is also applicable under this alternative view [Hammond and Summers 1972].

3.   The only significant homogeneity of variance result was for a simple effects test for mean pairwise absolute deviation. Log and square root tranformations of pairwise absolute deviation eliminated this homogeneity of variance problem. ANOVA and t test results before and after transformation were almost identical, thus only the nontransformed results are presented.

4.   The hypotheses suggest that training should have a significant positive effect on accuracy and consensus. Therefore, the p values for the training effect for these variables are one tailed. Experience and interaction have no directional hypothesis and thus have two-tailed p values. An exception occurs for consistency (Rs). The training procedure implemented in this study was not designed to improve Rs particularly, rather, it was intended to improve the G component of ra. Therefore, the p value for the training effect for Rs is two tailed, as are the Rs p values for experience and interaction.

5.   An additional performance measure, mean absolute error (MAE), was also examined. The results for MAE were very close to mean squared error, i.e., p values for the training effect were 0.037 for MSE and 0.060 for MAE. Thus, only the MSE results are shown.

REFERENCES

Ashton, R. H., *Human Information Processing in Accounting. Studies in Accounting Research No. 17* [American Accounting Association, 1982].

Brunswik, E., *The Conceptual Framework of Psychology* [University of Chicago Press, 1952].

Dawes, R. M., "A Case Study of Graduate Admissions: Applications of Three Principles of Human Decision Making," *American Psychologist* [February 1971], pp. 180-88.

Deane, B. H., K. R. Hammond and D. A. Summers, "Acquisition and Application of Knowledge in Complex Inference Tasks," *Journal of Experimental Psychology* [January 1972], pp. 20-26.

Glass, G. V. and J. C. Stanley, *Statistical Methods in Education and Psychology* [Prentice-Hall, 1970].

Goldberg, L. R., "Man Versus Model of Man: A Rationale, Plus Some Evidence, for a Method of Improving on Clinical Inferences," *Psychological Bulletin* [June 1970], pp. 422-432.

Hammond, K. R. and D. A. Summers, "Cognitive Control," *Psychological Review* 79(1) [1972], pp. 58-67.

Harrell, A. M., "The Decision-Making Behavior of Air Force Officers and the Management Control Process," *The Accounting Review* [October 1977], pp. 833-842.

Hoffman, P., "The Paramorphic Representation of Clinical Judgment," *Psychological Bulletin* [March 1960], pp. 116-131.

Jiambalvo, J., "Measures of Accuracy and Congruence in the Performance Evaluation of CPA Personnel: Replication and Extensions," *Journal of Accounting Research* [Spring 1982], pp. 152-161.

Jiambalvo, J., J. Watson and J. Baumler, "An Examination of Performance Evaluation Decision in CPA Firm Subunits," *Accounting, Organizations, and Society* 8(1) [1983], pp. 13-29.

Kessler, L. "The Effect of Different Types of Cognitive Feedback Upon the Prediction Achievement of Accounting Users: Some Experimental Evidence," Ph.D. Dissertation, University of Texas at Austin [1977].

Kessler, L. and R. Ashton, "Feedback and Prediction Achievement in Financial Analysis," *Journal of Accounting Research* [Spring 1981], pp. 146-162.

Kida, T. E., "Performance Evaluation and Review Meeting Characteristics in Public Accounting Firms,' *Accounting, Organizations, and Society* 9(2) [1984], pp. 137-147.

Maher, M., K. Ramanathan and R. Peterson, "Preference Congruence, Information Accuracy, and Employee Performance: A Field Study," *Journal of Accounting Research* [Autumn 1979], pp. 476-503.

Miller, J. A. H., T. R. Stewart, R. L. Cook and K. R. Hammond, *POLICY Reference Manual* [K. R. Hammond Associates, 1975].

Tucker, L. R., "A Suggested Alternative Formulation in the Developments by Hursch, Hammond, and Hursch and by Hammond, Hursch, and Todd," *Psychological Review* 71 [1964], pp. 528-530.

Winer, B. J., *Statistical Principles in Experimental Design* [McGraw-Hill, 1971].

Wright, A. "Performance Appraisal of Staff Auditors," *The CPA Journal* [November 1980], pp. 37-43.

Wright, A., "An Investigation of the Engagement Evaluation Process for Staff Auditors," *Journal of Accounting Research* [Spring 1982], pp. 227-239.

Wright, A., "Rating The Raters: Indications of Senior Performance in Evaluating Staff Auditors," *Advances in Accounting* [1985], pp. 185-198.

LEARNING STYLES OF PUBLIC ACCOUNTANTS:
MEASUREMENT AND APPLICABILITY
TO PRACTICE MANAGEMENT

David E. Mielke and Don E. Giacomino

ABSTRACT

A conceptualized model of the learning process, the Experiential Learning Model (ELM), depicts learning as a four-stage process. From this model a set of individual types by learning style can be generated. The Learning Style Inventory (LSI) test identifies four specific learning style preferences that can be compared relative to two learning score dimensions. This article outlines the basics of the ELM and describes the LSI testing procedures. Opportunities exist for applying the LSI and using the results for professional training, development, and recruiting. The primary purpose of this paper is to summarize the results of a study designed to measure learning style preferences of public accountants. Results for the study group and associated subgroups are compared with an "adult norm." Differences resulting from this comparison are interpreted with respect to their practical implications. The implications of the study for practice mangement are discussed in the final section of the paper.

Advances in Accounting, Volume 7, pages 241-256.
Copyright © 1989 by JAI Press Inc.
All rights of reproduction in any form reserved.
ISBN: 0-89232-960-2

Today's highly successful manager is distinguished not so much by any single set of knowledge or skills but by his ability to adapt to and master the changing demands of his job and career, i.e., by his ability to learn. *The same is true for successful organizations.*

—Kolb [1984, p. 27]

INTRODUCTION

Few, if any, partners in public accounting firms would argue that they do not face these same challenges. As managers of one of the largest and most important professions in the world, public accounting firm partners are charged with meeting the same challenges as these facing top managers of large corporations.

Public accounting is a service-oriented, people-oriented profession. CPAs aspiring to partnership must not only adapt to and master the changing technical demands of accounting, but also must recognize and adapt to increasing social demands placed on the profession. Growth and development come through learning. Knowledge of the learning process can enable CPA firm partners to enhance their own and their organization's ability to learn. The learning process is the focal point of this article.

This paper proposes that a conceptual model of the learning process and the related testing of learning skills are useful for training, development, and recruiting of public accounting professionals (accountants and other professionals involved in management services). To provide a basis for illustrating the use of learning-style testing, the authors measured learning styles of public accountants. Results of the study are summarized and compared with adult norm groups and implications of the study for accounting practice management are addressed.

THE EXPERIENTIAL LEARNING MODEL (ELM)

Kolb [1984] has proposed a conceptualized model of how people learn, the Experiential Learning Model. This model, derived from the social psychology studies of Kurt Lewin and others, emphasizes the role of experience in the learning process. Learning is a four-stage cycle (or process) whereby concrete experience serves as the basis for observation and reflection. A theory is developed from the observations, and new implications for action are deducted. These implications, in turn, lead to the creation of new experiences. The model is depicted in Exhibit 1.

Exhibit 1. The Experiential Learning Model

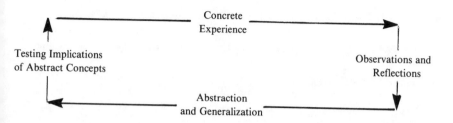

Effective learning requires four different abilities that parallel the stages given in Exhibit 1:

1. concrete experience abilities,
2. reflective observation abilities,
3. abstract conceptualization abilities, and
4. experimentation abilities.

The learner moves in varying degrees from actor to observer, from specific involvement to general analytic detachment. Most people develop learning styles that emphasize specific abilities. Some are more prone to active roles, whereas others tend to be more reflective. By identifying these learning abilities, public accounting firms can consider the potential for using this information for staff development and recruiting.

THE LEARNING STYLES INVENTORY (LSI)

The LSI tests for individual learning style preferences is a straightforward, easy-to-use process. This section discusses the makeup and scoring of the LSI and identifies the categories of learning styles (types of learners) that result from the scoring. Finally, the example LSI questionnaire is used to illustrate the interpretation of results.

Exhibit 2 is an example of an LSI form (Kolb [1976]).

Six scores are derived from the LSI:

- Concrete Experience (CE)
- Reflective Observation (RO)
- Abstract Conceptualization (AC)
- Abstract Conceptualization-Concrete Experience (AC-CE)
- Active Experimentation-Reflective Observation (AE-RO)

Exhibit 2.   Learning-Style Inventory

This inventory is designed to assess your method of learning. As you take the inventory, give a high rank to those words that best characterize the way you learn and a low rank to the words that are least characteristic of your learning style.

You may find it hard to choose the words that best describe your learning style because there are no right or wrong answers. Different characteristics described in the inventory are equally good. The aim of the inventory is to describe how you learn, not to evaluate your learning ability.

Instructions

There are nine sets of four words listed below. *Rank order* each of four words, assigning a 4 to the word that best characterizes your learning style, a 3 to the word that next best characterizes your learning style, a 2 to the next most characteristic word, and a 1 to the word that is least characteristic of you as a learner. Be sure to assign a different rank number for each of the four words in each set. Do not make ties.

1. ___ discriminating   ___ tentative   ___ involved   ___ practical
2. ___ receptive   ___ relevant   ___ analytical   ___ impartial
3. ___ feeling   ___ watching   ___ thinking   ___ doing
4. ___ accepting   ___ risk-taking   ___ evaluative   ___ aware
5. ___ intuitive   ___ productive   ___ logical   ___ questioning
6. ___ abstract   ___ observing   ___ concrete   ___ active
7. ___ present-   ___ reflecting   ___ future-   ___ pragmatic
        oriented   oriented
8. ___ experiencee   ___ observation   ___ conceptual-   ___ experi-
                                                  ization   mentation
9. ___ intense   ___ reserved   ___ rational   ___ responsible

---

Classifying individuals into learning style types requires measuring the relative position of the first four scores in two dimensions. The first dimension has concrete experience (CE) and abstract conceptualization (AC) at opposite ends of the axis. The second axis has reflective observation (RO) and active experimentation at opposite ends. By combining the first four scores along these two dimensions the individual's relative position on these axes can be determined. The fifth score (AC-CE) indicates the degree to which the individual emphasizes abstractions over concreteness, and the sixth score (AE-RO) indicates the degree to which experimentation is emphasized relative to reflection.

Kolb [1976] identified four types of learning styles using these measures:

- *The converger:* Abstract conceptualization and active experimentation are the dominant learning abilities of the converger. This type emphasizes practical application of ideas and organizes knowledge through hypothetical-deductive reasoning. Research has shown this style to be characteristic of many engineers.
- *The diverger:* Learning strengths for this type are opposite those of the converger. The diverger is better at generating ideas. Concrete experience and reflective observation are dominant. Personnel managers tend to exhibit this style of learning.
- *The assimilator:* This type's dominant learning styles are abstract conceptualization and reflective observation. The assimilator likes integrating observations into models that are logically precise, though not necessarily practical. People from the applied sciences frequently fit into this category. In business, R&D personnel are often assmiliators.
- *The accommodator:* Accommodators are actively involved, their strengths are concrete experience and active experimentation. This individual more easily adapts to immediate circumstances and likely has an educational background in business or other technical areas. In business, marketing and sales personnel often fit this mold.

Each of these learning types is depicted in Exhibit 3. The mean values used in this exhibit are the adult norms determined by Kolb [1976] in a study of 1933 individuals. These adult norm values are discussed in the following sections.

Exhibit 3. Learning Types

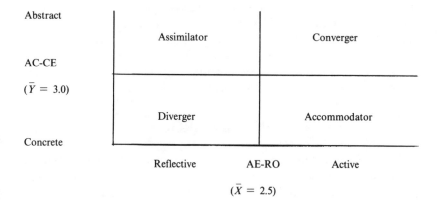

$(\bar{X} = 2.5)$

Exhibit 4. Scoring the LSI

Learning Style	Column Number	Set Numbers*
Concrete Experience (CE)	1	2, 3, 4, 5, 7, 8
Reflective Observation (RO)	2	1, 3, 6, 7, 8, 9
Abstract Conceptualization (AC)	3	2, 3, 4, 5, 8, 9
Active Experimentation (AE)	4	1, 3, 6, 7, 8, 9
AC-CE	3-1	
AE-RO	4-2	

* Nonscored words are ignored.

ILLUSTRATIVE EXAMPLE

Scoring requires the classification of each of the words in each set as CE, RO, AC, or AE. Each four-word set has one word related to each of the four learning skills. Notice, each column of words does not represent one specific learning style. Ordering of words within each four-word set is random, to prevent the individual from successfully manufacturing a desired classification.

In the first column, the words *receptive, feeling, acceptable, intuitive, present-oriented,* and *experience,* are classified as Concrete Experience. The sum for CE is the sum of the rankings for sets 2, 3, 4, 5, 7, and 8. The method used to determine learning skills scores is shown in Exhibit 4.

An initial study relating to the accounting profession by Baker et al. [1986] surveyed a group of 110 senior accounting majors using the LSI. They found that the learning styles of the accounting students differed from other academic majors and Kolb's adult norm group. The accounting major learning style preferences were more comparable with graduate students and business managers than with undergraduate students. In addition, a wide dispersion of preferences existed within this single class of students.

Although empirical testing of the LSI has been limited, studies to date have shown that actions of the business managers involved were consistent with the Experiential Learning Model. The results of the following study provide some insight as to the learning preferences of public accountants and provide support for application to practice management.

SURVEY GROUP

With the firms' cooperation, the LSI was sent to 500 public accountants employed at three public accounting firms in a midwestern city. Included with the LSI was a questionnaire requesting demographic data such as rank in the firm (partner, principal, manager, senior, or staff), sex, area (tax, audit, management advisory services, or small business), certifications (CPA, CMA, CIA, other, or none), and others. A total of 291 (58%) accountants completed the questionnaire and test instruments and were included in the study.

These firms were selected because they had the highest number of professional employees relative to the public accounting firms in the area. It was expected that the larger firms would have more individuals in various subgroupings and classifications of interest for the study.

RESULTS

The scores for each of the four learning stages and the two primary dimensions were computed for each of the respondents. The means and standard deviations for these six items are presented in Table 1, along with Kolb's [1976] "Adult Norms" survey results. In addition, the survey group was divided into subgroups according to rank, area, and sex. Selected information from these subgroups is also included in Table 1. Although no statistical analysis was done comparing our sample results with Kolb's, *T* tests were done between some subgroups. These results are discussed later.

A rigorous statistical comparison between Kolb's adult norms and this sample is not done because of the large number of potential variables between the groups, such as the timings of the administration of the LSI and the different attributes of each group. A relative comparison is used to point out potential differences that may exist between an "adult norm" group and accounting firm employees.

Four observations should be noted from the data contained in Table 1. First, for the entire group the scores for the reflective observation (RO) and concrete experience (CE) stages are relatively low compared to Kolb's adult norms. In addition, the scores for the abstract concepts (AC) and active experimentation (AE) stages are relatively higher, resulting in high scores on both the AC-CE and AE-RO dimensions. These relationships between the adult norms and the various subgroups are generally consistent, except that those individuals in the audit and female subgroupings have relatively higher scores for the CE stage and lower scores for the AC stage, resulting in relatively lower scores on the AC-CE dimension. For the group as a whole, this reliance on the last two stages of the learning cycle may reflect the maturity of the learning process of individuals resulting from their college education and job experience and because of the many screenings they have successfully completed. The relatively lower scores on the AC-CE dimension for the adult and female subgroupings may reflect relatively less job experience for individuals in these classifications. In general, the individuals in these subgroups had fewer years in public accounting than the members of other subgroups.

Table 1.   Learning Style Inventory Scores[3a]

	n	CE	RO	AC	AE	AC-CE	AE-RO
Adult Norms	1933	14.50	13.10	17.60	15.90	3.00	2.50
Survey Group	291	14.21	12.81	17.65	16.67	3.45	3.85
		(2.94)	(3.54)	(3.86)	(3.03)	(5.90)	(5.89)
Selected Groups							
Rank							
Partners	29	13.55	12.00	17.62	17.48	4.07	5.48
		(2.40)	(2.76)	(2.74)	(3.52)	(4.38)	(5.68)
Staff	124	14.15	13.01	17.49	16.64	3.35	3.63
		(2.69)	(3.49)	(3.89)	(2.98)	(5.66)	(5.62)
Total Subgroup[b]	153						
Area							
Tax	60	13.62	11.80	18.58	166.93	4.97	5.13
		(3.22)	(3.55)	(4.39)	(2.74)	(6.84)	(5.32)
Audit	136	14.54	13.13	17.23	16.65	2.69	3.53
		(2.77)	(3.52)	(3.62)	(3.18)	(5.33)	(6.00)
Total Subgroup[b]	196						
Sex							
Male	212	13.99	12.72	17.92	16.61	3.93	3.89
		(2.95)	(3.46)	(3.80)	(3.08)	(5.94)	(5.87)
Female	79	14.80	13.08	16.95	16.82	2.15	3.75
		(2.85)	(3.74)	(3.94)	(2.91)	(5.63)	(5.97)
Total	291						

[a] Means are given first, with standard deviations in parentheses.
[b] The subgroup totals represent only a portion of the total survey group. Individuals ranked as managers or seniors in the "Rank" subgroup and individuals in the MAS or Small Business "Area" subgroup were not included in the respective selected categories.

The second observation is that partners show relatively higher concentrations in the more advanced abstract concepts and active experimentation learning stages than do staff members. T tests were conducted to determine whether a significant difference exists between the two subgroups on the AC-CE and AE-RO dimensions. Although neither was significant at the 0.05 level, the results on the AE-RO dimension were significant at 0.113. These differences may reflect the additional job experience and screenings that the partners have successfully completed. The job experience may have enabled and required partners to focus more on the application of concepts to new business situations.

Tax accountants have relatively higher scores than auditors on both the AC-CE and AE-RO dimensions. T tests were conducted comparing the scores on the two dimensions for the tax and audit subgroups. The significant difference

Table 2. Learning Style Inventory Score Breakdowns for the Tax and Audit Subgroups[3a]

	n	CE	RO	AC	AE	AC-CE	AE-RO
Tax Partners	6	12.83 (1.72)	9.67 (1.03)	19.67 (2.58)	18.50 (2.43)	6.83 (3.87)	8.83 (2.32)
Audit Partners	12	14.25 (2.93)	12.75 (3.19)	17.42 (3.03)	16.58 (4.40)	3.17 (5.01)	3.83 (6.90)
Tax Staff	31	14.23 (2.74)	12.13 (3.52)	17.65 (4.63)	16.87 (3.07)	3.42 (6.68)	4.74 (5.18)
Audit Staff	60	14.48 (2.65)	13.35 (3.44)	17.07 (3.80)	16.58 (3.11)	2.58 (5.47)	3.23 (5.82)
Male Audit	43	13.53 (3.31)	12.02 (3.50)	18.58 (4.63)	16.74 (2.79)	5.05 (7.23)	4.72 (5.38)
Male Audit	96	14.24 (2.76)	13.18 (3.58)	17.34 (3.44)	16.51 (3.42)	3.10 (5.19)	3.33 (6.31)
Female Tax	17	13.82 (3.05)	11.24 (3.72)	18.59 (3.84)	17.41 (2.62)	4.76 (5.95)	6.18 (5.16)
Female Audit	40	15.25 (2.71)	13.00 (3.41)	16.95 (4.06)	17.00 (2.55)	1.70 (5.60)	4.00 (5.20)

[a] Means are given first, with standard deviations in parentheses. Individuals in the MAS and Small Business subgroups were not included in these breakdowns.

in the AC-CE scores was significant at the 0.05 level. The significant difference for the AE-RO dimension was significant at 0.076. In addition, the partners and staff in the tax area have relatively higher scores on these two dimensions than the partners and staff, respectively, in the audit area. Table 2 presents these results. *T* tests comparing the staff in the tax area and the staff in the audit area were conducted and the significant differences in the AC-CE and AE-RO scores were both significant at the 0.05 level. *T* tests were not conducted comparing the scores of the partners in each subgroup because of the limited sample size in these cells.

A final point is that both the male and female subgroups have higher concentrations in the abstract concepts and active experimentation levels in the learning process, but the scores are significantly different in the concrete experience level. The result is that the male subgroup tends more toward the abstract concepts end of the AC-CE dimension than does the female subgroup. A *T* test is significant at the 0.05 level. Further comparisons of males (females) in tax and males (females) in auditing indicate that each tax subgroup has relatively higher scores for both the AC-CE and AE-RO than the respective subgroupings in the audit area. This information is shown in Table 2. These significant differences may occur because the audit and female subgroups generally have less years in public accounting and are younger in age. The difference between partner and staff scores may also result from these changes during an individual's lifetime.

A limitation of the methodology used in this survey is that it does not accommodate longitudinal analysis. Therefore, changes that may occur over an individuals' lifetime cannot be directly assessed. Differences in learning styles noted for various subgroups may have resulted from other factors. These factors include the following: (1) changes in CPA firm training over the years, (2) changes in CPA firm recruiting, (3) changes in the audit process models applied by firms over the years, (4) changes in college education over the years, and (5) changes in the public accounting environment that have taken place over the years. However, Kolb [1976, pp. 7-10] does present some theoretical support that an individual's learning style may change over his lifetime—from more concrete to more abstract. Future research incorporating a longitudinal analysis would provide interesting information regarding these changes.

DISCUSSION/ANALYSIS

As previously discussed, Kolb categorized individuals by the predominance of their learning preferences. Table 3 breaks down the sample group and subgroups into these four categories, namely, convergers, divergers, assimilators, and accommodators. These categories are based on the mean values for the adult norms for the AC-CE and AE-RO dimensions. The mean values as shown in Table 1 are 3.00 and 2.50, respectively. For example, using Table 1 and Exhibit III, an individual with an AC-CE score greater (less) than 3.00 and an AE-RO score greater (less) than 2.50 is classified as a converger (diverger). Individuals with an AC-CE score greater (less) than 3.00 and an AE-RO score less (greater) than 2.50 are assimilators (accommodators).

The first observation from Table 3 is that 121 (63%) of the subjects are convergers. The accommodators are the next largest group with 68 (23%). The divergers and assimilators are close, but each represent less than 20% of the total subjects. Another way to view these results is to categorize the sample in terms of an active versus reflective learning style. The convergers and accommodators prefer active experimentation and represent 65% of the sample. Also, in this sample, 58.4% prefer abstract versus concrete learning styles. This abstract preference is demonstrated by the converger and assimilator categories. Thus, the public accountants in our sample demonstrate greater active and abstract learning preferences as compared to the general adult population.

Table 3. Breakdowns of Learning Style Preferences
Based on Adult Norm Mean Scores[a]

	Convergers	Assimilators	Divergers	Accommodators
	(AC-CE) 3.0	(AC-CE) 3.0	(AC-CE) 3.0	(AC-CE) 3.0
	(AE-RO) 2.5	(AE-RO) 2.5	(AE-RO) 2.5	(AE-RO) 2.5
Overall Sample	121	49	53	68
	(41.6)	(16.8)	(18.2)	(23.4)
Rank				
Partner	14	4	3	8
	(48.3)	(13.8)	(10.3)	(27.6)
Staff	51	21	22	30
	(41.4)	(16.9)	(17.7)	(24.3)
Area				
Tax	36	7	9	8
	(60.0)	(11.7)	(15.0)	(13.3)
Audit	41	31	26	38
	(30.1)	(22.8)	(19.1)	(28.0)
Sex				
Male	90	39	36	47
	(42.5)	(18.4)	(17.0)	(22.1)
Female	31	10	17	21
	(39.2)	(12.7)	(21.5)	(26.6)

[a] Means are given first, with standard deviations in parentheses.

Table 3 also presents the breakdowns into the four categories of learning preferences for the rank, area, and sex subgroups. Convergers are the largest group for both partners and staff (48.3 and 41.4%, respectively) with accommodators being the next largest category for each subgroup (27.6 and 24.3%, respectively). The least common styles are the assimilators (16.9%) and divergers (17.7%) in the staff group. These percentages decrease to 13.8 and 10.3%, respectively, as the rank increases to partner. It appears from this survey that there is a decrease in "reflective" individuals (the assimilators and diverger styles) and an increase in the task-oriented, "active" types (convergers and accommodators) as the rank increases.

As previously discussed, a longitudinal analysis was not conducted, however, this trend toward concentration is consistent with Kolb's premise that an individual's learning style may change over his (her) lifetime. Thus, as public accountants become older and become partners, their learning styles may change from reflective observation to active experimentation. An alternative explanation for the difference between staff and partner concentrations is that a more active learning style may lead to success in public accounting, aiding individuals with that preference to become partners. Thus, an active learning style may serve as a screening mechanism whereby individuals who have difficulty learning through active experimentation have difficulty becoming partners. Thus, learning style preferences may be a contributing factor to employee turnover in public accounting. This seems like a reasonable explanation, since success in public accounting may depend, at least in part, on the ability to focus acquired knowledge on specific problems and to solve those problems—an ability characteristic of an active experimentation learning style.

The analysis of the tax subgroup clearly reflects a dominance of convergers over other learning styles. Tax subgroup data in Table 3 disclose that 36 (60%) of the tax practitioners display the coverger learning style, with a balanced representation in the remaining three learning style categories. The high proportion of convergers in the tax subgroup is consistent with the characteristics that might be commonly attributed to tax specialists, that is, they display an ability to focus acquired knowledge on specific problems. Convergers are also described as preferring to work with things rather than with people and tending to have narrow technical interests.

In contrast, the audit subgroup has a relatively even distribution of individuals in each classification, with a somewhat lower representation in the diverger category. The relatively even distribution of learning preferences seems consistent with the general nature of the audit area, which may include a broader range of assignments requiring a more diverse set of individuals who have more diverse learning abilities. For example, many audit staffs have industry specialists whose specific learning styles may aid their work in specific applications. Because divergers are characterized as typically having broad cultural interests and often specialize in the arts, fewer of these individuals may be expected to work as public accountants.

The categorizations of the male and female subgroups into the four learning types are relatively consistent with the breakdowns for each other and the sample group as a whole. Assimilators represent a smaller group of females. Assimilators are described as preferring that a theory be logically sound and precise, and when facts do not reflect a theory these individuals may likely disregard the facts in favor of the theory. It would be expected that, in general, accountants would not disregard facts and that fewer accountants would be divergers.

In general, the results of analyzing and comparing subgroups reveal that differences exist between them. A majority of partners prefer an active learning style (convergers and accommodators) with a particularly large number of convergers. The staff, audit area, and the sex subgroups show more diversity in learning preferences.

The more well-balanced a person's learning approach, the easier it will be for that person to learn in a variety of environments. The more people rely on specific learning styles to learn, the more difficulty they may have in acquiring new learning and problem-solving skills in environments that use learning techniques different from their dominant one. Therefore, it appears that individuals in the tax area and partners would have the most difficulty, whereas the staff and auditors would have less difficulty, learning in new situations.

However, because the purpose of specialization is to gain expertise in a single area, the learning style concentrations in the tax area and for partners may be consistent with public accounting firm objectives. Tax accountants are usually specialists within their firms and would not, in general, be expected to participate in a wide variety of accounting assignments. As individuals gain experience, increase the number of years with the firm, and become partners, they also, in general, become specialists, whether in tax, auditing, or other functional areas. Industry specialists usually develop with experience and tenure in a firm. Thus, concentrations in specific learning styles may be expected and may not necessarily present a problem for public accounting firms.

Some might feel that to be successful in public accounting new employees should be able to learn in a variety of circumstances, since there are potentially a myriad of different learning environments in this field. The results of this survey show that at the staff level a relative diversity of learning styles exists. However, if a measure of success in the accounting profession is whether a person reaches the partner level, then the results also show that, in general, an individual must prefer an active learning style. It may be even more important to be successful in the tax area (become a tax partner) to prefer the learning style of a converger. The preferred learning styles may either develop with age or may result from screenings. That is, individuals, for example, who prefer a more reflective learning style may have difficulty performing in their jobs or may dislike public accounting and leave the firm. Thus, fewer of these types of learners are represented in these subgroups. Future research incorporating longitudinal studies might provide additional insights regarding this issue.

IMPLICATIONS OF THIS STUDY

A CPA firm may be able to facilitate a desired change in individual learning style through staff training and development. By comparing the LSI profiles of partners with the profiles of staff accountants, seniors, and managers, the firm could identify desired changes in learning styles. Training sessions could emphasize teaching methods that tend to strengthen specific learning styles. Learning style profiles may differ among areas of specialization within a firm. Tax practitioners could conceivably evidence learning skills different from those of audit or MAS personnel.

During the initial interviewing process, CPA firms can administer the LSI to applicants. Little time is required, and individuals should show no reluctance to complete the rankings. Quick, easy scoring of the results allows timely feedback. As data are accumulated, firms can develop profiles of a large number of applicants. They could be classified on the basis of learning style, with breakdowns of information for those accepting offers, those rejecting offers, and those to whom offers were not extended. For larger firms, test results could also be broken down by type of education (accountants, engineers, EDP).

Another use of the LSI would involve administering the test to current professionals in all ranks and areas of specialization. Thus, a profile could be drawn identifying the dominant learning styles for each rank and area of specialization. If learning styles differ at various ranks or between those retained and those who leave, management may have some insight as to the implications for recruiting.

Kolb and Goldman [1973], in a large study of M.I.T. seniors, performed associations between the LSI and students' ratings of 16 different situations that facilitated their learning. The learning situations included lectures, seminars, readings on theory, individual projects, examinations, talks by experts, homework, and others. The found significant results between the ratings and the students' learning style preferences. If these associations between learning style preferences and teaching methods hold for individuals in public accounting as well, the design of training courses taking advantage of these associations may be important to accounting firms. Since distinct learning style preferences for accountants were found relative to the adult norms, and additional differences were found in various subgroups, training methods may be adapted to fit these different subgroups.

Significant findings of Kolb for accounting firms are that active experimenters dislike lectures and prefer small group discussions, projects, and student feedback. In contrast, reflective observers tend to prefer lectures to aid their learning. Students who prefer abstract concepts prefer case studies and readings on theory. Finally, concrete students tend to prefer a defined set of guidelines and find theoretical readings of little help to their learning.

The fact that learning styles do differ and that an association exists between style and learning situations means that training sessions may have to provide a variety of learning approaches. This would be most important for staff members and auditors, who demonstrate the most diversity in their learning preferences. The significant difference found between males and females on the AC-CE dimension may require a variety of methods to best promote the learning in these subgroups, or may suggest separate programs for each. For example, the majority (65%) of the individuals in this study prefer active learning styles. As a result, training sessions might stress small group discussions and projects and avoid concentration on lectures. In particular, the use of case studies may aid the learning of these individuals. These methods may be of particular importance when designing tax training programs and sessions for partners, since they show the highest concentration in the active learning categories.

Learning styles of the teachers may also be an important ingredient for teaching effectiveness. Sadler et al. [1975] found an association between teaching styles and student learning preferences; in general, students gave higher teaching evaluations to teachers who demonstrated teaching styles similar to their learning style preferences. Thus, accounting firms may increase the satisfaction with their training programs by matching the teaching styles of their trainers with the learning styles of their trainees.

Further research may indicate whether learning styles of public accountants change over time or remain relatively constant, and whether learning styles influence success or tenure with the firms. If they remain relatively constant and learning style is found to affect turnover, the adminstration of the LSI may assist the firms in their hiring process. Alternatively, training programs could be designed to help change learning styles and promote a more active approach.

The results of this study indicate that the accounting firms in this survey are doing a good job of placing individuals in the tax area. An active learning style is characteristic of the tax area, and both the staff and partners in tax have higher active scores than the respective ranks in the audit area. The same relationship holds for males and females in tax relative to the males and females in audit.

The findings of this study relate specifically to the survey group; therefore, care must be exercised in generalizing the results to other groups. However, the survey and testing procedures followed in this study could be applied to other accounting firms and locations and the results similarly analyzed. The implications can assist public accounting firms in the development of appropriate teaching strategies and instructional materials. In addition, conclusions based on the LSI on an individual-by-individual basis must be tempered with the understanding that although the LSI is valid on the group level it may not be as valid on the individual level. There are many other aspects of an individual's learning process that can influence the results. As seen in this study, investigation of learning style characteristics for public accounting firms can provide useful insights for their professional training, development, and recruiting programs.

REFERENCES

Baker, R. E., J. R. Simon and F. P. Bazelli, "An Assessment of the Learning Style Preferences of Accounting Majors," *Issues in Accounting Education* 1(1) [Spring, 1986].

Kolb, D. A., *Learning Style Inventory: Technical Manual* [McBer & Co., 1976].

Kolb, D. A., "On Management and the Learning Process," in D.A. Kolb, I. N. Rubin and J. McIntyre (eds.), *Organizational Psychology: A Book of Readings,* 2nd ed. [Prentice Hall, 1984], p. 27.

Kolb, D. A. and M. Goldman, "Toward a Topology of Learning Styles and Learning Environments: An Investigation of Learning Styles and Discipline Demands on Academic Performance,

Social Adaptation and Career Choices of M.I.T. Seniors," Working Paper No. 652-73, M.I.T. Sloan School of Management [1973].

Sadler, G. R., M. Plovnick and F. C. Snope, "Learning Styles and Teaching Implications," *Journal of Medical Education* 50 [1975].

Advances in Accounting

Edited by **Bill N. Schwartz**
School of Business and Management
Temple University

Volume 1, 1984, 290 pp. $63.50
ISBN 0-89232-397-3

REVIEW: "Professor Schwartz and his associate editors, Philip Reckers and Arnold Wright, have produced a new, high-quality accounting publication that contains articles from some of the most respected names in academic and professional practice. The papers tend to be methodologically rigorous but are also quite readable and relevant to the concerns of the profession today — a combination of qualities seldom seen in accounting journals produced by academics. The editors have grouped the articles into three categories: financial and managerial accounting, accounting education, and auditing. The broad range of topics in this collection will prove interesting to the average reader."
                    —JOURNAL OF ACCOUNTANCY

JAI PRESS

J A I   P R E S S

Bernstein, American Institute for Certified Public Accounts. **The Economic Status of Accounting Educators: An Empirical Study,** Merrill T. Lewis, W. Thomas Lin, and Doyle Z. Williams, University of Southern California. **The Contributions of the Financial Accounting Standards Board to Accounting Education,** Paul B.W. Miller, University of Utah. **PART II. AUDITING. Intent to Turnover Among Higher Level Employees in Large CPA Firms,** Ralph L. Benke, Jr., James Madison University and John Grant Rhode, University of San Francisco. **Evaluation of Research on Expectancy Theory Predictions of Auditor Effect Judgements,** Steven Kaplan, Arizona State University. **The Impact of Selected Behavioral Variables on Disclosure Decisions,** Philip M.J. Reckers, Arizona State University. **Observations on Needed Research in Auditing: Materiality and Audit Risk,** Abraham D. Akresh, Laventhol and Horovath, Philadelphia. **Decision Support Systems and Auditing,** Jean Bedard, Glen L. Gray, and Theodore J. Mock, University of Southern California. **Probability Elicitation in Auditing: Additional Evidence on the Equivalent Prior Sample Method,** Ira Solomon, University of Illinois, Lawrence A. Tomassini, University of Teaxs at Austin, Marshall B. Romney, Brigham Young University and Jack L. Krogstad, Creichton University.

Volume 2, 1985, 289 pp. $63.50
ISBN 0-89232-514-3

REVIEW: "This hardbound collection of articles contains materials on financial and managerial accounting, auditing and accounting education. Most of this year's editionn is devoted to the last two areas. There are interesting pieces on the uses of Financial Accouting Standards Board statements and annual reports as teaching aids in the classroom and a study of recent graduates from a PhD program in accounting, which examines, among other things, the length of time necessary to complete the coursework and thesis. The section on auditing contains articles that will be of interest to practitioners, especially the work that examines the proficiency of senior auditors in evaluating their staff. All of the articles begin with an abstract and most have well-written summary and conclusion sections."

—JOURNAL OF ACCOUNTANCY

CONTENTS: List of Contributors. PART I. FINAN-
CIAL AND MANAGERIAL. A Taxonomic Approach
to Defining Industrial Social Costs, *Martin Freedman,
State Universtiy of New York at Binghamton and A.J.
Stagliano, George Mason University.* Materiality in
Commercial Bank Inflation Accounting, *Patricia A.
Frishkoff and Mary Ellen Phillips, Oregon State
University.* A Theoretical and Empirical Procedure for
the Measurement of the Economic Income of Corpora-
tions, *A.J. Merrett and G.D. Newbould, Cleveland State
University.* PART II. Education. A Profile of an
Accounting Doctoral Program: A Study of Recent
Graduates, *James W. Deitrick, University of Texas at
Austin, C. Wayne Alderman, Auburn University and
David L. Sayers, University of Nebraska.* FASB
Statement in the Classroom: A Study of Readability,
*William P. Stevens and Kathleen C. Stevens, DePaul
University and William A. Raabe, University of
Wisconsin, Milwaukee.* Consulting as an Instructional
Tool in Accounting, *Mohamed Elmutassim Hussein,
University of Connecticut.* A Computer-Assisted
Teaching Aid for Bayesian Variables Audit Sampling,
*Edward Blocher, University of North Carolina, Chapel
Hill.* Annual Reports: A Pedagogical Tool for Interme-
diate Accounting, *Jeffrey L. Harkins, Universtiy of
Idaho and John Mills, University of Nevada, Reno.*
PART III. AUDITING. Improving Auditor Judgement
Through Research: A Problem and Some Potential
Solutions, *Stanley F. Biggs, University of Connecticut.*
Rating the Raters: Indications of Seniors' Performance
in Evaluating Staff Auditors, *Arnold Wright, Boston
University.* The Expectation of Accounting Errors in
Medium-Sized Manfacturing Firms, *James R. Coakley,
Air Force Institute of Technology and James K.
Loebbecke, University of Utah.* The Death (Perhaps
Timely) of an Audit Report: Some Empirical Results,
*Kurt Pany and Douglas A. Johnson, Arizona State
University.* An Empirical Study of the Effects of Time
Pressure on Audit Time Allocations, *George F. Kermis,
Canisius College and S. Mahapatra, California State
University, Long Beach.* Bayesian Inference in Substan-
tive Testing: An Ease-of-Use Criterion, *Mohammad J.
Abdolmohammadi, Boston University.*

Volume 3, 1986, 358 pp. $63.50
ISBN 0-89232-655-7

in Governmental Accounting: A Review of Research and Policy, *James L. Chan, Ronald D. Picur, University of Illinois at Chicago.* The MFOA Certification of Conformance and Municipal Borrowing Costs, *Earl D. Benson, Western Washington University, Barry R. Marks, University of Houston at Clearlake, and K.K. Raman, North Texas State University.* A Comparison of Financial Ratios: Historical Cost Versus Price-Level Adjusted Disclosures, *Kung H. Chen, University of Nebraska, Lincoln.* PART II. EDUCATION SECTION, *Bill N. Schwartz, Associate Editor.* Capital Budgeting Under Risk and Inflation: A Pedagogical Guide, *Robert E. Jensen, Trinity University.* Treatment of the Material Price Variance, *Leonrad A. Robinson, Loudell Ellis Robinson, University of Alabama in Birmingham.* Vertical and Lateral Considerations of Undergraduate Accounting Honors Programs, *Mark W. Dirsmith J. Edward Jetz, Ronald J. Teichman, The Pennsylvania State University.* PART III. AUDITING SECTION, *Arnold Wright, Associate Editor.* Red Flagging Management Fraud-A Validation, *W. Steve Albrecht, Marshall B. Romney, Brigham Young University.* An Empirical Examination of the Effect of Orientation Information on Audit Judgements, *Steven E. Kaplan, Philip M.J. Reckers, Arizona State University.*

Volume 4, 1987, 328 pp. $63.50
ISBN 0-89232-685-9

CONTENTS: List of Contributors. Part I. FINANCIAL/MANAGERIAL SECTION. An Inquiry into the Utility of a Parallel System for Providing Insights into the Development of An Accounting Conceptual Systems, *G.A. Swanson, Tennessee Technological University.* Non-Economic Contributors to Tax Evasion: A Replication, *Steven E. Kaplan, Arizona State University and Philip M.J. Reckers, Arizona State University.* The Information Content of Unfunded Pension Obligations for Municipal Bond Ratings: An Empirical Evaluation, *Barry R. Marks, University of Houston at Clear Lake and K.K. Raman, North Texas State University.* International Accounting Research, *Kathleen R. Bindon, University of Alabama and Helen Gernon, University of Oregon.* Methodological Note: Using the Repeated Measures Model in Accounting

Volume 5, 1987, 233 pp. $63.50
ISBN 0-89232-788-X

Southern California, Alan A. Cherry, Loyola Mary-
mount University and Stewart S. Karlinsky, University
of Southern California. **Inflation Adjusted Data and
Security Prices: Some Empirical Evidence,** Heibatollah
Sami, Temple University and Jerry E. Trapnell,
Louisiana State University. **An Examination of the
Relationship of Unfunded Vested Pension Liabilities and
Selected Elements of Firm Value,** Robert S. Kemp, Jr.,
University of Virginia. **The Choice of Management
Accounting Normative Models: A Synthesis,** Awni
Zebda, University of Alabama. **Practitioner's Note.
Current Classification Criteria of New Financial
Instruments,** Michael D. Atchison and Robert Sanborn,
University of Virginia. **PART II. EDUCATION
SECTION. The Race - a View From the "Pits" of
Accounting,** Sarah A. Reed, Texas A&M University and
Bruce S. Koch, North Texas State University. **A Fifty
Cent Test: An Approach to Teaching Integrity,** Mark
Dirsmith and J. Edward Ketz, The Pennsylvania State
University. **Methods of Applying LIFO in Practice,**
Keith G. Stanga, The University of Tennessee. **Peer
Assessment vs. Citation Analysis of Contributions to the
Accounting Literature,** J. Louis Heck, Villanova
University and Junn C. Huang, San Francisco State
University. **Accounting Education: Practitioner's Views
on the Value of a Five-Year Program,** Rita P. Hull, John
O. Everett and Steven D. Hall, Virginia Commonwealth
University. **PART III. AUDITING SECTION. Artifical
Intelligence in Auditing: Assumptions and Preliminary
Development,** A. Faye Borthick, The University of
Tenneessee. **An Empirical Analysis of Audit Withdrawal
Decisions,** Richard G. Schroeder, University of Texas at
El Paso and Kathryn Verreault, University of Lowell.
**The Effect of Audit Billing Arrangement on Underreport-
ing of Time and Audit Quality Reduction Acts,** Timothy
Kelly and Loren Margheim, University of San Diego.

Volume 6, 1988, 276 pp. $63.50
ISBN 0-89232-892-4

CONTENTS: List of Contributors. Part I. FINANCIAL
AND MANAGERIAL. Confessions of a Failed
Empiricist, Robert R. Sterling, University of Utah. An
Evaluation of Conceptual Framework: Can It Resolve
the Issues Related to Accounting for Income Taxes?, J.
Edward Ketz and Walter K. Kunitake, The Pennsylvania
State University. Discounting Deferred Taxes: A New

Approach, *Bruce O. Bublitz, University of Kansas and Gilroy J. Zuckerman, North Carolina State University.* A Proposed Procedure for Incorporating Interindustry Relationships in the Design and Analysis of Empirical Forcasting Studies, *Clarence E. Feies, University of Arkansas.* Coalition Costs Through Queueing Theory for Shapely Cost Allocations, *Charles J. Davis, California State University, Sacramento and James T. Mackey, York University.* Municipal Bond Market Risk Measures and Bond Ratings, *Hassan Hefzi and A. James Ifflander, Arizona State University and David B. Smith, Claremont-McKern College.* A Note on the Estimation of Current Cost Depreciation, *Keith A. Shriver, Arizona State University.* Evaluating the Effects of Multicollinearity: A Note on the Use of Ridge Regression, *Earl R. Wilson, University of Missouri and R. Penny Marquette, University of Akron.* Part II. EDUCATION. Factors Motivating Academic Research in Accounting, *M. Abdolmohammadi and K. Menon, Boston University and T. Oliver, Northeastern University and S. Umapathy, Babson College.* Job Statisfaction of Academic Accountants in Southern Business Administration Association Schools, *Terry L. Campbell, The Pennsylvania State University , William W. McCartney, Doris M. Taylor and LeRoy A. Franklin, University of Central Florida.* Graduate Education and CPA Examination Performance: Some Empirical Evidence, *W. Marcus Dunn and Thomas W. Hall, University of Texas at Arlington.* An Empirical Study of Structural and Controllable Factors Affecting Faculty Evaluations, *Charles W. Mulford and Arnold Schneider, Georgia Institute of Technology.* Part III. AUDITING. Accounting and Review Services: Perceptions of the Message within the CPA's Report, *Alan G. Mayper, Texas A&M University, Robert B. Welker, University of Central Florida and Casper E. Wiggins, Texas A&M University.* An Empirical Examination of CPA Perceptions of Communication Barriers between Auditor and Client, *Steven P. Golen, Arizona State University, Stephen W. Looney, Louisiana State University, and Richard A. White, University of South Carolina.* An Analysis of Auditor Judgement in Nonstatistical Sampling, *William J. Read, Bentley College.* Forecasting Accounting Information for Auditor's Use in Analytical Reviews, *Arlene C. Wilson, Auburn University, William Glezen and Timothy P. Cronan, University of Arkansas.*

Volume 7, 1989, 256pp. $63.50
ISBN 0-89232-960-2

JAI PRESS

University. **The Relationship of Communication Satisfaction to Turnover Intentions and Job Satisfaction for Certified Public Accountants,** *Terry Gregson, University of Hawaii and Dennis M. Bline, University of Texas at San Antonio.* **Staff Performance Evaluation by Auditors: The Effect of Training on Accuracy and Consensus,** *Roy W. Regel, University of Montana and Dennis Murray, University of Colorado at Denver.* **Learning Styles of Public Accountants: Measurement and Applicability to Practice Mangement,** *David E. Mielke and Don E. Giacomino, Maruqette University.*

Supplement 1, In preparation, Summer 1989
ISBN 1-55938-047-0   Approx. $63.50

Guest Editor: **Jagdish S. Gangolly,** *State University of New York at Albany.* Associate Guest Editors: **Marcos Massoud,** *Claremont McKenna College* and **Dennis B. Kneier,** *Touche Ross & Co.*

CONTENTS. Foreword. INSTITUTIONAL PERS-PECTIVES. **Are Audit Fees Sufficiently Risk Adjusted?,** *Wanda A. Wallace, Texas A&M University.* **Corporate Capital Structure and Auditor 'Fit',** *John W. Eichense-her, Michigan State University and David Shields, Rice University.* **Auditors' Incompatible Economic Incen-tives,** *Joseph H. Callaghan, Michigan State University, H. Fred Mittelstaedt, Arizona State University and James A. Yardley, Virginia Polytechnic Institute and State University.* **Perceptions of Bankers and Analysts of the CPA's Responsibilities for Audited Financial Statements,** *Richard E. Ziegler and Philip E. Fess, University of Illinois.* **CPA as Financial Planners: Responsibilities Under the Investment Advisers Act of 1940,** *Larry M. Parker, Case Western Reserve University and Michael J. Tucker, George Mason University.* AUDIT RISK AND INTERNAL CONTROLS. **Risk Concepts and Risk Assessment in Auditing,** *Theodore J. Mock, University of Southern California and Mary T. Washington, University of California, Irvine.* **A Knowledge-Based Theory of the Audit Planning Process,** *Kirk P. Kelly, Canisius College.* **Adaptation and Use of Reliability Concepts in Internal Control Evaluation,** *Bin N. Srinidhi, New York University and M.A. Vasarhelyi, AT&T Bell Laboratories.* **Measurement of the Relaibility Parameters of Internal Accounting Control Compo-**

JAI PRESS INC.

55 Old Post Road - No. 2
P.O. Box 1678
Greenwich, Connecticut 06836-1678
Tel: 203-661-7602

JAI PRESS

the ACCOUNTING REVIEW

Quarterly Journal
of the
American Accounting Association

Managing Editor and Editor
WILLIAM R. KINNEY, JR.
University of Texas at Austin

Editors
ROBERT LIBBY
University of Michigan
ROBERT P. MAGEE
Northwestern University
GERALD L. SALAMON
Indiana University

Consulting Editors
JOEL S. DEMSKI
Yale University
ROBERT W. HOLTHAUSEN
University of Chicago

VOL. LXIII   JULY 1988   No. 3

MAIN ARTICLES